Securities Industry Essentials Exam

1st Edition

License Exam Manual

At press time, this edition contains the most complete and accurate information currently available. Owing to the nature of license examinations, however, information may have been added recently to the actual test that does not appear in this edition. Please contact the publisher to verify that you have the most current edition.

This publication is designed to provide accurate and authoritative information in regard to the subject matter covered. It is sold with the understanding that the publisher is not engaged in rendering legal, accounting, or other professional services. If legal advice or other expert assistance is required, the services of a competent professional should be sought.

SECURITIES INDUSTRY ESSENTIALS EXAM LICENSE EXAM MANUAL, 1ST EDITION
©2018 Kaplan, Inc.

If you find imperfections or incorrect information in this product, please visit www.kaplanfinancial.com and submit an errata report.

Published in April 2018 by Kaplan Financial Education.

Printed in the United States of America.

ISBN: 978-1-4754-6334-7

Contents

Introduction

Thank you for choosing Kaplan for your educational needs and welcome to the Securities Industry Essentials (SIE) License Exam Manual (LEM). This manual applies adult learning principles to give you the tools you'll need to pass your exam on the first attempt.

Why Do I Need to Pass the SIE?

All individuals interested in pursuing employment as representative-level registrants must take the SIE. Individuals do not have to be associated with a FINRA member firm to be eligible to take the SIE. However, passing the SIE alone will not qualify an individual for registration with FINRA. An individual who has passed the SIE will also need to pass the appropriate specialized knowledge examination associated with the registration category pertaining to the individual's job function to be eligible for registration with FINRA.

Specialized knowledge examinations are available for the following representative categories:

- Investment Company and Variable Contracts Products Representative (Series 6)
- General Securities Representative (Series 7)
- Direct Participation Programs Representative (Series 22)
- Equity Trader (Series 55)
- Investment Banking Representative (Series 79)
- Private Securities Offerings Representative (Series 82)
- Research Analyst (Series 86/87)
- Operations Professional (Series 99)

Are There Any Prerequisites?

There are no prerequisite exams to pass before sitting for the SIE.

What Is the SIE Exam Like?

The SIE exam is a 1 hour and 45 minute (105 minutes), 75 question exam. Each exam will contain 10 pretest questions, randomly distributed and unscored. Therefor each exam contains 75 scored and 10 unscored questions. The SIE is administered by FINRA and offered as a computer-based exam at Prometric testing centers around the country.

What Score Must I Achieve to Pass?

All candidate test scores are placed on a common scale using a statistical adjustment process known as equating. Equating scores to a common scale accounts for the slight variations in difficulty that may exist among the different sets of exam items that candidates receive. This allows for a fair comparison of scores and ensures that every candidate is held to the same passing standard regardless of which set of exam items they received. Be sure to check the Exam-tips & Content Updates link on your Dashboard for any updates to the passing requirement.

What Topics Will I See on the Exam?

The questions you will see on the SIE exam do not appear in any particular order. The computer is programmed to select a new, random set of questions for each exam taker, selecting questions according to the preset topic weighting of the exam. Each SIE candidate will see the same number of questions on each topic but a different mix of questions. The SIE exam is divided into four sections:

Test Topic	# of Questions	% of Exam
Knowledge of Capital Markets	12	16%
Understanding Products and their Risks	33	44%
Understanding Trading, Customer Accounts and Prohibited Activities	23	31%
Overview of Regulatory Framework	7	9%

When you complete your exam, you will receive a printout that identifies your performance in each area.

PREPARING FOR THE EXAM

How Is the License Exam Manual Organized?

The License Exam Manual consists of units and unit tests. In addition to the regular text, each unit also has some unique features designed to help with quick understanding of the material. When additional emphasis is valuable to your comprehension, the following distinctions are made.

TAKE NOTE

Each Take Note provides special information designed to amplify important points.

TEST TOPIC ALERT

Each Test Topic Alert reviews content that is especially likely to appear on the exam.

EXAMPLE

Examples provide practical applications that convert theory into understanding.

QUICK QUIZ 1.A   Quick Quizzes are a quick interactive review of what you just read. These ensure you understand and retain the material.

Additional Study Resources

To accompany and supplement your License Exam Manual, your study package may contain additional study resources. Be sure to spend some time on your homepage, view the best practices video, and understand all that is available to help you study.

SecuritiesPro Qbank. Coordinating with the LEM, the SecuritiesProTM QBank includes a large number of questions that are similar in style and content to those you will encounter on the exam. You may use it to generate tests by a specific unit or combination of units. The QBank also allows you to create Weighted Mock Exams that mimic your test. There is no limit on the number of QBank exams you can create.

Practice and Mastery Exams. Depending on the study package purchased, you may also have a fixed Practice Exam or a fixed Practice and Mastery Exam. These exams are designed to closely replicate the true exam experience, both in terms of the degree of difficulty and topical coverage. They provide scores and diagnostic feedback, but you will not be given access to, or be able to obtain from Kaplan, correct answers or question explanations. The Practice and Mastery Exams are sound indicators of potential actual exam scores—the better you do on these exams, the more likely you are to pass your actual exam. These may be taken just once each.

Video Library. You may also have access to various topics from our video library. These short, engaging videos cover key topics from your manual. If your package includes access to our video library, please review the topics as you complete your reading assignments in the study manual.

Exam Tips & Content Updates Link. Don't forget to monitor your Exam-tips & Content Updates. When rules and regulations change, or we want to share new information regarding your exam, it's posted there.

What Topics Are Covered in the Course?

The License Exam Manual consists of four units, each devoted to the sections defined by FINRA that you will need to know to pass the SIE exam. Each unit is divided into study sections devoted to more specific areas with which you need to become familiar.

Unit	Topic
1	Knowledge of Capital Markets
2	Understanding Products and Their Risks
3	Understanding Trading, Customer Accounts, and Prohibited Activities
4	Overview of the Regulatory Framework

How Much Time Should I Spend Studying?

Plan to spend approximately 7–9 hours reading the material and carefully answering the questions in the License Exam Manual. Spread your study time over 3-4 weeks before the date on which you are scheduled to take the SIE exam. Your actual time may vary depending on your reading rate, comprehension, professional background, and study environment.

What Is the Best Way to Structure My Study Time?

The following schedule is suggested to help you obtain maximum retention from your study efforts. Remember, this is a guideline only, because each individual may require more or less time to complete the steps included.

Step 1. Read a unit and complete all exercises. Review rationales for all questions whether you got them right or wrong (two to three hours per unit).

Step 2. In the SecuritiesPro™ QBank, create a minimum of two 40 question exams for each unit as you go. Carefully review all rationales. Use the reference number to locate additional or related information on the test topic in your LEM if needed (two to three hours per Unit).

- Do not become too overwhelmed or bogged down in any one unit. You don't want to lose sight of the finish line because you're having trouble with one hurdle. Keep moving forward. It's a steady pace that wins the race.

- View rationales after each question initially and spend time studying each rationale in order to learn the concepts. Later, you will want to create exam scenarios in which scores and rationales are viewed at the end of each exam.

- Perfection is not the goal during the reading phase; scores in the mid-to-high 60s is good initially.

Step 3. When you have completed all the units in the License Exam Manual and their unit tests, using the Securities Pro QBank, concentrate on comprehensive exams covering all the material. With your comprehensive testing, it is best to view correct answers and rationales only after the test is completed. Plan to spend at least one week testing prior to a scheduled class. (abouttwo hours for every 100 questions.)

- You should complete at least 10 Weighted Mock Exams prior to class. Review your answers and rationales. Also, review your LEM and video library as needed.

- Your goal is to consistently score in the 80s.

Step 4. Complete online Practice and Mastery exams. You should complete each exam while observing the time limits for the actual exam. Upon completing the exam, you will receive a diagnostic report that identifies topics for further review (about two hours per exam). We recommend taking the Practice Exam prior to a scheduled class and the Mastery Exam afterward.

Note: After completing Practice, Mastery, and Mock exams be sure to review your Performance Tracker so you can identify areas of weakness. You can then create focused exams on topics as needed. Also, review your video library for additional help.

How Well Can I Expect to Do?

The exams administered by FINRA are not easy. You must display considerable understanding and knowledge of the topics presented in this course to pass the exam and qualify for registration.

If you study diligently, complete all sections of the course, and consistently score in the 80s on the tests, you should be well prepared to pass the exam. However, it is important for you to realize that merely knowing the materials will not enable you to pass unless you can apply your knowledge to the questions you are given and understand the essence of the information behind the question.

TEST-TAKING TIPS

Passing the exam depends not only on how well you learn the subject matter but also on how well you take exams. You can develop your test-taking skills—and improve your score—by learning a few test-taking techniques:

- Read the full question
- Avoid jumping to conclusions—watch for hedge clauses
- Interpret the unfamiliar question
- Look for key words and phrases
- Identify the intent of the question
- Memorize key points
- Use a calculator
- Beware of changing answers
- Pace yourself

Each of these pointers is explained below, including examples that show how to use them to improve your performance on the exam.

Read the Full Question

You cannot expect to answer a question correctly if you do not know what it is asking. If you see a question that seems familiar and easy, you might anticipate the answer, mark it, and move on before you finish reading it. This is a serious mistake. Be sure to read the full question before answering it. Mistakes are often made when assuming too much (or too little).

Avoid Jumping to Conclusions—Watch for Hedge Clauses

The questions on FINRA exams are embellished with distractors as choices. To avoid being misled by seemingly obvious answers, make it a practice to read each question and each answer twice before selecting your choice. Doing so will provide you with a much better chance of doing well on the exam.

Watch out for hedge clauses embedded in the question. (Examples of hedge clauses include the terms *if, not, all, none,* and *except.*) In the case of *if* statements, the question can be answered correctly only by taking into account the qualifier. If you ignore the qualifier, you will not answer correctly.

Qualifiers are sometimes combined in a question. Some that you will frequently see together are *all* with *except* and *none* with *except*. In general, when a question starts with *all* or *none* and ends with *except*, you are looking for an answer that is opposite to what the question appears to be asking.

Interpret the Unfamiliar Question

Do not be surprised if some questions on the exam seem unfamiliar at first. If you have studied your material, you will have the information to answer all the questions correctly. The challenge may be a matter of understanding what the question is asking.

Very often, questions present information indirectly. You may have to interpret the meaning of certain elements before you can answer the question. Be aware that the exam will approach a concept from different angles.

Look for Key Words and Phrases

Look for words that are tip-offs to the situation presented. For example, if you see the word *prospectus* in the question, you know the question is about a new issue. Sometimes a question will even supply you with the answer if you can recognize the key words it contains. Few questions provide blatant clues, but many offer key words that can guide you to selecting the correct answer if you pay attention. Be sure to read all instructional phrases carefully. Take time to identify the key words to answer this type of question correctly.

Identify the Intent of the Question

Many questions on FINRA exams supply so much information that you lose track of what is being asked. This is often the case in story problems. Learn to separate the story from the question.

Take the time to identify what the question is asking. Of course, your ability to do so assumes you have studied sufficiently. There is no method for correctly answering questions if you don't know the material.

Memorize Key Points

Reasoning and logic will help you answer many questions, but you will have to memorize a good deal of information. Some memorization will be automatic as you go over the material and answer questions; some you will simply have to do systematically.

Use of a Calculator

Any math required to answer a question will be simple math: add, subtract, multiply, and divide. We recommend using a calculator for math. You may ask for a calculator or ask if you can use your own. If using your own, only simple math functions are allowed (add, subtract, multiply, and divide).

Avoid Changing Answers

If you are unsure of an answer, your first hunch is the one most likely to be correct. Do not change answers on the exam without good reason. In general, change an answer only if you:

■ discover that you did not read the question correctly; or

■ find new or additional helpful information in another question.

Pace Yourself

Some people will finish the exam early and some will not have time to finish all the questions. Watch the time carefully (your time remaining will be displayed on your computer screen) and pace yourself through the exam.

Do not waste time by dwelling on a question if you simply do not know the answer. Make the best guess you can, mark the question for *Record for Review,* and return to the question if time allows. Make sure that you have time to read all the questions so that you can record the answers you do know.

THE EXAM

How Do I Enroll in the Exam?

To take the exam, you should make an appointment with a Prometric Testing Center as far in advance as possible of the date on which you would like to take the exam.

You may schedule your appointment at Prometric 24 hours a day, 7 days a week on the Prometric secure website at **www.prometric.com**. You may also use **www.prometric.com** to reschedule or cancel your exam, locate a test center, and get a printed confirmation of your appointment. To speak with a Prometric representative by phone, please contact the Prometric Contact Center at **1-800-578-6273**.

What Should I Take to the Exam?

Bring one form of personal identification with your signature and photograph as issued by a government agency. No personal items, food, or drink, including coffee and water, are permitted inside the testing room. Personal items include but are not limited to: pens, pagers, cellular phones, watches, hats, non-medical electronic devices, outerwear, purses, and wallets. Personal items must be kept in your assigned locker or returned to your car prior to the start of your exam. As the testing vendor is not responsible for any personal items, they encourage you to bring only your identification into the center.

Erasable note boards and pens will be provided to you upon admittance to the testing room. If you need additional note boards or pens, please alert your proctor. The note boards and pens must be returned at the end of your exam or continuing education session.

If you need a calculator for your testing session, please see the Test Center Administrator. You will be provided with a non-programmable, non-printing calculator.

Additional Trial Questions

During your exam, you may see extra trial questions. These are potential exam-bank questions being tested during the course of the exam. These questions are not included in your final score.

Exam Results and Reports

At the end of the exam, your score will be displayed, indicating whether you passed.

1

Knowledge of Capital Markets

In this unit, you will be introduced to the securities industry regulatory bodies and their responsibilities as well as an overview of different markets and how securities are registered in the United States to be offered for sale in those markets. The role of different types of broker-dealers and the underwriting process will unfold, showing how capital is initially raised. A number of factors can impact these markets, including both foreign and domestic policies. Here, our domestic fiscal and monetary policies, such as those enacted by our lawmakers and those taken in particular by the Federal Reserve Bank (FRB), will be discussed.

Finally, a look at how the cycles of prosperity and decline associated with all economies impact our capital markets will be examined. ■

When you have completed the unit you should be able to:

- **define** the roles of the regulatory agencies;

- **differentiate** between the different types of market participants;

- **differentiate** between market types;

- **interpret** factors impacting the securities market;

- **identify** the components of the business and economic cycles;

- **relate** actions taken by the Federal Reserve Board to the securities market; and

- **identify** characteristics of different types of securities offerings.

1. 1   REGULATORY ENTITIES, AGENCIES, AND MARKET PARTICIPANTS

LEARNING OBJECTIVES:
- Define the roles of the regulatory agencies
- Differentiate between the different types of market participants

In this section, we will discuss the regulatory bodies who govern the securities industry, starting with the Securities and Exchange Commission (SEC).

1. 1. 1   THE SECURITIES AND EXCHANGE COMMISSION (SEC)

Created under the Securities Exchange Act of 1934, the **Securities and Exchange Commission (SEC)** is the securities industry's primary regulatory body. Broker-dealers that transact securities business with customers or with other broker-dealers must apply and be approved for registration with the SEC. Additionally, the SEC regulates all exchanges and trading markets.

TAKE NOTE   Although a broker-dealer must register with the SEC, the broker-/dealer may not claim that this registration in any way implies that the SEC has passed upon or approved the broker-dealer's financial standing, business, or conduct. Any such claim or statement is misrepresentation.

1. 1. 1. 1   Broker-Dealer Registration and Compliance

Broker-dealers must comply with SEC rules and regulations when conducting business. A broker-dealer that does not comply is subject to:
- censure;
- limits on activities, functions, or operations;
- suspension of its registration (or one of its associated person's license to do business);
- revocation of registration; or
- fine.

1. 1. 2   SELF-REGULATORY ORGANIZATIONS (SROS)

Self-regulatory organizations (SROs) function under the SEC's oversight. Each SRO is accountable to the Commission for enforcing federal securities laws, as well as supervising securities practices within an assigned jurisdiction. The largest of these SROs and their jurisdictions follow.

1. 1. 2. 1   FINRA

Financial Industry Regulatory Authority (FINRA)—FINRA regulates all matters related to investment banking (securities underwriting), trading in the OTC market, trading in NYSE-listed securities, and the conduct of FINRA member firms and associated persons. FINRA also regulates investment companies and limited partnership transactions.

FINRA's purpose and objectives are to:

■ promote the investment banking and securities business, standardize principles and practices, promote high standards of commercial honor, and encourage the observance of federal and state securities laws;

■ provide a medium for communication among its members and between its members, the government, and other agencies;

■ adopt, administer, and enforce rules designed to prevent fraudulent and manipulative practices as well as to promote just and equitable principles of trade; and

■ promote self-discipline among members and investigate and resolve grievances between the public and members and between members.

1. 1. 2. 2   Chicago Board Options Exchange (CBOE)

The **CBOE** regulates all matters related to trading standardized options and related contracts listed on that exchange.

1. 1. 2. 3   Municipal Securities Rulemaking Board (MSRB)

The **MSRB** regulates all matters related to the underwriting and trading of state and municipal securities. The MSRB regulates but does not have enforcement powers—it depends on other SROs (e.g., FINRA) for the enforcement of its rules. In this light, it should be noted that it has no regulatory power over the municipalities who issue municipal securities.

EXAMPLE   The city of New Orleans is issuing municipal bonds. To do so they it is utilizing the services of several broker dealers acting as underwriters (syndicate members) to sell the new bonds. It's important to recognize that the MSRB has no enforcement power regarding their municipal securities rules. Those rules will be enforced by FINRA. FINRA will ensure that the broker- dealers underwriting these new bonds abide by all securities rules and regulations (including those of the MSRB) regarding the sale of new securities to the public.

1. 1. 3   OTHER REGULATORS AND AGENCIES

In addition to those securities regulators noted in the previous section, there are federal and state regulatory agencies to be familiar with as well.

1. 1. 3. 1   Department of the Treasury/IRS

The U.S. Department of the Treasury (USDT) is an executive department and the treasury of the United States federal government. The Department is administered by the Secretary of the Treasury, who is a member of the Cabinet. One of the department's functions is to oversee the collection of taxes. The collection of taxes and enforcement of tax laws is a function of the Internal Revenue Service (IRS) which is a bureau of the Department of the Treasury

1. 1. 3. 2   State Regulators

FINRA recommends that you learn as much as possible about any investment professionals you work with or are considering. FINRA encourages investors to also consult their *state* securities *regulator* or associations such as the North American Securities Administrators Association (NASAA). NASAA is a voluntary association whose members provide insight from their unique perspective to the SEC and SROs as they move forward in their rulemaking process. NASAA actively advocates pro-investor policies, provides investor education, and offers resources for the regulatory community and securities industry professionals.

1. 1. 3. 3   The Federal Reserve

The **Federal Reserve Board (FRB)** consists of 12 regional Federal Reserve Banks and hundreds of national and state banks that belong to the system. The FRB determines monetary policy and takes actions to implement its policies, including:

■   acting as an agent of the U.S. Treasury;

■   regulating the U.S. money supply;

■   setting reserve requirements for members;

■   supervising the printing of currency;

■   clearing fund transfers throughout the system; and

■   examining members to ensure compliance with federal regulations.

Because the FRB, through its actions, determines how much money is available for businesses and consumers to spend; its decisions are a critical aspect of the U.S. economy.

1. 1. 3. 4   Securities Investor Protection Act and Corporation (SIPC)

The **Securities Investor Protection Corporation** (SIPC) was created under the **Securities Investor Protection Act of 1970**. The corporation is a nonprofit membership organization. SIPC members pay assessments into a general insurance fund that is used to meet customer claims in the event of a broker-dealer bankruptcy.

TAKE NOTE

All broker-/dealers registered with the SEC must be SIPC members except:

■   banks that deal exclusively in municipal securities;

■   firms that deal exclusively in U.S. government securities; and

■   firms that deal exclusively in redeemable investment company securities.

If the SEC or any self-regulatory organization (SRO) finds indications that a broker-dealer is in financial difficulty, SIPC will be notified immediately. If SIPC determines that the member has failed or is in imminent danger of failing, it may petition a federal court to take action by appointing a trustee to liquidate the firm and protect its customers. A customer can be broadly defined as anyone who has cash or securities in the possession of a broker-dealer.

The court, upon receipt of SIPC's petition, will issue a protective decree if the broker-dealer is, in fact, insolvent and will then promptly appoint a trustee for the liquidation of the broker-dealer's business.

Once a trustee has been appointed, the member firm is prohibited from engaging in business as a broker-dealer. It also is prohibited from attempting to conceal assets, file false statements, or alter securities records to defraud the trustee or SIPC.

1. 1. 3. 4. 1   SIPC Coverage and Disclosures

The basic coverage under SIPC is no more than $500,000 per separate customer, not per separate account. Of that $500,000 total, SIPC covers no more than $250,000 in cash. How an account is titled will determine if it represents a separate customer.

Sample SIPC Customer Coverage Limits

Examples of Customer Coverage Limits	
John Doe—cash account John Doe—margin account	1 customer = $500,000 coverage
John and Mary Doe— joint account	1 customer = $500,000 coverage
John Doe as custodian for Jane Doe	1 customer = $500,000 coverage

TAKE NOTE

Cash and margin accounts for the same customer are combined for the purposes of determining SIPC coverage. However, only the equity in a margin account is covered, not the full market value.

If a broker-dealer fails, any customer with claims in excess of SIPC coverage limits becomes a general creditor of the broker-dealer for the uncovered amount. It should also be noted here that commodities and commodities futures contracts are not covered by SIPC, nor are futures contracts or losses related to currencies, because they are not considered securities.

Regarding disclosures, broker-dealers must include their SIPC membership on all advertising but may not imply that SIPC coverage is more than it actually is or that its benefits are unique to only that broker-dealer. The term *SIPC* may not appear larger than the firm's own name. Also, all member firms must post a sign on its premises that indicates SIPC membership.

In addition, SIPC members must provide written disclosure to customers that they may obtain information about SIPC, including the SIPC brochure, by contacting SIPC. This disclosure must be made to new customers at the time an account is opened and to all customers at least once each year thereafter.

1. 1. 3. 5   Federal Deposit Insurance Corporation (FDIC)

Created during the Great Depression of the 1930s in response to widespread bank failures and massive losses to bank customers, the **Federal Deposit Insurance Corporation** (FDIC) is an independent agency of the United States federal government that preserves public confidence in the banking system by insuring deposits. The funds for the agency are provided in the same way as the funds for a private insurance company, premiums are paid by all participating institutions.

In the event of the failure of a member financial institution, the FDIC may do any of several things. Usually, customer deposits and loans of the failed institution are sold to another institution, and in this way the depositors become customers of the new institution.

The FDIC provides deposit insurance guaranteeing the safety of a depositor's accounts in member banks up to $250,000 for each deposit ownership category in each insured bank.

EXAMPLE
Mr. Jones has $200,000 deposited with an FDIC member bank. Mr. and Mrs. Jones have $450,000 deposited in a joint account at the same bank. Titled differently, each of these accounts is recognized as a separate account and each is entitled to FDIC insurance. If the bank were to fail, Mr. Jones's account would be covered in full and the joint account titled Mr. and Mrs. Jones would be covered up to the $250,000 maximum.

The FDIC covers the traditional types of bank deposit accounts including checking and savings accounts, money market deposit accounts and certificates of deposit (CDs) and self-directed IRA accounts. Investment products that are not deposits, such as mutual funds, annuities, life insurance policies, and stocks and bonds are not covered by FDIC deposit insurance.

1. 1. 4 MARKET PARTICIPANTS AND THEIR ROLES

In the following sections we will briefly discuss the different market participants, their roles in securities industry, and how they may interact.

1. 1. 4. 1 Investors

An investor is someone who provides money or resources for an enterprise, such as a corporation, with the expectation of financial or other gain. Investors can be categorized in different ways.

A **retail investor** is an individual who makes investments such as the purchase of securities for his or her own personal account rather than for an organization.

An **institutional investor** is an entity that pools money to purchase securities and other investment assets. *Institutional investors* can include banks, insurance companies, pensions, hedge funds, and mutual funds.

An **accredited investor** is defined as one who:

- has a net worth of $1 million or more, not including net equity in a primary residence; or
- has had an annual income of $200,000 or more in each of the two most recent years (or $300,000 jointly with a spouse) and who has a reasonable expectation of reaching the same income level during the current year.

Officers and directors of an issuer of securities are also considered accredited.

1. 1. 4. 2 Broker-Dealers

Each member firm broker-dealer operates under an individualized membership agreement with FINRA or other self-regulatory organization (SRO). The membership agreement explains what lines of business the broker-dealer undertakes. Some broker-dealers are referred to as full service BDs offering all types of investment products, such as stocks, bonds, mutual funds, options and many others, while some limit the products they offer to only a few. BDs can also incorporate proprietary trading, that is to trade in the account of the BD known as market making into their business model, and there are some who only make markets choosing not to deal with or accommodate customer retail accounts.

1. 1. 4. 2. 1   Carrying Firms (Clearing)

A **carrying firm** carries customer accounts and accepts funds and securities from customers. Carrying and clearing firms typically rank among the larger broker-dealers. They have the capability to do trade executions, clear and settle transactions, take custody of customer funds and securities, and handle all back office tasks such as sending trade confirmations and statements.

A firm carrying customer funds and securities clearly has a line of business that is inherently risky, and it is required to maintain levels of net capital higher than that of firms who do not accept custody of funds or securities.

TAKE NOTE

Carrying firms must segregate customer funds and securities held in their custody from the firm's capital and securities.

1. 1. 4. 2. 2   Introducing Firms (Fully Disclosed Firms)

A **fully disclosed firm**, or **introducing BD**, is one that introduces its customers to a clearing firm. The clearing firm holds funds and securities of the introducing firm's customers and performs related functions, such as sending confirmations and statements for its correspondent firms. Essentially, the clearing firm acts as the introducing firm's back office. Because the risk associated with holding customer funds and securities is not present, net capital requirements are lower for introducing BDs than they are for self-clearing or carrying BDs.

TAKE NOTE

An introducing firm may receive customer checks, but they must be made out to the clearing firm.

EXAMPLE

Firms sometimes referred to as "full service" firms, are carrying or clearing firms who clear their own transactions. Smaller regional BDs are typically introducing or fully disclosed firms who introduce their transactions to larger carrying firms in order to clear their transactions. In other words, firms like Merrill Lynch, in addition to clearing to their own transactions, may accept transactions from other smaller, fully disclosed firms, and in so doing so, are acting as the smaller firms' clearing firm.

1. 1. 4. 2. 3   Prime Brokers

To understand a prime broker's role you must first understand what a prime account is. This type of account allows a customer—generally an institution—to select one member firm (the prime broker) to provide custody and other services, while other firms—called executing brokers—handle all trades placed by the customer.

To open a prime brokerage account for a customer, a member (the prime broker) must sign an agreement with the customer, spelling out the terms of the agreement as well as names of all executing brokers the customer has contracted with. The prime broker will then enter into written agreements with each executing broker named by the customer. The customer receives trade confirmations and account statements from the prime broker, who facilitates the clearance and settlement of the securities transactions. Responsibility for compliance of certain trading rules rests with the executing brokers.

The key advantage of a prime brokerage account is that it usually provides a client with the ability to trade with multiple brokerage houses while maintaining a centralized master account with all of the client's cash and securities. A prime brokerage account often includes a list of specialized services, such as securities lending, margin financing, trade processing, cash management, and operational support. Prime brokerage accounts are likely to be offered to a broker-dealer's more active trading clients, such as hedge funds, who may require a number of executing broker outlets to conduct their transactions and who can benefit by having margin requirements that are netted across all of the prime broker's positions.

1. 1. 4. 3 Investment Advisers

Anyone who, as part of his or her business, gives investment advice for compensation, must register as an investment adviser under the Investment Advisers Act of 1940. Broker-dealers who provide advice for a fee are subject to registration under this act. Agents of investment advisers must register and pass the Series 65 exam or Series 66 exam (for representatives with a Series 7). Providing advice and not charging separately for it (i.e., acting as a registered representative) does not require registration as an adviser.

EXAMPLE   A registered representative who is registered under the Securities Act of 1934 and has been charging commissions for transactions now wants to charge separately for investment advice regardless of whether a transaction takes place or not. In order to do so, even though already registered under the Act of 1934, the RR would now need to register under the Investment Advisors Act of 1940 by passing the appropriate exam (Series 65 or 66).

1. 1. 4. 4 Municipal Advisors

A municipal advisor is a person who:

■ provides advice to or on behalf of a municipal entity with respect to municipal products or the issuance of municipal securities, including advice with respect to the structure, timing, terms, and other similar matters concerning such financial products or issues; or

■ undertakes a solicitation of a municipal entity.

1. 1. 4. 5 Issuers and Underwriters

An entity, such as a corporation or municipality, might offer or proposes to offer its securities for sale to the investing public for the purpose of raising capital. These entities are known as issuers of securities. Underwriters are groups of broker-dealers or investment bankers that work with an issuer to bring its securities to the market and sell them to the investing public.

1. 1. 4. 6   Traders and Market Makers

Any entity, individual or institution, willing to accept the risk of holding a particular security in its own account to facilitate trading and provide liquidity in that security is known as a market maker or trader. Market makers generally stand ready to buy or sell (make markets) in securities with the ultimate goal of being profitable.

1. 1. 4. 7   Custodians and trustees

An institution or a person responsible for making all investment, management, and distribution decisions in an account maintained in the best interests of another is known as a custodian. One example would be the custodian for the account of a minor.

By contrast, a trustee is an institution or a person responsible for making all investment, management, and distribution decisions in an account maintained in the best interests of another who has been legally appointed to do so. An example would be the fiduciary appointed to manage assets in a trust.

1. 1. 4. 8   Transfer agents

The transfer and registration of stock certificates are two distinct functions that, by law, cannot be performed by a single person or department operating within the same institution. Issuers typically use commercial banks and trust companies to handle these functions. The transfer agent for a corporation is responsible for:

■ ensuring that its securities are issued in the correct owner's name;

■ canceling old and issuing new certificates;

■ maintaining records of ownership; and

■ handling problems relating to lost, stolen, or destroyed certificates.

1. 1. 4. 9   Depositories and Clearing Corporations

A clearing agency is an intermediary between the buy and sell sides of a transaction. The clearing agency receives and delivers payments and securities on behalf of both parties. Any organization that fulfils this function, including a securities depository, is considered a clearing agency. Conceptually, this is similar to the way a bank clears checks between two parties.

In addition to broker-dealers, commercial banks can act as clearing agencies and depositories as well as corporations that are set up for the purpose of clearing securities transactions and taking custody of funds and securities. Among them are the National Securities Clearing Corporation (NSCC) and securities depositories such as the Depository Trust and Clearing Company (DTCC). DTCC is the world's largest securities depository. It provides custody services for virtually all securities except those subject to transfer or ownership restrictions, which are known as "restricted" securities.

TAKE NOTE

The Depository Trust and Clearing Company (DTCC) is a member of the Federal Reserve System. Not in the retail banking business (one can't open a savings or checking account there), it exists to serve the custody needs of security industry participants not only in the United States but in more than 60 countries worldwide.

Another is the Options Clearing Corporation (OCC). OCC is the clearing agent for listed options contracts; that is those listed for trading on U.S. options exchanges. Its primary functions are to standardize, guarantee the performance of, and issue option contracts. The OCC determines when new option contracts should be offered to the market on an underlying security. It designates the contract specifications such as strike prices and expiration months for new contracts utilizing standards to maintain uniformity and liquidity.

QUICK QUIZ 1.A

LEARNING OBJECTIVES

■ Define the roles of the regulatory agencies

■ Differentiate between the different types of market participants

1. The federal regulatory body that governs the securities industry is the

A. Financial Industry Regulatory Authority
B. Securities and Exchange Commission
C. NYSE
D. Federal Reserve Board

2. A fully disclosed broker-dealer

A. self clears the transactions of their customers
B. is known as a clearing agent
C. is like the Depository Trust Company in that it can take custody of funds and securities
D. is an introducing firm clearing its transactions through a carrying firm

3. An intermediary between the buy and sell sides of a transaction is known as a

A. custodian
B. transfer agent
C. clearing agent
D. depository

4. For the Depository Trust and Clearing Company (DTCC) all of the following are true EXCEPT

A. It is a member of the Federal Reserve System.
B. It acts as a retail bank servicing savings and checking accounts
C. It serves for the purpose of providing custody of securities
D. It is a worldwide clearing agent

5. Your broker-dealer acts as a prime broker for an institutional account. In this arrangement, your broker-dealer is likely to be providing which of the following services?

A. Execution of all transactions
B. Maintenance of a trading floor operation on an exchange
C. Ensuring that all exchange-trading rules are complied with
D. Clearing and transaction settlement services for executing brokers

6. An individual or institution willing to hold securities positions in its own proprietary account for the purpose of providing liquidity to the marketplace is a
   A. market maker
   B. broker
   C. trustee
   D. custodian

7. An entity such as a corporation wishing to offer securities for sale to the public for the purpose of raising capital is
   A. an underwriter
   B. an issuer
   C. a trustee
   D. a transfer agent

8. A nonprofit organization requiring members to pay assessments into a general insurance fund used to meet customer claims in the event of a broker-dealer bankruptcy is
   A. SEC
   B. DTCC
   C. FDIC
   D. SIPC

9. The Federal Deposit Insurance Corporation (FDIC) provides insurance guaranteeing the safety of a depositor's accounts in FDIC member banks for each deposit up to
   A. $150,000
   B. $200,000
   C. $250,000
   D. $500,000

10. Determining monetary policy and taking actions to implement those policies is the responsibility of
    A. Federal Reserve Board (FRB)
    B. Depository Trust and Clearing Corporation (DTCC)
    C. Internal Revenue Service (IRS)
    D. Securities Investors Protection Corporation (SIPC)

1. 2 MARKET STRUCTURE

LEARNING OBJECTIVES:
■ Differentiate between market types

The term **market** is used to describe any physical place or electronic venue where buyers and sellers can come together for the purpose of trading assets. Markets can be found in nearly every nation in the world and while some are small, such as local farmer's markets, others like stock exchanges have billions of dollars in transactions daily.

1. 2. 1 TYPES OF MARKETS

A number of different assets such as equities (stocks), bonds, currencies, and derivative products like options can be offered and traded in the financial markets. Financial markets can be expected to have transparent pricing, basic regulations on how trading is to be conducted, costs and fees, and prices of securities determined by market forces such as supply and demand.

1. 2. 1. 1 Capital Markets

Capital markets are broadly defined as the stock and bond markets. In capital markets, both public and private sectors sell securities in order to raise funds. Consider that government entities like states and other municipalities and corporations require funding to finance their operations and to engage in their own short- and long-term initiatives. To do this, a company, for example, can raise capital through the sale of securities such as stocks and bonds issued in the company's name. These can be bought and sold (traded) in the capital markets by individuals and institutions alike.

1. 2. 1. 2 Primary and Secondary Markets

The primary market is where securities are sold to the investing public in what are known as issuer transactions. In other words, the issuer of the securities receives the proceeds generated by the sale of the securities. By contrast, the secondary markets are where securities trade between investors. Secondary market transactions have one investor selling securities to another, and the issuer is not involved in the transaction. Stock exchanges are an example of a secondary market, where investors buy securities from and sell securities to each other throughout the trading day.

1. 2. 1. 3 Third Market

The third market, or Nasdaq Intermarket, is a trading market in which exchange-listed-securities are traded in the OTC market. Broker-dealers registered as OTC market makers in listed securities can do transactions in the third market. All securities listed on the NYSE and most securities listed on the regional exchanges are eligible for OTC trading as long as the trades are reported to the Consolidated Tape within 10 seconds of execution.

1. 2. 1. 4 Fourth Market

The fourth market is a market for institutional investors in which large blocks of stock, both listed and unlisted, trade in transactions unassisted by broker-dealers. These transactions take place through electronic communications networks (ECNs). ECNs are open 24 hours a day and act solely as agents.

QUICK QUIZ 1.B

LEARNING OBJECTIVES
- Differentiate between market types

1. Magnolia Steel Corporation needs to build a refinery plant. It is estimated to cost $750 million to complete. What market can be used to raise the money needed to build the new plant?
   A. Currency market
   B. Capital market
   C. Secondary market
   D. Money market

2. When securities are sold to the investing public in what are known as issuer transactions the transactions are being done in the
   A. primary market
   B. secondary market
   C. third market
   D. fourth market

3. If an investment company bought stock directly from a bank bypassing any intermediary or broker, this trade took place in which of the following markets?
   A. Primary
   B. Secondary
   C. Third.
   D. Fourth

4. Which of the following statements regarding the third market is TRUE?
   A. It refers to the trading of unlisted stocks directly between institutional investors.
   B. The services of a broker acting as an agent or intermediary are not used.
   C. It is composed of listed securities traded OTC.
   D. It is composed only of unlisted securities.

5. An investor enters an order to purchase shares of XYZ stock. Another investor enters an order to sell XYZ stock. These two orders meet on the floor of a U.S. stock exchange where they are executed. This transaction took place in the
   A. OTC market
   B. new issues market
   C. primary market
   D. secondary market

1. 3   ECONOMIC FACTORS

LEARNING OBJECTIVES:
- Interpret factors impacting the securities market

- Identify the components of the business and economic cycles

- Relate actions taken by the Federal Reserve Board to the securities market

A number of factors can impact the prices of individual securities and thus the securities markets as a whole. Simple concepts like supply and demand affect the prices of company's products and also the prices of their equity and debt securities.

The economic climate has both an enormous effect on the conditions of individual companies and, therefore, the securities markets. In addition to a company's earnings and business prospects, any changes in business cycles, the money supply, and Federal Reserve Board (FRB) actions affect securities prices and trading and the markets at large.

Finally, economic conditions abroad can influence the conditions domestically and, in turn, will also impact our securities markets. In the following sections, we will explore some of these factors.

1. 3. 1   THE FEDERAL RESERVE BOARD'S IMPACT ON BUSINESS ACTIVITY AND MARKET STABILITY

The FRB affects the money supply through its use of three policy tools:

- Open-market operations (buying/selling government securities)
- Changes in the discount rate (on loans to member banks)
- Changes in reserve requirements

In the following sections, we'll compare monetary policies (engaged in by the FRB) with fiscal policy (engaged in by our president and Congress), look at the open market activities of the FRB and finally discuss key interest rates.

1. 3. 1. 1   Monetary vs. Fiscal Policy

Two distinctive types of policies impact our economy—monetary and fiscal. Monetary policy is what the FRB engages in when it attempts to influence the money supply. The money supply is the capital available to be lent to consumers and ultimately spent in the economy. Fiscal policy refers to governmental budget decisions enacted by our President and Congress including increases or decreases in:

- federal spending
- money raised through taxes; and
- federal budget deficits or surpluses.

Fiscal policy is based on the assumption that the government can control such economic forces as unemployment levels and inflation by adjusting overall demand for goods and services.

Because the political process determines fiscal policy, it takes time for conditions and solutions to be identified and implemented. Due to the length of time it may take to enact fiscal policy decisions, fiscal policy is not considered the most efficient means to solve short-term economic problems.

TAKE NOTE   Monetary policies are those enacted by the FRB to influence the money supply. Fiscal policies are those enacted by our president and Congress such as tax laws and federal spending appropriations.

1. 3. 1. 1. 1   The Money Supply

Most people think of money as cash in their pockets. An economist takes a much broader view and includes loans, credit, and other liquid instruments. Economists divide money into three categories, as shown here.

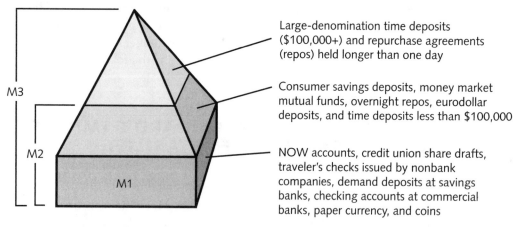

Large-denomination time deposits ($100,000+) and repurchase agreements (repos) held longer than one day

Consumer savings deposits, money market mutual funds, overnight repos, eurodollar deposits, and time deposits less than $100,000

NOW accounts, credit union share drafts, traveler's checks issued by nonbank companies, demand deposits at savings banks, checking accounts at commercial banks, paper currency, and coins

M1. The most readily available type of money, M1, consists of currency in circulation and demand deposits (checking accounts) that can be converted to currency immediately. It is the money that consumers use for ordinary purchases of goods and services. Most money (M1) is in demand deposits—that is, checking accounts. M1 is the largest and most liquid component of the money supply.

M2. In addition to M1, M2 includes some time deposits (less than $100,000) that are fairly easy to convert into demand deposits. These time deposits include savings accounts, nonnegotiable CDs, money market funds, and overnight repurchase agreements.

M3. In addition to M1 and M2, M3 includes time deposits of more than $100,000 and repurchase agreements with terms longer than one day.

1. 3. 1. 2   Open Market Activities and Impact on Economy

The Federal Reserve Board, acting as an agent for the U.S. Treasury Department, influences the money supply by buying and selling U.S. government securities (treasury bills, notes, and bonds) in the open market. These actions will expand or contract the money supply depending on which they are doing (buying or selling). The **Federal Open Market Committee** (FOMC) meets regularly to direct the government's open-market operations.

When the FOMC buys securities, it increases the supply of money in the banking system, and when it sells securities, it decreases the supply.

When the Fed wants to expand (loosen) the money supply, it buys securities from banks. The securities come out of the economy and the money goes into the economy as a direct credit in the respective banking institutions reserve accounts. The increase of reserves allows banks to make more loans and effectively lowers interest rates. Thus, by buying securities, the Fed pumps money into the banking system, expanding the money supply and reducing rates.

When the Fed wants to contract (tighten) the money supply, it sells securities to banks. Now cash comes out of the respective banks and the securities go in as each sale is charged against a bank's reserve balance. This reduces the bank's ability to lend money, which tightens credit and effectively raises interest rates. By selling securities, the Fed pulls money out of the system, contracting the money supply and increasing rates.

FRB buying or selling securities in the open market and its impact on the economy: BUYING—securities come out of the economy and money goes in. Money supply goes up, interest rates down, borrowing and spending for consumers is easier and the economy *expands*.

SELLING—securities go into the economy and money comes out. Money supply goes down, interest rates go up, borrowing and spending for consumers becomes more difficult and the economy *contracts*.

1. 3. 1. 3 Interest Rates

The cost of doing business is closely linked to the cost of money; the cost of money is called **interest**. In large measure, the supply and demand of money determines the rate of interest that must be paid to borrow it. When the money available for loans exceeds demand, interest rates fall and when the demand for money exceeds the supply, interest rates rise. The level of a specific interest rate can be tied to one or more benchmark rates, such as the federal funds rate, the prime rate, the discount rate, and the broker loan rate. Let's look at each of these now.

1. 3. 1. 3. 1 Federal Funds Rate

The **federal funds rate** is the rate the commercial money center banks charge each other for overnight loans of $1 million or more. It is considered a barometer of the direction of short-term interest rates, which fluctuate constantly and can be considered the most volatile rate in the economy.

1. 3. 1. 3. 2 Discount Rate

The **discount rate** is the rate the Federal Reserve charges for short-term loans to member banks. The discount rate also indicates the direction of FRB monetary policy: a decreasing rate indicates an easing of FRB policy; an increasing rate indicates a tightening of FRB policy.

EXAMPLE

If the FRB wants to ease its monetary policy to allow consumers to borrow more easily it can lower the discount rate. This allows member banks to borrow from the FRB at a lower rate, which in turn allows consumers to borrow money at a lower rate from the member banks. Consumers' ability to borrow at lower interest rates helps to fuel or push the economy forward as they are now in a position to purchase more goods and services.

Federal Reserve Policy Tactics

To expand credit during a recession to stimulate a slow economy:	To tighten credit to slow economic expansion and prevent inflation:
■ Buy U.S. government securities in the open market	■ Sell U.S. government securities in the open market
■ Lower the discount rate	■ Raise the discount rate
■ Lower reserve requirements	■ Raise reserve requirements

1. 3. 1. 3. 3   Prime Rate

The **prime rate** is the interest rate that large U.S. money center commercial banks charge their most creditworthy corporate borrowers for unsecured loans. Each bank sets its own prime rate, with larger banks generally setting a rate other banks use or follow. Banks lower their prime rates when the Federal Reserve Board (FRB or Fed) eases the money supply, and they raise rates when the Fed contracts the money supply.

1. 3. 1. 3. 4   Broker Loan Rate (Call Loan Rate)

The **broker loan rate is** the interest rate banks charge broker-dealers on money they borrow to lend to margin account customers. Margin accounts allow customers to purchase securities without paying in full. The amount not paid is essentially loaned to the customer by banks and broker-dealers. The broker loan rate is also known as the **call loan rate** or **call money rate**. The broker loan rate usually is a percentage point or so above other short-term rates. Broker call loans are callable on 24-hour notice.

TAKE NOTE

When a bank needs to borrow money, it can borrow from the Federal Reserve Bank, or it can borrow from another member bank like itself:

- Borrowing from the FRB: banks pay the *discount* rate

- Borrowing from another member bank: banks pay the *federal funds* rate

1. 3. 2   BUSINESS ECONOMIC FACTORS

In the normal course of events, some industries or corporations prosper as others fail. So, to determine the economy's overall direction, economists consider many aspects of business activity.

1. 3. 2. 1   Financial Statements

A corporation's **financial statements** provide a fundamental analyst with the raw material needed to assess that corporation's profitability, financial strength, and operating efficiency. By examining how certain static numbers from the statement relate to one another and how the resulting ratios relate to the company's competitors, the analyst can determine how financially viable the company is.

Companies issue quarterly and annual financial reports that include a balance sheet and income statement to their stockholders.

1. 3. 2. 1. 1   Balance Sheet

The **balance sheet** provides a snapshot of a company's financial position at a specific time. It identifies the value of the company's assets (what it owns) and its liabilities (what it owes). The difference between these two figures is the corporation's **equity**, or **net worth**.

A corporation can be compared to a homeowner who borrows money to buy a home. The homeowner's equity is the difference between the mortgage balance (liability) and the home's market value (asset value). A corporation can buy assets using borrowed money (liabilities) and equity raised by selling stock. The value of its assets must equal (balance with) the value of its liabilities and equity.

Although it is useful in determining a company's current value, the balance sheet cannot tell the analyst whether the company's business is improving or deteriorating.

The Balance Sheet Equation

| **Assets**
Current assets
Fixed assets
Other assets | **Liabilities**
Current liabilities
Long-term debt

Equity (net worth)
Preferred stock
Common stock
Additional paid-in capital
Treasury stock
Retained earnings |

TAKE NOTE

The basic balance sheet equation can be expressed in two ways:

Assets – liabilities = net worth

Assets = liabilities + net worth

1. 3. 2. 1. 2   Income Statement

The income statement summarizes a corporation's revenues and expenses for a fiscal period, usually quarterly, year-to-date, or the full year. It compares revenue with costs and expenses during the period.

Fundamental analysts use the income statement to judge the efficiency of a company's operation and its profitability.

Income Statement Entries

Net Sales

–	Cost of goods sold (COGS)
–	Operating costs (including depreciation)
=	Operating profit
+	Nonoperating income
=	Operating income (earnings before interest and taxes)
–	Interest expenses
=	Taxable income (pre-tax income)
–	Taxes
=	Net income after taxes
–	Preferred dividends
=	Earnings available to common
–	Common dividends
=	Retained earnings

1. 3. 2. 2   Business Cycles

Throughout history, periods of economic expansion have been followed by periods of economic contraction in a pattern referred to as the **business cycle**.

Business cycles go through four stages:

- Expansion
- Peak
- Contraction
- Trough

Expansion is characterized by increased business activity—increasing sales, manufacturing, and wages—throughout the economy. For a variety of reasons, an economy can expand for only so long; when it reaches its upper limit, it has reached its peak. When business activity declines from its peak, the economy is **contracting**. Economists call mild, short-term contractions **recessions**. Longer, more severe contractions are **depressions**. When business activity stops declining and levels off, it is known as a **trough**.

According to the U.S. Commerce Department, the economy is in a recession when a decline in real output of goods and services—the gross domestic product (GDP)—lasts for six months or more. It defines a depression as a severe downturn lasting for six quarters (18 months) or more.

The Four Stages of the Business Cycle

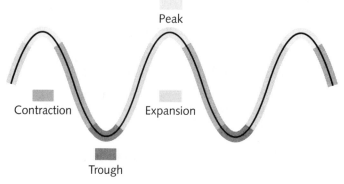

Expansions are characterized by:

- increased consumer demand for goods and services;
- increases in industrial production;
- rising stock prices;
- rising property values; and
- increasing gross domestic product.

Downturns in the business cycle tend to be characterized by:

- rising numbers of bankruptcies and bond defaults;
- higher consumer debt;
- falling stock prices;
- rising inventories (a sign of slackening consumer demand in hard times); and
- decreasing gross domestic product.

Finally, remember that while some investments, like stocks, tend to move with the economic cycles, there are investments, such as precious metals (e.g., gold), that historically have been counter cyclical.

1. 3. 2. 3   Indicators and Measures

Certain aspects of economic activity serve as barometers, or **indicators**, of business cycle phases. Additionally, there are specific measures like inflation that can be used to gauge our economy. These issues will be discussed next.

1. 3. 2. 3. 1   Leading Indicators

Leading indicators are spot checks of business activity that reliably predict trends in the economy. Positive changes in these indicators predict economic improvement. Negative changes predict economic contraction.

Leading indicators used most often include:

- money supply (M2);
- building permits (housing starts);
- average weekly initial claims for state unemployment compensation;
- average work week in manufacturing;
- new orders for consumer goods;
- machine tool orders;
- changes in inventories of durable goods;
- changes in sensitive materials prices;
- stock prices; and
- changes in business and consumer borrowing.

1. 3. 2. 3. 2   Coincident Indicators

Leading indicators reflect where the economy is going; coincident indicators confirm where it is. Coincident indicators are those measurable factors that vary directly and simultaneously with the business cycle. Widely used coincident indicators include:

- number of hours worked (as a proxy for personal income);
- employment levels;
- nonagricultural employment;
- personal income;
- industrial production;
- manufacturing and trade sales; and
- GDP.

1. 3. 2. 3. 3   Lagging Indicators

Lagging indicators are those factors that change after the economy has begun a new trend but serve as confirmation of the new trend. Lagging indicators help analysts differentiate long-term trends from short-term reversals that occur in any trend. Lagging indicators include:

- corporate profits;
- average duration of unemployment;
- labor cost per unit of output (manufacturing);
- ratio of inventories to sales;
- commercial and industrial loans outstanding; and
- ratio of consumer installment credit to personal income.

1. 3. 2. 3. 4 Inflation

Inflation is a general increase in prices. Mild inflation can encourage economic growth because gradually increasing prices tend to stimulate business investments. High inflation reduces a dollar's buying power, which hurts the economy.

1. 3. 2. 3. 5 Deflation

Deflation is a general decline in prices. Deflation usually occurs during severe recessions when unemployment is on the rise.

1. 3. 2. 3. 6 Stagnation

Economic stagnation refers to prolonged periods of slow or little economic growth, accompanied by high unemployment.

1. 3. 2. 3. 7 Stagflation

Stagflation is the term used to describe the unusual combination of inflation (a rise in prices) and high unemployment (stagnation). This generally occurs when the economy isn't growing and there is a lack of consumer demand and business activity, but prices for goods are still rising.

1. 3. 2. 4 Basic Effects on Bond and Equity Markets

Because business cycle phases have different effects on different industries, fundamental analysts look for companies in industries that offer better-than-average opportunities in the context of the business cycle. It is useful to distinguish between the four types of industries and investments: defensive, cyclical, growth, and special situation.

1. 3. 2. 4. 1 Defensive Industries

Defensive industries are least affected by normal business cycles. Companies in defensive industries generally produce nondurable consumer goods, such as food, pharmaceuticals, and tobacco, or supply essential services such as utility companies. Public consumption of such goods remains fairly steady throughout the business cycle. During recessions and bear markets, stocks in defensive industries generally decline less than stocks in other industries, but during expansions and bull markets, defensive stocks may advance less. Investments in defensive industries tend to involve less risk and, consequently, lower investment returns.

1. 3. 2. 4. 2 Cyclical Industries

Cyclical industries are highly sensitive to business cycles and inflation trends. Most cyclical industries produce durable goods, such as heavy machinery, and raw materials, such as steel and automobiles. During recessions, the demand for such products declines as manufacturers postpone investments in new capital goods and consumers postpone purchases of these goods, such as automobiles. Counter-cyclical industries, on the other hand, tend to turn down as the economy heats up and to rise when the economy turns down.

1. 3. 2. 4. 3 Growth Industries

Every industry passes through four phases during its existence: introduction, growth, maturity, and decline. An industry is considered in its **growth phase** if the industry is growing faster than the economy as a whole, because of technological changes, new products, or changing consumer tastes. Computers and bioengineering are current growth industries. Because many growth companies retain nearly all of their earnings to finance their business expansion, growth stocks usually pay little or no dividends.

1. 3. 2. 4. 4 Special Situation Stocks

Special situation stocks are stocks of a company with unusual profit potential resulting from nonrecurring circumstances. These situations might include new management, the discovery of a valuable natural resource on corporate property, patents pending, or the introduction of a new product.

1. 3. 2. 5 Principal Economic Theories

There are a number of different economic theories regarding how the economy should be viewed and how it should be impacted by government. Following, we'll explore three: Keynesian, Monetarist, and Supply-Side.

1. 3. 2. 5. 1 Keynesian Theory

The economist John Maynard Keynes held that active government involvement in the economy was vital to the health and stability of a nation's economy. Keynesians believe that demand for goods ultimately controls employment and prices. Insufficient demand for goods causes unemployment; too much demand causes inflation. Keynes believed it was the government's right and responsibility to manipulate overall demand (and therefore artificially manipulate the economy) by changing its own levels of spending and taxation.

According to Keynes, a government's fiscal policies determine the country's economic health. Fiscal policy involves adjusting the level of taxation and government spending. The government is expected to intervene in the economy as a major force in creating prosperity by engaging in activities that affect aggregate demand.

Government affects individual levels of spending and saving by adjusting taxes. Increasing taxes removes money from the private sector, which reduces private sector demand and spending. Government spending puts money back into the economy. To increase private sector demand for goods, the government reduces taxes, which increases people's disposable income.

1. 3. 2. 5. 2 Monetarist Theory

Milton Friedman is considered the originator of **monetarist economic theory**. Monetarists believe the quantity of money, the **money supply**, is the major determinant of price levels. Too many dollars chasing too few goods leads to inflation; conversely, too few dollars chasing too many goods leads to deflation.

Monetarists believe a well-controlled, moderately increasing money supply leads to price stability. Price stability allows business managers (considered to be more efficient allocators of resources than the government) to plan and invest, which in turn keeps the economy healthy.

Monetary economic policy is controlled by the Federal Reserve Board. Monetarists believe that the amount of money in the system is the major influence on economic performance. The reserve requirement, discount rate, and open market operations are the tools used by monetarists to regulate the economy.

1. 3. 2. 5. 3   Supply-Side Economic Theory

Supply-side economics holds that government should allow market forces to determine prices of all goods. Supply-siders believe the federal government should reduce government spending as well as taxes. In this way, sellers of goods will price them at a rate that allows them to meet market demand and still sell them profitably.

1. 3. 3   INTERNATIONAL ECONOMIC FACTORS

A number of factors outside the United States can have immediate and prolonged impact on our securities and trade markets, and thus our domestic economy. For instance, countries that are in debt to us but show signs of being unable to pay can send our financial markets into disarray. The flow of money between the United States and other countries is known as the **balance of payments**.

1. 3. 3. 1   U.S. Balance of Payments

The balance of payments may be a **surplus** (more money flowing into the country than out) or a **deficit** (more money flowing out of the country than in). A deficit may occur when interest rates in another country are high because money flows to where it earns the highest return.

The largest component of the balance of payments is the **balance of trade**—the export and import of goods and services.

On the U.S. credit side are sales of American products to foreign countries. In other words, if the United States is selling more goods to foreign countries (exporting) than our consumers are importing, we will have more money coming in than going out. This ultimately leads to a surplus. On the debit side are American purchases of foreign goods (importing) that cause American dollars to flow out of the country. This will ultimately lead to a deficit.

TAKE NOTE

When debits exceed credits, a deficit in the balance of payments occurs; when credits exceed debits, a surplus exists.

1. 3. 3. 2   Gross Domestic Product (GDP) and Gross National Product (GNP)

A nation's annual economic output, all of the goods and services produced within the nation, is known as its gross domestic product (GDP). The United States' GDP includes personal consumption, government spending, gross private investment, foreign investment, and net exports.

GDP is place based, whereas GNP is ownership based. Thus, if a foreigner creates a company in the U.S., this will count as GDP, but not GNP. Conversely, if a U.S. company opens a new plant abroad, this investment will be included in GNP, but not GDP.

1. 3. 3. 3   Exchange Rates

The value of one currency against another is known as the exchange rate. If the dollar is weak, foreign currency buys more U.S. goods, so exports increase.

Therefore, the value of the U.S. dollar against foreign currencies affects the balance of trade. More money flows into the United States—surplus. When the dollar is strong, foreign currency buys fewer U.S. goods. The dollar buys more foreign goods, so imports increase. More money flows out of the United States—deficit.

QUICK QUIZ 1.C

LEARNING OBJECTIVES

■ Interpret factors impacting the securities market

■ Identify the components of the business and economic cycles

■ Relate actions taken by the Federal Reserve Board to the securities market

1. Assuming all other factors to remain constant, an increase in imports would most likely cause GDP to

   A. increase
   B. decrease
   C. initially increase and then decrease
   D. remain the same

2. Which state of the business cycle is characterized by rising interest rates and higher wages?

   A. Contraction
   B. Expansion
   C. Recession
   D. Trough

3. An economic environment with little or no economic growth, but where inflation is present, is best described as

   A. Deflation
   B. Depression
   C. Stagflation
   D. Stagnation

4. It is generally agreed that the two primary policies impacting the U.S. economy are fiscal and monetary. Which of the following would be considered tools of fiscal policy?

   I. Government spending
   II. Operations of the FOMC
   III. Changing the reserve requirements
   IV. Taxation
   A. I and III
   B. I and IV
   C. II and III
   D. II and IV

5. Which of the following is added to M2 to arrive at M3?

   A. $100,000 and larger time deposits
   B. Currency in circulation
   C. Checking accounts
   D. Gold and silver bars in bank storage vaults

6. Which of the following actions of the FRB would likely have the effect of causing interest rates to increase?

   I. The FOMC buying securities
   II. Raising the reserve requirements
   III. Raising the discount rate
   IV. Raising the prime rate

   A. I and II
   B. II and III
   C. II and IV
   D. III and IV

7. Economic data shows that the gross domestic product (GDP) has been declining steadily over the past 2 quarters. This would suggest Recession is 6 consecutive months of economic decline. Depression is 6 consecutive quarters of economic decline.

   A. expansion.
   B. inflation.
   C. a depression.
   D. a recession.

8. All of the following would be considered a defensive industry security EXCEPT

   A. Tobacco stock.
   B. Food chain stock.
   C. Steel company stock.
   D. Utility company stock.

9. Which of the following would be a leading economic indicator?

   A. S&P 500 index.
   B. Industrial production.
   C. Duration of unemployment.
   D. Gross domestic product (GDP).

10. When a government actively manipulates the economy through tax and spending policies this is referred to as

    A. supply and demand economics.
    B. monetarist economics
    C. Keynesian economics
    D. supply side economics.

1. 4   OFFERINGS

LEARNING OBJECTIVES:

■ Identify characteristics of different types of securities offerings

■ An offering can be defined as the issue or sale of a security, such as stocks or bonds made available to the investing public.

1. 4. 1   ROLES OF PARTICIPANTS (E.G., INVESTMENT BANKERS, UNDERWRITING SYNDICATE, MUNICIPAL ADVISORS)

Earlier we learned that a corporation or municipality might offer its securities for sale to the investing public for the purpose of raising capital. Those offering the securities are known as the issuers of the securities and those who assist them in the endeavor are known as underwriters. Underwriters are groups of broker-dealers or investment bankers who will work with an issuer through the registration process and ultimately bring the securities to the market and sell them to the investing public. These underwriting groups are often referred to as underwriting **syndicates**, and often the members of these groups specialize in different types of underwritings. For instance, those who specialize in underwriting municipal bonds are municipal advisors.

1. 4. 2   TYPES OF OFFERINGS

Different types of offerings are identified by who is selling the securities and whether the selling entity already has publically offered securities in the markets. Corporate securities, those offered by corporations for sale to the investing public are sold to investors through either public or private securities offerings.

1. 4. 2. 1   Primary Offering

A primary offering is one in which the proceeds raised go to the issuing corporation. Primary offerings are done in the primary (new issues) market. The corporation increases its capitalization by selling stock (either a new issue or previously authorized but unissued stock). It may do this at any time and in any amount, provided the total stock outstanding never exceeds the amount authorized in the corporation's bylaws.

1. 4. 2. 2   Public vs. Private Securities Offering

We will distinguish the different characteristics of public and private offerings.

1. 4. 2. 2. 1   Public Securities Offering

Public offerings of securities are regulated under the Securities Act of 1933. In a public offering, securities are offered and sold to the investing public. To facilitate this, companies will utilize the services of investment bankers and broker-dealers known as underwriters of the securities. The offerings can be advertised to the public, raise relatively large amounts of capital via the sale of stocks or bonds, and may attract investors with smaller budgets and less investment sophistication. Typically, they are more tightly regulated under the Securities Act of 1933 and are subject to the more stringent federal registration and prospectus requirements than private securities offerings would be. Registration of securities to be offered to the public will be discussed later in this unit.

TAKE NOTE

The primary purpose of the Securities Act of 1933 is to require full and fair disclosure in connection with the sale of securities to the public. The Act of 1933 requires that a new issue, unless specifically exempted from the Act, must be registered with the Securities Exchange Commission (SEC) before public sale. All investors must receive a detailed disclosure document known as a prospectus prior to purchase.

1. 4. 2. 2. 2   Private Securities Offering

A private securities offering, sometimes referred to as a private placement, occurs when the issuing company, usually with the assistance of an investment bank, sells securities to private investors as opposed to the general investing public. Although private placement buyers tend to be institutional investors, securities may be sold to small groups of wealthy individuals who meet certain net worth and income criteria. Those who meet the criteria are known as accredited investors. Private placements are generally exempt from the registration requirements of the Securities Act of 1933.

TAKE NOTE

Public offerings are subject to the registration requirements of the Securities Act of 1933 while private securities offerings (private placements) are generally not. Offerings that are not subject to the registration requirements are known to be **exempt** offerings.

1. 4. 2. 3   Initial Public offering (IPO)

The first time an issuer distributes securities to the public, it is called an initial public offering (IPO). Because the issuer (the company) receives the proceeds from the investors who are investing in the company, all IPOs are primary issuer transactions.

Any subsequent issuance of new shares to the public is called a subsequent public offering (SPO) or additional public offering (APO).

EXAMPLE

The first time that ABC Shoe Co. issued shares to the public, ABC Shoe engaged in an IPO. Later, subsequent primary offerings (SPO) or additional public offerings (APO) were made to the public. The IPO as well as the SPO and the APO were all issuer transactions done in the primary market.

TAKE NOTE

An SPO or APO can also be known as a follow-on public offering (FPO). An FPO is an issuing of shares by a public company that is already listed on an exchange and therefore has already gone through the IPO process. FPOs are popular methods for companies to raise additional equity capital in the capital markets through a stock issue.

1. 4. 2. 3. 1   Initial Public Offering (IPO) Rules and Regulations

Designed to protect the integrity of the public offering process and public investors, the rules ensure that:

- members make a bona fide public offering of securities at the public offering price;
- members do not withhold securities in a public offering for their own benefit or use such securities to reward persons who are in a position to direct future business to the member; and
- industry insiders, such as members and their associated persons, do not take advantage of their insider status to gain access to new issues for their own benefit at the expense of public customers.

Essentially, the rules apply to IPOs of common stock. The rules prohibit member firms from selling a new issue to any account where restricted persons are beneficial owners. Before selling an IPO to any account, representatives are required to obtain a written representation from the account owner(s) that the account is eligible to purchase a new common stock issue at the public offering price. Restricted persons, those not allowed to purchase shares at the public offering price (POP) are defined as follows:

1. Member firms
2. Employees of member firms
3. Finders and fiduciaries acting on behalf of the managing underwriter, including attorneys, accountants, financial consultants, and so on
4. Portfolio managers, including any person who has the authority to buy or sell securities for a bank, savings and loan association, insurance company, or investment company
5. Any person owning 10% or more of a member firm

Furthermore, any immediate family member of any person in items 2–5 above is also restricted. Immediate family includes parents, in-laws, spouses, siblings, children, or any other individual to whom the person provides material support.

TAKE NOTE
Aunts and uncles as well as grandparents are not considered immediate family. If, however, one of these individuals lives in the same household as a restricted person, that individual would be a restricted person.

Finally, there is a de minimis exemption. If the beneficial interests of restricted persons do not exceed 10% of an account, the account may purchase a new equity issue. In other words, restricted persons will be able to have an interest in an account that purchases new equity issues as long as no more than 10% of the account's beneficial owners are restricted persons.

EXAMPLE
Mr. Smith is a restricted person. He is a member of an investment club and has a 5% interest in the investment club account. Because his interest in the club account does not exceed 10%, the investment club account is not considered to be a restricted account.

1. 4. 2. 4   Secondary Offering

As stated earlier, a primary offering takes place in the primary market and is one where the proceeds raised go to the issuing entity (corporation or governments). A secondary offering is one in which one or more stockholders in the corporation are selling all or a major portion of their holdings to the public. The proceeds of the sale are paid to the stockholders rather than to the corporation. Typically, secondary offerings occur in situations in which the founder of a business and perhaps some of the original financial backers determine there is more to be gained by selling their shares to the public rather than holding them.

Offerings and Markets

	New Issue (IPO) Market	Additional Issue Market
Primary Offering	Company is going public; underwriting proceeds go to the company	Company is already public; underwriting proceeds go to the company
Secondary Offering	Company is going public; underwriting proceeds go to the selling stockholders	Company is already public; underwriting proceeds go to the selling stockholders

TAKE NOTE

An offering can be a combination of a primary and secondary offering. These are known as split offerings. In a split offering, the corporation issues a portion of the shares offered to the public and existing shareholders offer the balance.

1. 4. 2. 5   Underwriting Commitments

Different types of underwriting agreements require different levels of commitment from the underwriters. This results in different levels of risk for the underwriters and the issuer.

1. 4. 2. 5. 1   Best Efforts Underwriting

A **best efforts underwriting** calls for the underwriters (syndicate) to buy securities from the issuer acting simply as an agent, not as the principal. This means that the underwriter is not committed to purchase the shares themselves, and is therefore not at risk. The underwriter is acting as an agent contingent on the underwriter's ability to sell shares in either a public offering or a private placement. The underwriter is not at risk for the shares, but the issuer is. If all of the shares cannot be sold, the issuer will not raise the needed capital.

Following are two types of best efforts underwritings to be familiar with.

- All-or-None (AON)—In an all-or-none (AON) underwriting, the issuing corporation has determined that it wants an agreement outlining that the underwriter must either sell all of the shares or cancel the underwriting. Because of the uncertainty over the outcome of an AON offering, any funds collected from investors during the offering period must be held in escrow pending final disposition of the underwriting.

- Mini-Max—A mini-max offering is a best efforts underwriting, setting a floor or minimum, which is the least amount the issuer needs to raise in order to move forward with the underwriting, and a ceiling or maximum on the dollar amount of securities the issuer is willing to sell. The underwriter must locate enough interested buyers to support the minimum (floor) issuance requirement. Once the minimum is met, the underwriter can expand the offering up to the maximum (ceiling) amount of shares the issuer specified.

1. 4. 2. 5. 2   Firm Commitment Underwriting

Firm commitment underwriting is a widely used type of underwriting contract. Under its terms, the underwriters contract with the issuer to buy the securities. Here the underwriters are acting as principals rather than agents. They are committing to purchase any unsold shares for the syndicate account. In this type of underwriting it is the underwriters who are at risk for any shares they cannot sell to the public, not the issuer. The issuer knows that ultimately all of the securities will be sold and all of the capital needed will be raised.

1. 4. 3   REGISTRATION OF SECURITIES AND THE SECURITIES ACT OF 1933

The Securities Act of 1933 is also referred to as the **Paper Act, Full Disclosure Act, New Issues Act, Truth in Securities Act**, and **Prospectus Act**. The act's main purpose is to ensure that the investing public is fully informed about a security and its issuing company when the security is first sold in the primary market. The 1933 Act protects investors who buy new issues by:

- requiring registration of new issues that are to be distributed interstate;
- requiring an issuer to provide full and fair disclosure about itself and the offering;
- requiring an issuer to make available all material information necessary for an investor to judge the issue's merit;
- regulating the underwriting and distribution of primary and secondary issues; and
- providing criminal penalties for fraud in the issuance of new securities.

1. 4. 3. 1   The Registration Statement

An issuer must file with the SEC a **registration statement** disclosing material information about the issue. Part of the registration statement is a **prospectus**, which must be provided to all purchasers of the new issue.

The registration statement must contain:

- a description of the issuer's business;
- the names and addresses of company officers and directors, their salaries, and a five-year business history of each;
- the amount of corporate securities company officers and directors own and identification of investors who own 10% or more of the company;
- the company's capitalization, including its equity and debt;
- a description of how the proceeds will be used; and
- whether the company is involved in any legal proceedings.

Underwriters (broker-dealers and investment bankers) may assist the issuer in preparing and filing the registration statement and prospectus. However, the accuracy and adequacy of these documents is the responsibility of the issuer.

1. 4. 3. 1. 1   The Cooling-Off Period

After the issuer files a registration statement with the SEC, a 20-day **cooling-off period** begins. The registration can become effective as early as 20 calendar days after the date the SEC has received it. In practice, however, the cooling-off period is seldom the minimum 20 days; the SEC usually takes longer to clear registration statements.

If it finds that the registration statement needs revision or expansion, the SEC may suspend the review and issue a deficiency letter to the issuer of the securities. The 20-day cooling-off period would resume when the issuer submits a corrected registration statement. Note that it resumes where it had left off and does not begin anew.

During the cooling-off period, no one can solicit sales of the securities. However, indications of interest may be taken and solicited with a preliminary prospectus known as a "red herring".

1. 4. 3. 1. 2   Tombstone Advertisements

Certain types of advertisements relating to a new issue are allowed to be run prior to the effective date. These are known as tombstone ads because of the *bare bones, minimum information* provided. Tombstone ads are an announcement and description of the securities to be offered.

Tombstone ads are the only form of advertising that is permitted from the time the registration statement is filed with the Securities Exchange Commission and the effective date of the offering. The effective date is the time the securities may then be sold to the public. Remember that this period between the registration filing with the SEC and the effective date is known as the cooling-off period. While tombstone ads may run to announce a new issue during the cooling-off period, they are not required and do not need to be filed with the SEC.

Tombstone ads may be placed by the issuer directly or with the assistance of the underwriters. They are limited to the following information:

- Name of the issuer
- Type of security being offered
- Number of shares to be sold
- Public offering price (or a range)
- Names of the underwriting members (when placed by the underwriters instead of the issuer)

All tombstone advertisements must contain the following advisory:

This announcement is neither an offer to sell nor a solicitation of an offer for any of these securities. This offer is made only by prospectus.

1. 4. 3. 2   Shelf Offering Registration

Through a shelf offering registration, an issuer who is already a publically traded company can register new securities without selling any of the shares until later or some of the shares initially, and waiting to sell the remaining portion of the shares. Once filed, the registration is good for two years and allows the issuer to sell portions of a registered shelf offering over a three-year period without having to reregister the security. This provision under the Securities Act of 1933 allows issuers to quickly raise capital when needed or when market conditions are favorable.

For securities offered via a shelf registration, a supplemental prospectus must be filed with the SEC before each sale.

1. 4. 3. 3 State Registration Requirements (Blue Sky)

In addition to federal securities regulations, each state has laws that pertain to the issuance and trading of securities. These state securities laws are known as blue sky laws because of a statement made by a Kansas Supreme Court justice who referred to "speculative schemes that have no more basis than so many feet of blue sky."

1. 4. 3. 3. 1 The Uniform Securities Act (USA)

The Uniform Securities Act provides a legal framework for the state registration of securities. It may be adopted by individual states and adapted to their needs. State registration requirements apply to broker-dealers, investment advisers, investment adviser representatives, and registered representatives. State securities administrators have the power to revoke any of these registrations if a violation of the state's law has occurred.

State laws require that broker-dealers with an office in the state, or those that direct calls into the state or receive calls from the state, be registered in that state. Registered representatives must register in a state if they are residents or if they solicit business in a state. Registrations must be renewed annually.

There are exemptions to state registration. The two most common are isolated nonissuer transactions and unsolicited transactions.

Isolated nonissuer transactions—These are transactions occurring in the secondary market (nonissuer) that occur infrequently (very few transactions per agent/representative per year; the exact number varies by state). These transactions generally do not involve securities professionals.

EXAMPLE   In the same manner that individuals placing a "for sale by owner" sign on their front lawns do not need a real estate license, one individual selling stock to another in a one-on-one transaction is engaging in a transaction exempt from oversight of the state Administrator because the issuer is not receiving any of the proceeds, and the parties involved are not trading as part of a regular practice.

Unsolicited transactions—These are transactions initiated by the client not the agent or representative.

EXAMPLE   If a client calls a registered agent and requests that the agent buy or sell a security, the transaction is an unsolicited brokerage transaction exempt from state registration. But, the state Administrator may, by rule, require that the customer acknowledge on a specified form noting the sale was unsolicited and that a signed copy of the form be kept by the broker-dealer for a specified period.

1. 4. 3. 3. 2   Registering Securities at the State Level

Much like securities to be sold require issuers to register them at the federal level with the SEC, securities to be sold within a state require registration at the state level. States have two ways to register (or blue sky) securities: coordination, and qualification. There is also a third provision used solely for those securities that are referred to as *federal covered*. The third provision is known as notice filing.

Coordination—The issuer files with the state at the same time it files with the SEC. Registration is effective at the time the federal filing becomes effective. Coordination can only be used for IPOs (securities that have not been previously registered with the SEC).

Qualification—If registration cannot be accomplished by coordination or filing, it must be registered by qualification. In this situation, the issuer must respond to any requirement the state specifies. This type of registration is effective only when so ordered by the state securities administrator. It is the most difficult way of registering securities in a state.

Notice filing—Under the National Securities Markets Improvements Act of 1996, certain categories of securities, such as those listed on national exchanges and investment companies registered under the Investment Company Act of 1940, are deemed to be federal covered. The effect of this designation is that states do not have jurisdiction over the registration requirements of these securities. However, the Act did provide that states could require the filing of a notice to sell securities in that state along with the payment of a filing fee.

1. 4. 4   OFFERING DOCUMENTS AND DELIVERY REQUIREMENTS

There are different offering documents intended to provide full disclosure to investors.

1. 4. 4. 1   Prospectus

The Securities Exchange Commission under the Act of 1933 requires full and fair disclosure of all material information and facts regarding the issuance of securities. This disclosure is done via a prospectus, which is required to provide investors enough information to make fully informed buying decisions.

1. 4. 4. 1. 1   Preliminary Prospectus

The **preliminary prospectus, or red herring**, can be used as a prospecting tool, allowing issuers and underwriters to gauge investor interest and gather indications of interest. There is no final price included in the preliminary prospectus. The preliminary prospectus must be made available to any customer who expresses interest in the securities during the cooling-off period, that is, between the SEC registration filing date and when the SEC clears the issue for sale, the effective date.

An indication of interest is an investor's declaration of potential interest in purchasing some of the issue from the underwriter after the security comes out of registration. An investor's indication of interest is not a commitment to buy because sales are prohibited until after the registration becomes effective (the **effective date**). In that light, it should be recognized that indications of interest are neither binding on buyers nor sellers.

During the cooling-off period, underwriters may not:

■ make offers to sell the securities;

■ take orders; or

■ distribute sales literature or advertising material.

However, they may:

■ take indications of interest;

■ distribute preliminary prospectuses; or

■ publish tombstone advertisements to provide information about the potential availability of the securities.

1. 4. 4. 1. 2   *Final Prospectus*

When the registration statement becomes effective, the issuer amends the preliminary prospectus and adds information, including the final offering price for the **final prospectus**. Registered representatives may then take orders from those customers who indicated interest in buying during the cooling-off period.

A copy of the final prospectus must precede or accompany all sales confirmations. The prospectus must include the:

■ description of the offering;

■ offering price;

■ selling discounts;

■ offering date;

■ use of the proceeds;

■ description of the underwriting, but not the actual contract;

■ statement of the possibility that the issue's price may be stabilized;

■ history of the business;

■ risks to the purchasers;

■ description of management;

■ material financial information;

■ legal opinion concerning the formation of the corporation; and

■ SEC disclaimer.

The SEC does not approve or endorse any offering for sale, they simply clear, or release the offering for sale. The standard SEC disclaimer reads as follows:

"These securities have not been approved or disapproved by the SEC nor have any representations been made about the accuracy or the adequacy of the information."

The Three Phases of Underwriting

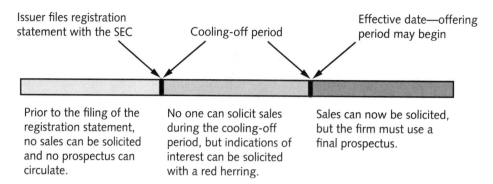

Issuer files registration statement with the SEC

Cooling-off period

Effective date—offering period may begin

Prior to the filing of the registration statement, no sales can be solicited and no prospectus can circulate.

No one can solicit sales during the cooling-off period, but indications of interest can be solicited with a red herring.

Sales can now be solicited, but the firm must use a final prospectus.

1. 4. 4. 2 Prospectus Delivery Requirements

A final prospectus must be delivered to all buyers in the secondary market for a specified time following the effective date. This is termed the **prospectus delivery requirement period**. For initial public offerings (IPOs), this period is:

- 90 days if the security is to be quoted on the OTC *Pink* or over the OTCBB (non-Nasdaq); or

- 25 days if the security is to be listed on an exchange or quoted over Nasdaq.
  For additional issue offerings, the following apply:

- If the security is listed or quoted over Nasdaq, a prospectus must be delivered only in connection with purchases at the public offering price. Once the distribution is complete, there is no obligation to deliver a prospectus in secondary market transactions.

- If the security is non-Nasdaq, the prospectus delivery requirement period is 40 days.

TAKE NOTE

The securities industry has adopted an access equals delivery model for meeting prospectus delivery obligations. A prospectus will be deemed to precede or accompany a security for sale if the final prospectus has been filed with the SEC. In other words, an investor can see a copy of the final prospectus by logging on to the SEC's website. The access equals delivery rule applies to the final prospectus and aftermarket prospectus delivery obligations. It does not apply to preliminary prospectuses, which still must be printed, nor does it apply to mutual funds, which must provide investors with a paper prospectus.

1. 4. 5 REGULATORY FILING REQUIREMENTS AND EXEMPTIONS

When securities are required to be registered in order to be sold to the public they are known as **non-exempt** securities (not exempt from registration and must be registered). However, there are exemptions from the registration requirements and we will discuss those now.

1. 4. 5. 1   Exempt Securities

Certain securities are exempt from the registration statement and prospectus requirements of the 1933 Act, either because of the issuer's level of creditworthiness or because another government regulatory agency has jurisdiction over the issuer.

These exempt securities include:

- U.S. government securities;
- municipal bonds;
- commercial paper and banker's acceptances that have maturities of less than 270 days;
- insurance policies and fixed annuity contracts (but not variable annuities);
- national and state bank (not bank holding company) securities;
- building and loan (S&L) securities;
- charitable, religious, educational, and nonprofit association issues;
- interests in railroad equipment certificates; and
- banks

TAKE NOTE   The bank exemption applies only to the securities of banks, not to the securities of bank holding companies.

Insurance policies are not included in the definition of security; however, variable annuities, variable life insurance, and variable universal life insurance are funded by separate accounts investing in securities, therefore these products must be registered as securities with the SEC.

1. 4. 5. 2   Exempt Transactions

Securities offered by industrial, financial, and other corporations may qualify for exemption from the registration statement and prospectus requirements of the 1933 Act under one of the following exclusionary provisions:

- Regulation A+: small and medium corporate offerings
- Regulation D: private placements
- Rule 147: securities offered and sold exclusively intrastate
- Regulation S: offers and sales made outside the United States by U.S. issuers

1. 4. 5. 3   Exempt Securities and Transactions Full Disclosure Documents

Earlier we learned about the full disclosure document (prospectus) required for non-exempt securities (those that must register). Exempt securities also have disclosure documents, though they are not called a prospectus. For example, the **official statement** serves as a disclosure document and contains any material information an investor might need about a municipal bond issue. The official statement, which must be signed by an officer of the issuer, is the municipal securities industry's equivalent of the corporate prospectus.

In a Regulation A+ offering, the issuer files an abbreviated **notice of sale**, or **offering circular**, with the SEC. Investors are provided with this offering circular rather than a full prospectus.

LEARNING OBJECTIVES

■ Identify characteristics of different types of securities offerings

1. A major distinction of a secondary offering is

   A. the transaction takes place in the secondary market
   B. the securities are not offered to the general public
   C. money raised in a secondary offering is more heavily regulated than other offerings
   D. proceeds are not received by the issuer of the securities

2. How many primary offerings can a corporation issue?

   A. 1
   B. 2
   C. 3
   D. Unlimited

3. What federal law regulates the initial sale of securities to the public?

   A. The Securities Act of 1933
   B. The Securities & Exchange Act of 1934
   C. The Investment Company Act of 1940
   D. The Truth in Investing Act

4. A tombstone advertisement includes all of the following information EXCEPT

   A. the offering price
   B. the name of the issuer
   C. the risks associated with the offering
   D. the number of shares to be sold

5. Mark the following as true or false.

   A. ___The final prospectus may be delivered via the internet prior to a sale.

   B. ___ A shelf registration is good for five years.

   C. ___ The access equals delivery rule is not applicable to the preliminary prospectus.

   D. ___ APOs of listed securities do not require delivery of a prospectus.

   E. ___ Once the SEC approves a registration, the cooling-off period ends and an effective date is established.

6. The Uniform Securities Act (USA) is the template from which state securities laws are derived. Under the USA, a broker-dealer would have to register with the state under all of the following conditions EXCEPT

   A. there was an office in the state
   B. calls were directed to prospects in the state
   C. the broker-dealer made a market in municipal bonds issued by the state
   D. calls were received from clients in the state

7. An issuer wishing to raise additional capital engages the services of an underwriter who proposes limiting the sale to the six New England states. In doing so, it is most likely that the registration method to be used will be

   A. coordination
   B. qualification
   C. notice filing
   D. solely with the SEC

8. The Uniform Securities Act provides for a number of exemptions from registration on the state level. There are securities which are exempt and transactions which are exempt. Among the most popular exempt transactions are

   I.   United States Treasury bonds
   II. isolated non-issuer transactions
   III. municipal bonds
   IV. unsolicited transactions

   A. I and III
   B. I and IV
   C. II and III
   D. II and IV

QUICK QUIZ ANSWERS AND RATIONALES

QUICK QUIZ 1.A

1. **B.** Created under the Securities Exchange Act of 1934, the Securities and Exchange Commission (SEC) is the securities industry's primary regulatory body.

2. **D.** A fully disclosed broker-dealer is not a clearing firm. They cannot take custody of funds and securities. Instead, they introduce their business to other firms who are known as carrying/clearing firms. These carrying/clearing firms act as the fully disclosed BD's clearing agent.

3. **C.** A clearing agency is an intermediary between the buy and sell sides of a transaction. The clearing agency receives and delivers payments and securities on behalf of both parties.

4. **B.** The Depository Trust and Clearing Company (DTCC) is a member of the Federal Reserve System. Not in the retail banking business (one can't open a savings or checking account there), it exists to serve the custody needs of security industry participants not only in the United States but in more than 60 countries worldwide.

5. **D.** The prime broker would supply clearing services, as well as back office support including cash management, account statements, and transaction reports. Executions and related functions are handled by executing brokers contracted with by the client.

6. **A.** Market makers or traders are will to accept the risk of holding securities in proprietary accounts for the purpose of providing liquidity to the market place.

7. **B.** Any entity offering or proposing to offer securities to the public for the purpose of raising capital is an issuer.

8. **D.** The Securities Investors Protection Corporation (SIPC) was created under the Securities Investor Protection Act of 1970. The corporation is a nonprofit membership organization. SIPC members pay assessments into a general insurance fund that is used to meet customer claims in the event of a broker-dealer bankruptcy.

9. **C.** The FDIC provides insurance for depositor's accounts at its member banks up to $250,000.

10. **A.** The Federal Reserve Board (FRB) consists of 12 regional Federal Reserve Banks and hundreds of national and state banks. The board has the responsibility of implementing the monetary policies it develops.

QUICK QUIZ 1.B

1. **B.** Capital markets such as the stock market and the bond market are a source of financing for corporations, municipalities, and governments. Money can be raised by issuing equities or debt and offering the securities to investors in an initial public offering (IPO) or an additional public offering (APO) in the capital markets.

2. **A.** When an issuer of securities engages in transactions to sell those securities to the investing public, the transactions are being done in the primary market. The primary market is where the issuer of the securities receives the proceeds generated by the sale of the securities.

3. **D.** The fourth market is where direct trades between institutions, pension funds, broker-dealers, and other financial entities occur, utilizing electronic communications networks (ECNs). There are no brokers involved in these transactions.

4. **C.** The third market refers to when listed securities (those listed on U.S. exchanges) are traded in the over-the-counter (OTC) market.

5. **D.** The secondary markets are where securities trade between investors. Secondary market transactions have one investor selling securities to another. Unlike the primary market, and the issuer is not involved in the transaction. Stock exchanges are an example of a secondary market, where investors buy securities from and sell securities to each other.

QUICK QUIZ 1.C

1. **B.** Imports involve domestic residents' spending money on foreign goods. Therefore, the outflow of money creates a negative factor in the computation of gross domestic product.

2. **B.** Expansion is characterized by increased business activity—increasing sales, manufacturing, and wages—throughout the economy. Along with the increased demand for money comes an increase in the cost of money (interest rates).

3. **C.** Stagflation generally occurs when the economy isn't growing and there is a lack of consumer demand and business activity, yet prices for goods are still rising.

4. **B.** Fiscal policy is under the control of the president and Congress and consists of federal spending and taxation.

5. **A.** One of the key additions to M2 in order to reach M3 is the negotiable time deposits of $100,000 or more, generally known as jumbo CDs.

6. **B.** When the FRB raises the reserve requirements, it reduces the available funds for banks to lend. Having fewer dollars to lend will lead to higher interest rates. When the discount rate is increased, it costs more for banks to borrow, and that increase is passed along to consumers. The FRB does not set the prime rate and it is only when the FOMC sells securities that the money supply shrinks.

7. **D.** A recession is recognized as 6 consecutive months of economic decline while a depression is 6 consecutive quarters of economic decline.

8. **C.** Steel is cyclical and is not considered defensive; defensive stocks are generally less affected by the business cycle.

9. **A.** Broad stock market indices are generally leading indicators, moving ahead of the overall economy. GDP and industrial production are coincident indicators that show us where the economy is presently, and the duration of unemployment claims is a lagging indicator.

10. **C.** Keynesian economics adheres to active government intervention in the marketplace to insure economic growth and stability. Using Keynesian economics this is achieved by manipulating the levels of government spending and taxation.

QUICK QUIZ 1.D

1. **D.** In a secondary offering, one or more stockholders in the corporation are selling all or a major portion of their holdings to the public. The proceeds of the sale are paid to the stockholders rather than to the corporation.

2. **D.** A corporation can only have one initial public offering (IPO), but there is no limit on the number of subsequent public offerings (SPOs) or additional public offerings (APOs) issued. IPOs, SPOs, and APOs are all primary offerings that benefit an issuer.

3. **A.** The Securities Act of 1933 is designed to ensure the investing public is fully informed about securities when purchasing them in the primary market, which is where the initial sale of securities from an issuer to the public takes place.

4. **C.** The *bare bones* tombstone advertisement does not identify risks associated with the investment. That information is found in the prospectus

5. **A.** T

   B. F

   C. T

   D. T

   E. F

6. **C.** The Uniform Securities Act does not require registration of a broker-dealer because the firm buys and sells securities issued by the state. However, if there is a place of business in the state, or calls are received from or directed to the state, registration is generally required.

7. **A.** An issue sold in more than one state must be registered with the SEC as well as each of the states. The best way to do that is to *coordinate* the registration using the method known, logically, as coordination.

8. **D.** It is true that U.S. government securities and municipal securities are exempt from registration, but that is because they are exempt securities. The question asks for exempt transactions and there are only two choices that refer to transactions, both of which are exempt: isolated non-issuer and unsolicited transactions.

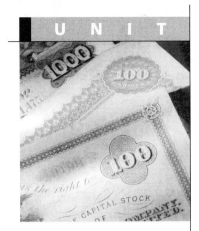

2

Understanding Products and Their Risks

I n this unit you will become familiar with specific securities products. These products can generally be broken down into two categories; equity and debt. Here we will examine a number of each, looking at their unique characteristics enabling you to differentiate one from the other. We'll also touch on derivative products, those that have value derived from another security, for example options.

Recognizing that there are a number of different types of risk that can impact securities investments is important. We'll look at the most common of these risks and how they can affect not only individual securities but entire portfolios as well. ■

When you have completed the unit you should be able to:

- **compare** the characteristics of equity and debt securities;

- **recognize** the basic option contract characteristics;

- **calculate** premiums, breakeven points, and maximum gain and loss for simple option positions;

- **compare** the characteristics of different investment products;

- **define** different investment risks; and

- **identify** risks associated with different investment products.

2. 1   PRODUCTS

LEARNING OBJECTIVES:

■   compare the characteristics of equity and debt securities

■   recognize the basic option contract characteristics

■   calculate premiums, breakeven points, and maximum gain and loss for simple option positions

■   compare the characteristics of different investment products

Investment products come in a number of forms and can represent different types of participation in the issuing company's business. For example, equity securities represent ownership in an issuing company and debt securities represent a loan to the issuing company, while a number of derivative products such as options represent neither. In the following sections, we'll define and take a closer look at the characteristics of the most common and utilized investment products.

2. 1. 1   EQUITIES

Individual investors, by purchasing shares of stock in a company, can participate in the company's prosperity. They can benefit from an increase in the price of the shares (capital appreciation) and by sharing in earnings through the receipt of dividends (distributed profits). Essentially, these shares represent ownership in the corporation.

2. 1. 1. 1   Common stock

A company issues stock to raise capital. Investors who buy the stock also buy a share of ownership in the company's net worth. Net worth is calculated by taking the business' assets less its liabilities (creditors' claims). The resulting net worth belongs to the business owners (its stockholders).

Each share of stock entitles its owner to a portion of the company's earnings and dividends and a proportionate vote in major management decisions. Most corporations are organized in such a way that their stockholders regularly vote for and elect individuals to a board of directors to oversee company business. By electing a board of directors, stockholders have a say in the company's management but are not involved in the day-to-day details of its operations.

EXAMPLE   If a corporation issues 100 shares of stock, each share represents an identical 1/100—or 1%—ownership position in the company. An investor who owns 10 shares of stock would own 10% of the company; an investor who owns 50 shares of stock would own 50% of the company.

2. 1. 1. 1. 1   Benefits of Owning Common Stock

Common shareholders enjoy a number of benefits including voting rights, the opportunity for capital appreciation, and current income as well as limited liability. Following, we'll explore these benefits.

Rights of Common Stockholders—Common stockholders have the right to vote for corporate directors. Frequently, it is not possible for the stockholder to attend the stockholder's meetings to personally cast a vote. An absentee ballot, known as a **proxy**, is made available for those shareholders who want to vote but can't attend the shareholder meeting. Those voting by proxy can generally do so by mail or online. Common stock is freely transferable to anyone who wants to buy it or receive it as a gift. In this regard, shareholders have the right to sell or give away their shares without permission of the corporation. Without this feature, there would be no stock markets.

Common stockholders have a right to limited access to the corporation's books. For the most part, common stockholders have the right to examine the minutes of meetings of the board of directors and the right to examine the list of stockholders. Usually, this right is not exercised unless the performance of the corporation's management declines seriously. They also have the right to receive an audited set of financial statements of the company's performance each year (annual reports).

Finally, common stockholders usually have the preemptive right to maintain their proportionate share of ownership in the corporation. The word *preempt* means to put oneself in front of another. If a corporation wants to issue additional shares, existing shareholders have the right to purchase those shares in an amount that would keep their proportionate ownership in the corporation unchanged.

Growth (capital gains)—An increase in the market price of securities is capital appreciation. Historically, owning common stock has provided investors with returns in excess of the inflation rate. For this reason, most investors with a long-term investment horizon have included common stock in their portfolios as a hedge against inflation. Of course, it must be mentioned that stock prices can decline, particularly over the short run.

Income—Many corporations pay regular quarterly cash dividends to stockholders. Dividends are declared by the board of directors (BOD) and may increase over time as profitability increases. Dividends, which can be a significant source of income for investors, are a major reason many people invest in stocks.

Issuers may also pay stock dividends (additional shares in the issuing company) or property dividends (shares in a subsidiary company or a product sample).

Limited liability—One of the most important features of equity ownership is limited liability. In the event of a corporation's bankruptcy, when corporate assets are not adequate to meet corporate obligations, personal assets are not at risk. One cannot be forced to sell any personal assets to help pay the debts of the business.

If an individual invests $5,000 in the stock of a corporation that goes bankrupt, the investor may lose the entire $5,000 invested if the company is not salvaged, but the investor will not be forced to pay out any more monies to take care of additional debts. Shareholders are personally at risk only for the amount that was invested. By contrast, a partner or sole proprietor risks not only the amount personally invested in the business but also personal assets should the business not be able to pay off its obligations.

In summation, why would you include common stock in a client's portfolio?

- Potential capital appreciation
- Income from dividends
- Hedge against inflation
  In doing so, the client would be incurring the following risks:
- Market
- Business difficulties leading to possible reduction or elimination of the dividend and even bankruptcy leading to loss of principal

2. 1. 1. 1. 2   Risks of Owning Common Stock

Regardless of their expectations, investors have no assurances that they will receive the returns they expect from their investments. The risks of owning common stock are listed following.

Market risk—The chance that a stock will decline in price is one risk of owning common stock (known as market risk). A stock's price fluctuates daily as perceptions of the company's business prospects change and influence the actions of buyers and sellers. Investors have no assurance whatsoever that they will be able to recoup the investment in a stock at any time. The price of a stock when an investor wishes to sell shares may be higher or lower than when the shares were initially purchased.

Decreased or no dividend income—A risk of stock ownership is the possibility of dividend income decreasing or ceasing entirely if the company loses money. The decision to pay a dividend rests with the board of directors and it is not guaranteed.

Low priority at dissolution—If a company enters bankruptcy, the holders of its bonds and preferred stock have priority over common stockholders. A company's debt and preferred shares are considered senior securities. Common stockholders have residual rights to corporate assets upon dissolution. If after debt holders and preferred shareholders are paid, only then would common shareholders be paid if there were any funds left to divide among them.

TAKE NOTE

In owning common equity, the investor stands to lose current income through dividend reduction or suspension, as well as capital loss, should the market price decline. In return, however, the shareholder has limited liability; that is, the liability is limited to the amount invested.

2. 1. 1. 1. 3   Bankruptcy

Bankruptcy is a general term for a federal court procedure that allows both individuals and businesses to get relief from their debts or make a plan to repay their creditors. For those entitled to file for bankruptcy, the court will protect them from creditors during the bankruptcy proceedings. Though there are different classifications (chapters) of bankruptcy, they can be broken down into two basic types: reorganization and liquidation.

Limiting our discussion of bankruptcy to businesses and corporations rather than individuals, the primary difference between a reorganization and a liquidation is that, in a reorganization, the entity will likely be able to retain property and continue doing business but must submit and stick to a plan that will allow the repayment of some or all of its existing debts within a specified time frame. Liquidation, on the other hand, means that keeping property or continuing business will not occur and all property will be taken and sold to repay all debts.

2. 1. 1. 1. 4   Liquidation

In the event a company liquidates, the priority of claims on the company's assets that will be sold are as follows:

- IRS (taxes) and employees (unpaid wages)
- Secured debt (bonds and mortgages)
- Unsecured liabilities and general creditors (suppliers and utilities)
- Subordinated debt (debt holders who agreed to be paid back last of all debt holders in the event a liquidation ever needed to occur)

- Preferred stockholders
- Common stockholders

While the priority standing can differ slightly depending upon which chapter of bankruptcy a company is filing under, the basic structure should be noted as being divided into three simple categories: taxes and wages, debt holders (bonds), and equity holders (stocks).

TAKE NOTE

In the corporate liquidation priority, common shareholders are paid last of all bond and stockholders. Consider that only in cases where there are funds remaining after all others are paid do common stockholders receive anything; such cases can be rare.

---

2. 1. 1. 2   Preferred stock

Preferred stock is an equity security because it represents a class of ownership in the issuing corporation. Although it is an equity security, it does share some characteristics with a debt security. Like debt securities, the rate of return on a preferred stock is fixed rather than subject to variation as with common stock. A preferred stock's annual dividend represents its fixed rate of return. This is a key attraction for income oriented investors. Normally a preferred stock is identified by its annual dividend payment stated as a percentage of its par value. Always assume preferred par value is $100 unless stated differently.

EXAMPLE

A preferred stock with a par value of $100 that pays $6 in annual dividends is known as a 6% preferred ($6 dividend / $100 par). The dividend of a preferred stock with no par value is stated as a $6 no-par preferred.

Two final characteristics of preferred stock are that unlike common shareholders, preferred shareholders generally have no voting rights nor do they have preemptive rights. With few exceptions the right to vote for board members or on other corporate issues is reserved for common shareholders.

TAKE NOTE

All corporations issue common stock, but not all corporations issue preferred stock.

---

2. 1. 1. 2. 1   Benefits of Owning Preferred Stock

Although preferred stock does not typically have the same growth potential as common stock, preferred stockholders have some advantages over common stockholders.

Dividend preference—When the Board of Directors declares dividends, owners of preferred shares must be paid prior to any payment to common shareholders.

Priority at dissolution over common stock—If a corporation goes bankrupt, preferred stockholders have a priority claim over common stockholders on the assets remaining after creditors have been paid.

2. 1. 1. 2. 2   Risks of Owning Preferred Stock

Although they enjoy some preferences, owners of preferred stock face risks as well.

Purchasing power risk—The potential that, because of inflation, the fixed income produced will not purchase as much in the future as it does today.

Interest rate sensitivity—Like a fixed income security, when interest rates rise, the value of preferred shares declines. (This will be discussed in greater detail later in this unit.)

Decreased or no dividend income—Like common stock ownership, there is the possibility of dividend income decreasing or ceasing entirely if the company loses money. The decision to pay a dividend rests with the Board of Directors (BOD) and it is not guaranteed.

Priority at dissolution—While preferred shareholders are paid before common shareholders if a company enters bankruptcy, they are paid behind all creditors.

In summation, why would you include preferred stock in a client's portfolio?

- Fixed income from dividends
- Prior claim ahead of common stock
- Convertible preferred sacrifices income in exchange for potential appreciation (discussed shortly)

In doing so, the client would be incurring the following risks:

- Possible loss of purchasing power
- Interest rate (money rate) risk
- Business difficulties leading to possible reduction or elimination of the dividend and even bankruptcy leading to loss of principal

2. 1. 1. 2. 3   Types or Preferred

Separate categories of preferred may differ in several ways, including dividend rate and profit participation privileges. However, all maintain preference over common stock.

Straight (noncumulative)—Straight preferred has no special features beyond the stated dividend payment. Missed dividends are not paid to the holder.

Cumulative—Cumulative preferred stock accrues payments due its shareholders in the event dividends are reduced or suspended.

Dividends due cumulative preferred stock accumulate on the company's books until the corporation's board of directors decides to pay them. When the company resumes dividend payments, cumulative preferred stockholders receive current dividends plus the total accumulated dividends—dividends in arrears—before any dividends may be distributed to common stockholders.

EXAMPLE   In 2011, RST Corp. had both common stock and cumulative preferred stock outstanding. The common paid a dividend of $1, and the preferred paid a $2 dividend. Because of financial difficulties, the company stopped paying dividends during 2011. After resolving its problems in 2015, the company resumed dividend payments and paid the cumulative preferred shareholders an $8 dividend for dividends in arrears for years 2011, 2012, 2013, and 2014 plus the current year's (2015) $2 dividend ($10 total) before paying any dividends to the common stockholders.

Callable preferred—Corporations often issue callable (or redeemable) preferred, which a company can buy back from investors at a stated price after a specified date. The right to call the stock allows the company to replace a relatively high fixed dividend obligation with a lower one when the cost of money has gone down. This is similar to refinancing a mortgage.

When a corporation calls a preferred stock, dividend payments cease on the call date. In return for the call privilege, the corporation may pay a premium exceeding the stock's par value at the call, such as $103 for a $100 par value stock.

Convertible preferred—A preferred stock is convertible if the owner can exchange the shares for a fixed number of shares of the issuing corporation's common stock.

Convertible preferred is generally issued with a lower stated dividend rate than nonconvertible preferred of the same quality because the investor may have the opportunity to convert to common shares and enjoy greater capital gain potential. The concept of a convertible security will be discussed in greater detail later in this unit when we cover convertible bonds.

TAKE NOTE

Because the value of a convertible preferred stock is linked to the value of a common stock, the convertible preferred share price tends to fluctuate in line with the common.

Adjustable-rate preferred—Some preferred stocks are issued with adjustable (or variable) dividend rates. Such dividends are usually tied to the rates of other interest rate benchmarks, such as Treasury bills and money market rates, and can be adjusted as often as quarterly. Because the payment adjusts to current interest rates, the price of the stock remains relatively stable.

TEST TOPIC ALERT

For investors looking for income through preferred stocks, this would be their least appropriate choice.

Participating preferred—In addition to fixed dividends, participating preferred stock offers its owners a share of corporate profits that remain after all dividends and interest due other securities are paid. The percentage to which participating preferred stock participates is noted on the stock certificate.

EXAMPLE

If a preferred stock is described as XYZ 6% preferred participating to 9%, the company pays its holders up to 3% in additional dividends in profitable years if the Board of Directors (BOD) declares so.

2. 1. 1. 3   Control and Restricted Securities (SEC Rule 144)

SEC Rule 144 regulates the sale of control and restricted securities, stipulating the holding period, quantity limitations, manner of sale, and filing procedures.

Control securities are those owned by directors, officers, or persons who own or control 10% or more of the issuer's voting stock.

If an unaffiliated individual owns 7% of the voting stock of XYZ, that person is not a control person. However, if that person's spouse owns 4% of the voting stock, then both would be considered control persons. In other words, if there is a 10% or more interest held by immediate family members, then all those family members owning voting stock are control persons.

Restricted securities are those acquired through some means other than a registered public offering. A security purchased in a private placement is a restricted security. Restricted securities may not be sold until they have been held fully paid for six months. According to Rule 144, after holding restricted stock fully paid for six months, an affiliate may begin selling shares but is subject to the volume restriction rules as enumerated following. In any 90-day period, an investor may sell the greater of:

- 1% of the total outstanding shares of the same class at the time of sale; or
- the average weekly trading volume in the stock over the past four weeks on all exchanges or as reported through Nasdaq.

After the six-month holding period, affiliated persons are subject to the volume restrictions for as long as they are affiliates. For unaffiliated investors, the stock may be sold completely unrestricted after the six-month holding period has been satisfied.

Selling shares under Rule 144 effectively registers the shares. In other words, buyers of stock being sold subject to Rule 144 are not subject to any restrictions if they choose to resell.

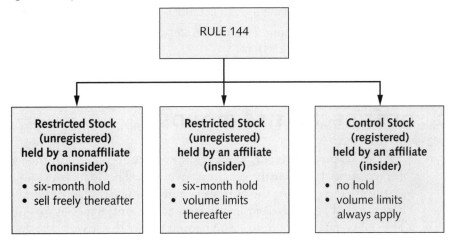

2. 1. 1. 4 Penny Stocks

A penny stock is an unlisted (not listed on a U.S. stock exchange) security trading at less than $5 per share. Equity securities defined as penny stocks are considered highly speculative. In this light, SEC rules require that customers, before their initial transaction in a penny stock, be given a copy of a risk disclosure document. The member must receive a signed and dated acknowledgment from the customer that the document has been received. Not surprisingly, the penny stock disclosure document fully describes the risks associated with penny stock investments.

Regardless of activity in the account, if the account holds penny stocks, broker-dealers must provide a monthly account statement to the customer. This must indicate the market value and number of shares for each penny stock held in the account as well as the issuer's name.

2. 1. 1. 4. 1 Penny Stock Cold-Calling Rules

SEC rules regarding cold-calling customers also state that when a broker-dealer's representative contacts a potential customer to purchase penny stocks (this is a solicitation to buy like those occurring during a cold call), the representative must first determine suitability on the basis of information about the buyer's financial situation and objectives. The customer must sign and date this suitability statement before any initial penny stock trades can be effected. In addition, the broker-dealer must disclose:

- the name of the penny stock;
- the number of shares to be purchased;
- a current quotation; and
- the amount of commission that the firm and the representative received.

TAKE NOTE

The provisions of the penny stock rules apply only to solicited transactions like those that might occur during a cold-call. Unsolicited transactions (those not recommended by the broker-dealer or registered representative) are exempt.

2. 1. 1. 4. 2 Established Customer Exemption

Established customers are exempt from the suitability statement requirement but not from the disclosure requirements. An **established customer** is someone who:

- has held an account with the broker-dealer for at least one year (and has made a deposit of funds or securities); or
- has made at least three penny stock purchases of different issuers on different days.

2. 1. 2 DEBT SECURITIES (BONDS)

Debt capital represents money borrowed by corporations, the federal government, or local governments (municipalities) from investors. The loan is evidenced by a bond which is a certificate representing the borrowers indebtedness to the investor. These certificates state the borrower's obligation to pay back a specific amount of money on a specific date to the investor. They also state the borrower's obligation to pay the investor a specific rate of interest for the use of the funds.

When an investor buys a bond, the investor is lending the borrowing entity money for a set period of time at a fixed annual interest rate. The investor, in the position of lender, is acquiring no ownership in the entity as he would when purchasing stock, but instead is now a creditor of the borrowing entity.

2. 1. 2. 1 Bond Characteristics

Before we explore bonds from different issuers (corporate, federal government, and municipal governments) let's introduce some basic bond characteristics.

2. 1. 2. 1. 1 Maturities

Each bond has its own maturity date. This is the date the investor receives the loan principal back. While common maturities are in the 5–30 year range some can be much shorter (short-term debt securities) and others longer. Maturities come in different types: term, serial, and balloon.

- Term—A **term bond** is structured so that the principal of the whole issue matures at once. Because the entire principal is repaid at one time, issuers may establish a sinking fund account to accumulate money to retire the bonds at maturity.

- Serial—A **serial bond issue** schedules portions of the principal to mature at intervals over a period of years until the entire balance has been repaid.

- Balloon—An issuer sometimes schedules its bond's maturity using elements of both serial and term maturities. The issuer repays part of the bond's principal before the final maturity date, as with a serial maturity, but pays off the major portion of the bond at maturity. This bond has a **balloon**, or **serial and balloon**, maturity.

2. 1. 2. 1. 2   Coupons

The coupon represents the interest rate the issuer has agreed to pay the investor. At one time, bonds were actually issued with interest coupons attached that the investor would detach and turn in to receive the interest payments. While bonds are no longer issued with physical coupons attached, the interest rate the bond pays is still called the coupon rate. It is also referred to as the stated or nominal yield. It is calculated from the bond's par value, usually stated as a percentage of par. Par value, also known as face value for a bond, is normally $1,000 per bond, meaning each bond will be redeemed for $1,000 when it matures. Therefore a bond with a 6% coupon is paying $60 in interest per year (6% × $1,000 Par value = $60)

TAKE NOTE

Interest is generally paid on a semi-annual basis. Using the previous example, the 6% coupon bond would pay $30 in interest every six months, a total of $60 per year.

2. 1. 2. 1. 3   Pricing

Once a bond is trading in the secondary markets they can trade at a price of par, a premium to par, or a discount to par. If par equals $1,000, an example of a premium bond might be one trading at $1,200 and an example of a discount bond might be one trading at $800.

2. 1. 2. 1. 4   Market Forces Affecting Bond Prices

Bond prices can be impacted by the usual market forces that impact securities in general, such as supply and demand. However, because they are debt instruments they have a particular sensitivity to changes in market interest rates. Remember that the interest rate the issuer pays is the cost of borrowing money. In that light, it makes sense that bond prices will rise and fall as interest rates fluctuate.

Generally, bond prices have an inverse relationship to interest rates. If interest rates go up, bond prices for those trading in the secondary markets will go down. Conversely, if interest rates are falling, bond prices for those trading in the secondary market will be going up. Think about it this way. If interest rates in the market place were at 6%, wouldn't a bond currently paying 8% trading in the secondary market look attractive? It would, and as investors were attracted to it, its price would push upward. On the other hand, if interest rates in the market place were at 6%, wouldn't a bond currently paying only 4% look less attractive? It would, and as investors moved to sell it, its price would move downward.

Though the price of the bond will react to market forces (interest rate sensitivity and general supply and demand) the coupon is always the same. The coupon is a fixed percentage of par value; a 6% coupon pays $60 of annual interest no matter what the current market value of the bond is.

2. 1. 2. 1. 5 Yields

A bond's yield expresses the cash interest payments in relation to the bond's value. Yield is determined by the issuer's credit quality, prevailing interest rates, time to maturity, and any features the bond may have, such as a call feature that we'll discuss shortly. As noted earlier, a bond can be traded at prices other than par, so the price discount or premium from par is taken into consideration when calculating a bond's overall yield. You can look at a bond's yield in several ways.

■ Nominal yield—Coupon, nominal, or stated yield is set at the time of issue. Remember that the coupon is a fixed percentage of the bond's par value.

■ Current yield—Current yield (CY) measures a bond's annual coupon payment (interest) relative to its market price, as shown in the following equation:
Annual coupon payment ÷ market price = current yield

■ Yield to maturity—A bond's **yield to maturity** (YTM) reflects the annualized return of the bond if held to maturity. In calculating yield to maturity, the bondholder takes into account the difference between the price that was paid for a bond and par value received when the bond matures. If the bond is purchased at a discount, the investor makes money at maturity; in other words, the discount amount increases the return. If the bond is purchased at a premium, the investor loses money at maturity; in other words, the premium amount decreases the return.

If a bond is purchased for $900 (a discount) and is held to maturity, at maturity the investor will receive $1,000 (par). The amount of the discount ($100) increases the investor's return. On the other hand, if a bond is purchased for $1,100 (a premium) and is held to maturity, at maturity the investor will receive $1,000 (par) and the amount of the premium paid ($100) reduces the investor's return.

■ Yield to call—Some bonds are issued with what is known as a call feature. A bond with a call feature may be redeemed before maturity at the issuer's option. Essentially, when a callable bond is called in by the issuer, the investor receives the principal back sooner than anticipated (before maturity). Yield to call (YTC) calculations reflect the early redemption date and consequent acceleration of the discount gain if the bond was originally purchased at a discount, or the accelerated premium loss if the bond was originally purchased at a premium.

Recognizing the relationship these yields have to one another is important and it will depend on if a bond is trading at par, a premium, or a discount. This is visualized in the following diagram where you should note that while the coupon (nominal or stated) yield never changes regardless of price, the CY, YTM, and YTC do.

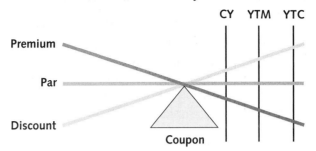

Current Yield, Yield to Maturity, and Yield to Call

2. 1. 2. 1. 6 Features

Bonds can be issued with different features attached. Among the most common are the following;

- Call feature—As noted previously, a call feature allows an issuer to call in a bond before maturity. Issuers will generally do this when interest rates are falling. From the issuers' perspective, why pay 6% interest to investors on an existing bond if current interest rates have fallen to 4%? It is better to call in the 6% bond and simply issue a new bond paying the lower current interest rate. This feature benefits the issuer.

- Put feature—A put feature for a bond is the opposite of a call feature. Instead of the issuer calling in a bond before it matures, with a put feature the investor can put the back to the issuer before it matures. Investors will generally do this when interest rates are rising. From the investors' perspective, why accept 6% interest on a bond one owns if current interest rates have risen to 8%? It is better to put the 6% bond back to the issuer, take the principal returned, and invest it in a new bond paying the current interest rate of 8%. This feature benefits the bondholder.

- Convertible—Much like our discussion of convertible preferred stock, convertible bonds are issued by corporate issuers allowing the investor to convert the bond into shares of common stock. Giving the investor the opportunity to exchange a debt instrument for one that gives the investor ownership rights (shares of common stock) is generally considered a benefit for the investor.

TAKE NOTE

When bonds are issued with features that benefit the issuer, like a call feature, the issuer generally will need to pay a slightly higher coupon rate of interest to make the bond attractive to new investors. Conversely, when bonds are issued with features that benefit the bondholder, like put or conversion features, the issuer can usually pay a slightly lower coupon rate of interest as the feature will compensate for the lower return.

2. 1. 2. 2 Treasury Securities

The U.S. Treasury Department determines the quantity and types of government securities it must issue to meet federal budget needs. The marketplace determines the interest rates those securities will pay.

The federal government is the nation's largest borrower as well as the best credit risk. Securities issued by the U.S. government are backed by its full faith and credit, based on its power to tax. In this light, securities issued by the U.S. government are considered to be among the highest in quality regarding safety of principal. These securities are classified as bills, notes, and bonds which distinguish each issue's term to maturity (short, intermediate, and long-term).

Finally, government securities issued by the U.S. Treasury are all issued in book-entry form, meaning that no physical securities (paper certificates) exist.

2. 1. 2. 2. 1 Treasury Bills (T-Bills)

U.S. Treasury bills are direct short-term debt obligations of the U.S. government. They are issued weekly with maturities of 4 weeks, 13 weeks, 26 weeks, and at times, 52 weeks. Though the maximum maturity for T-bills is subject to change, they are always short term instruments; that is one year or less.

Treasury bills pay no interest in the way other bonds do; rather, they are issued at a discount from par value and redeemed at par. For example, an investor might purchase a $10,000, 26-week T-bill at a price of $9,800. She would receive no regular interest check, but, at maturity, the Treasury would send her a check for $10,000. The difference between the $9,800 she paid and the $10,000 she received would be considered her interest income even though she never received a separate interest check.

TAKE NOTE

Key points to remember regarding T-bills include:

- Treasury bills are the only Treasury security issued at a discount;

- Treasury bills are the only Treasury security issued without a stated interest rate;

- Treasury bills are highly liquid; and

- 13-week (also referred to as 90-day) Treasury bills are used in market analysis as the stereotypical "risk-free" investment.

2. 1. 2. 2. 2 Treasury Notes (T-Notes)

U.S. Treasury notes are direct debt obligations of the U.S. government. They pay semiannual interest as a percentage of the stated par value and they mature at par value. T-Notes have intermediate maturities (2–10 years).

2. 1. 2. 2. 3 Treasury Bonds (T-Bonds)

U.S. Treasury bonds are direct debt obligations of the U.S. government. They pay semiannual interest as a percentage of the stated par value and mature at par value. These government obligations have long-term maturities, greater than 10 years and up to 30 years.

Testable Features of Treasury Bills, Notes, and Bonds

Marketable Government Securities			
Type	**Maturity**	**Pricing**	**Form**
T-bills	Less than 1 year	Issued at a discount; priced on discount basis	Book entry
T-notes	2–10 years (intermediate-term)	Priced at percentage of par	Book entry
T-bonds	Greater than 10 years (long-term)	Priced at percentage of par	Book entry

2. 1. 2. 2. 4 *Treasury Receipts and STRIPS*

Treasury Receipts—Brokerage firms can create a type of bond known as a **Treasury receipt** from U.S. Treasury notes and bonds. Broker-dealers buy Treasury securities, place them in trust at a bank and sell separate receipts against the principal and coupon payments, essentially, separating the coupon interest payments from the principal. Although the Treasury securities held in trust collateralize the Treasury receipts, unlike Treasury securities, Treasury receipts are not backed by the full faith and credit of the U.S. government.

Treasury STRIPS (Separate Trading of Registered Interest and Principal of Securities)— The Treasury Department has its own version of receipts known as Treasury STRIPS. The Treasury Department designates certain issues as suitable for stripping into interest and principal components. Banks and broker-dealers perform the actual separation of interest coupon and principal and trading of the STRIPS.

TEST TOPIC ALERT

Treasury STRIPS are backed in full by the U.S. government. Treasury Receipts are not.

2. 1. 2. 3 U.S. Government Agency Issues

In addition to the U.S.-Treasury-issued securities, T-bills, T-notes, and T-bonds, the U.S. Congress authorizes the following agencies of the federal government to issue debt securities:

- Farm Credit Administration
- Government National Mortgage Association (GNMA or Ginnie Mae)
  Other agency-like organizations operated by private corporations include the following:
- Federal Home Loan Mortgage Corporation (FHLMC or Freddie Mac)
- Federal National Mortgage Association (FNMA or Fannie Mae)
- Student Loan Marketing Association (SLMA or Sallie Mae)

The term agency is sometimes used to refer to entities that are not technically government agencies, but that do have ties to the government. For example, Fannie Mae is privately owned but government sponsored.

TAKE NOTE

The settlement of agency-issued securities occurs regular way—two business days (T+2). These securities are generally known as asset-backed or mortgage-backed securities.

2. 1. 2. 3. 1   Farm Credit System

The Farm Credit System (FCS) is a national network of lending institutions that provides agricultural financing and credit. The system is a privately owned, government-sponsored enterprise that raises loanable funds through the sale of Farm Credit Securities to investors. These funds are made available to farmers through a nationwide network of banks and Farm Credit lending institutions. The Farm Credit Administration (FCA), a government agency, oversees the system.

2. 1. 2. 3. 2   Government National Mortgage Association (GNMA)

The Government National Mortgage Association (GNMA) is a government-owned corporation that supports the Department of Housing and Urban Development. Ginnie Maes are the only agency securities backed by the full faith and credit of the federal government.

2. 1. 2. 3. 3   Federal Home Loan Mortgage Corporation (Freddie Mac)

The Federal Home Loan Mortgage Corporation (FHLMC) is a public corporation. It was created to promote the development of a nationwide secondary market in mortgages by buying residential mortgages from financial institutions and packaging them into mortgage-backed securities for sale to investors.

2. 1. 2. 3. 4   Federal National Mortgage Association (Fannie Mae)

The Federal National Mortgage Association (FNMA) is a publicly held corporation that provides mortgage capital. FNMA purchases conventional and insured mortgages from agencies such as the FHA and the VA. The securities it creates are backed by FNMA's general credit.

2. 1. 2. 4   Corporate bonds

Corporate debt securities, like any other loan, may be either secured or unsecured. Secured debt securities are backed by various kinds of assets owned by the issuing corporation, whereas unsecured debt securities are backed only by the reputation, credit record, and financial stability of the corporation. The latter is commonly referred to as being backed by the corporation's full faith and credit.

2. 1. 2. 4. 1   Mortgage Bonds

Just as the owner of a home pledges a real asset (the home and land) as collateral for a loan (the mortgage), a corporation will borrow money backed by real estate and physical assets of the corporation. Just as a home ordinarily would have a market value greater than the principal amount of its mortgage, the value of the real assets pledged by the corporation will be in excess of the amount borrowed under that bond issue. If the corporation develops financial problems and is unable to pay the interest on the bonds, those real assets pledged as collateral are generally sold to pay off the mortgage bondholders. Having the real assets as collateral for the loan puts the purchaser of a mortgage bond in a position of safety. This is a secured loan.

2. 1. 2. 4. 2   Equipment Trust Certificates

Corporations, particularly railroads and other transportation companies, finance the acquisition of capital equipment used in the course of their business. For example, railroads will issue equipment trust certificates to purchase their rolling stock and locomotives. Title to the newly acquired equipment is held in trust, usually by a bank acting as trustee, until the certificates have been paid in full. When the railroad has finished paying off the loan, it receives clear title to its equipment from the trustee. If the railroad does not make the payments, the lender repossesses the collateral and sells it for his benefit. Again, this is in an example of secured loan; the obligation to pay the investor is secured by the equipment.

2. 1. 2. 4. 3   Collateral Trust Bonds

Sometimes a corporation wants to borrow money and has neither real estate (to back a mortgage bond) nor equipment (to back an equipment trust) to use as collateral. Instead, it deposits securities it owns into a trust to serve as collateral for the lenders. The securities it deposits can be securities in other corporations or those of partially or fully owned subsidiaries as long as the securities are marketable, that is readily able to be liquidated. Collateral trust certificates are secured by the securities deposited, and obviously, the better the quality of the securities, the better the quality of the certificate.

2. 1. 2. 4. 4   Debentures

A debenture is a debt obligation of the corporation backed only by its word and general creditworthiness. Debentures are written promises of the corporation to pay the principal at its due date and interest on a regular basis. Although this promise is as binding as a promise for a secured bond such as a mortgage bond, debentures are not secured by any pledge of property. They are sold on the general good faith and credit of the company, unsecured.

TAKE NOTE   Although debentures are unsecured, there are issuers whose credit standing is so good that their debentures might be considered safer than secured bonds of less creditworthy companies.

2. 1. 2. 4. 5   Guaranteed Bonds

Guaranteed bonds are backed by a company other than the issuing corporation such as a parent company. The value of the guarantee is only as good as the strength of the company making that guarantee.

TEST TOPIC ALERT   Never be fooled by the apparent strength of the word "guaranteed" as it relates to guaranteed bonds. These are unsecured debt securities.

2. 1. 2. 4. 6   Income Bonds

Income bonds, also known as adjustment bonds, are used when a company is reorganizing and coming out of bankruptcy. Income bonds pay interest only if the corporation has enough income to meet interest on debt obligations and if the board of directors declares that the interest payment be made. Obviously, income or adjustment bonds fall under the heading of unsecured debt securities.

TEST TOPIC ALERT

Income bonds are a true oxymoron. If an investor is seeking income; an *income bond* is not likely a suitable recommendation.

2. 1. 2. 4. 7   Senior of Subordinated Debt

The word senior is used to describe the relative priority of a security claim. For example, every preferred stock has a senior claim to common stock. In this regard, it is important to know that every debt security has senior claim to preferred stock. Secured bonds have a senior claim to unsecured bonds.

Sometimes the term *subordinated* is used to describe a class of debt securities. This means "belonging to a lower or inferior class or rank; secondary." It is usually used in describing a type of debenture. A subordinated debenture has a claim that is behind (junior to) that of any other creditor. However, no matter how subordinated the debenture, it is still senior to any stockholder.

EXAMPLE

Here is an example of the order or priority a trustee would follow if liquidating a corporation's securities due to bankruptcy:

■ Secured creditors' debt instruments (mortgage bonds, equipment trust certificates, collateral trust bonds, and mortgages)

■ Unsecured creditors' debt instruments (general creditors such as suppliers and utilities, debenture holders, guaranteed bonds, and income bonds)

■ Subordinated debt (debt holders who agree to be paid back last of all debt holders in the event a liquidation ever needs to occur)

■ Preferred stockholders

■ Common stockholders

2. 1. 2. 5   Municipal Securities

Municipal bonds are securities issued either by state or local governments or by U.S. territories, authorities, and special districts. Investors that buy such bonds are lending money to the issuers for the purpose of public works and construction projects (e.g., roads, hospitals, civic centers, sewer systems, and airports). Municipal securities are considered second in safety of principal only to U.S. government and U.S. government agency securities, but the safety of any particular issue is based on the issuing municipality's financial stability.

Two categories of municipal securities exist: general obligation (GO) bonds and revenue bonds.

2. 1. 2. 5. 1   General Obligation (GO) Bonds

General obligation bonds (GOs) are municipal bonds issued for capital improvements that benefit the entire community. Typically, these projects do not produce revenues, so principal and interest must be paid by taxes collected by the municipal issuer. Because of this backing, general obligation bonds are known as **full faith and credit issues** and are backed by the municipality's taxing power. Bonds issued by states are backed by income taxes, license fees, and sales taxes. Bonds issued by towns, cities, and counties are backed by property (**ad valorem**) taxes, license fees, fines, and all other sources of direct income to the municipality. School, road, and park districts may also issue municipal bonds backed by property taxes.

Finally, the amount of debt that a municipal government may incur can be limited by state or local statutes to protect taxpayers from excessive taxes. Debt limits can also make a bond safer for investors. The lower the debt limit, the less risk of excessive borrowing and default by the municipality. If an issuer wishes to issue GO bonds that would put it above its statutory debt limit, a public referendum is required. In this light, GO bonds are often associated with requiring voter approval.

2. 1. 2. 5. 2   Revenue bonds

Revenue bonds can be used to finance any municipal facility that generates sufficient income. These municipal bonds are considered to be self-supporting debt because principal and interest payments are made exclusively from revenues generated by the project or facility for which the debt was issued, such as:

- utilities (water, sewer, and electric);
- housing (public housing projects);
- transportation (airports and toll roads);
- education (college dorms and student loans);
- health (hospitals and retirement centers);
- industrial (industrial development and pollution control); and
- sports (stadium facilities).

Keeping in mind that revenue bonds are not supported by the issuers' authority to tax, they are not subject to statutory debt limits and therefore do not require voter approval.

2. 1. 2. 5. 3   Short-term Municipal Obligations (Anticipation Notes)

Municipal anticipation notes are short-term securities that generate funds for a municipality that expects other revenues soon. Usually, municipal notes have less than 12-month maturities, although maturities may range from three months to three years. They are repaid when the municipality receives the anticipated funds. Municipal notes fall into several categories.

- Municipalities issue tax anticipation notes (TANs) to finance current operations in anticipation of future tax receipts. This helps municipalities to even out cash flow between tax collection periods.
- Revenue anticipation notes (RANs) are offered periodically to finance current operations in anticipation of future revenues from revenue producing projects or facilities.
- Tax and revenue anticipation notes (TRANs) are a combination of the characteristics of both TANs and RANs.
- Bond anticipation notes (BANs) are sold as interim financing that will eventually be converted to long-term funding through a sale of bonds.

■ Tax-exempt commercial paper is often used in place of BANs and TANs for up to 270 days, though maturities are most often 30, 60, and 90 days.

■ Construction loan notes (CLNs) are issued to provide interim financing for the construction of housing projects.

■ Variable rate demand notes have a fluctuating interest rate and are usually issued with a put option.

■ Grant anticipation notes (GANs) are issued with the expectation of receiving grant money from the federal government.

2. 1. 2. 5. 4   Taxable Municipals

Some municipal issues are taxable, such as Build America Bonds. Build America Bonds (BABs) were created under the Economic Recovery and Reinvestment Act of 2009 to assist in reducing costs to issuing municipalities and stimulating the economy. While bonds to fund municipal projects have traditionally been sold in the tax-exempt arena, BABs are taxable obligations. Bondholders pay tax on interest received from BABs, but tax credits are provided in lieu of the tax-exempt status usually afforded the interest on municipal securities. These bonds attracted investors who would normally not buy tax-exempt municipal bonds, and expanded the pool of investors to include those in lower-income tax brackets, investors funding retirement accounts where tax-free securities would normally not be suitable, public pension funds, and foreign investors. Two types of Build America Bonds are issued: tax credit BABs and direct payment BABs.

■ Tax Credit BABs: These types of BABs provide the bondholder with a federal income tax credit equal to 35% of the interest paid on the bond in each tax year. If the bondholder lacks sufficient tax liability to fully use that year's credit, the excess credit may be carried forward.

■ Direct Payment BABs: Direct payment BABs provide no credit to the bondholder but instead provide the municipal issuer with payments from the U.S. Treasury equal to 35% of the interest paid by the issuer.

TAKE NOTE

The BABs program expired on December 31, 2010, without being renewed. However, in the short time that municipalities were permitted to issue BABs, billions of dollars of capital had been raised to fund municipal projects throughout the United States, and many of these issues will remain outstanding for years. Finally, it should be noted that the program could be reinstated at some time in the future, and the types of BABs offered and the credits they provide could be amended as well.

2. 1. 2. 5. 5   Section 529 Plans

A section 529 plan is a specific type of education savings account available to investors. The plans allow money saved to be used for qualified expenses for K-12 and post-secondary education. Qualified expenses include tuition at an elementary or secondary public, private or religious school, for up to $10,000 per year. Because they are state sponsored, they are defined as a municipal fund security. As such, the sale of these plans must be accompanied or preceded by an official statement or offering circular (similar to a prospectus) in the same way other municipal securities sales would be.

There are two basic types of 529 plans: prepaid tuition plans for state residents and savings plans for residents and nonresidents. Prepaid plans allow resident donors to lock in current tuition rates by paying now for future education costs. The more popular option is the savings plan, which allows donors to save money to be used later for education expenses.

Any adult can open a 529 plan for a future college student. The donor does not have to be related to the student. With a 529 plan, the donor can invest a lump sum or make periodic payments. When the student is ready for college, the donor withdraws the amount needed to pay for qualified education expenses (e.g., tuition, room and board, and books).

Contributions, which are considered gifts under federal tax law, are made with after-tax dollars, and earnings accumulate on a tax-deferred basis. Withdrawals are tax free at the federal level if they are used for qualified education expenses. Most states permit tax-free withdrawals as long as the donor has opened an in-state plan. In addition, many states allow contributions into in-state plans to be tax deductible. Therefore, if one of your customers wishes to open an out-of-state plan, you must advise the customer that certain tax advantages, such as the one just noted, may not be available to out-of-state donors.

Other relevant points regarding Section 529 plans are as follows.

- Overall contribution levels can vary from state to state.

- Assets in the account remain under the donor's control even after the student becomes of legal age.

- There are no income limitations on making contributions to a 529 plan.

- Plans allow for monthly payments if desired by the account owner.

- Account balances left unused may be transferred to a related beneficiary.

- Rollovers are permitted from one state's plan to another state's plan but no more than once every 12 months.

2. 1. 2. 5. 6   *Local Government Investment Pools (LGIPs)*

States establish local government investment pools (LGIPs) to provide other government entities, such as cities, counties, school districts or other state agencies, with a short-term investment vehicle to invest funds. The LGIPs are generally formed as a trust in which municipalities can purchase shares or units in the LGIP's investment portfolio.

While not a money market fund, most LGIPs operate similar to one. For instance, an LGIP may be permitted to maintain a fixed $1.00 Net Asset Value (NAV). Maintaining a stable NAV, similar to a money market mutual fund, facilitates liquidity and minimum price volatility.

LGIPs are not required to register with the SEC and are not subject to the SEC's regulatory requirements, given that LGIPs fall within the governmental exemption, just as municipal securities do. Therefore, investment guidelines and oversight for LGIPs can vary from state to state.

With no SEC registration required, there is no prospectus. However, LGIP programs do have disclosure documents, which generally include information statements, investment policy, and operating procedures. The information statement typically details the management fees associated with participation in the LGIP.

2. 1. 2. 5. 7   *Achieving a Better Life Experience (ABLE) Accounts*

ABLE accounts are tax-advantaged savings accounts for individuals with disabilities and their families. They were created as a result of the passage of the Achieving a Better Life Experience Act of 2014. The beneficiary of the account is the account owner, and income earned by the accounts is not taxed.

The ABLE Act limits eligibility to individuals with significant disabilities where the age of onset of the disability occurred before turning age 26. In this light, remember that one need not be under the age of 26 to be eligible to establish an ABLE account. One could be over the age of 26, but as long as the onset of the disability occurred before age 26 they are eligible to establish an ABLE account.

If an individual meets the age/onset criteria and is also receiving benefits either through Social Security insurance (SSI) and/or Social Security disability insurance (SSDI), they are automatically eligible to establish an ABLE account. Only one ABLE account per person is allowed.

Contributions to these accounts, which can be made by any person including the account beneficiary themselves, as well as family and friends, must be made using after-tax dollars and is not tax deductible for purposes of federal income taxes. Some states, however, do allow income tax deductions for contributions made to an ABLE account. Contributions by all participating individuals are limited to a specified dollar amount per year, which may be adjusted periodically to account for inflation.

2. 1. 2. 6 Money Market Instruments

In the financial marketplace, a distinction is made between the **capital market** and the **money market**. The capital market serves as a source of intermediate-term to long-term financing, usually in the form of equity or debt securities with maturities of more than one year.

The money market, on the other hand, provides very short-term funds to corporations, banks, broker-dealers, government municipalities, and the U.S. federal government.

Money market instruments are fixed-income (debt) securities with short-term maturities, typically one year or less. Because of their short-term maturities they are considered to be highly liquid. These securities also provide a relatively high degree of safety. Consider that because they are short term, they have little time to default. In return for the safety, investors forgo a higher return for the lower returns generally associated with money market securities.

Finally, investors who purchase money market securities generally do not receive interest payments; instead, these securities are typically issued at a discount and mature at face value. The return is the difference between the discounted purchase price and the face value received at maturity.

In the following sections we'll discuss the most widely used money market securities.

2. 1. 2. 6. 1 Certificate of Deposit (CD)

Banks issue and guarantee certificates of deposit (CDs) with fixed interest rates and minimum face values of $100,000 (Jumbo CDs), although face values of $1 million or more are common. Most mature in one year or less. Some that can be traded in the secondary market are known as negotiable CDs. Only these negotiable CDs are considered to be money market instruments.

A negotiable CD is a bank's version of an unsecured promissory note in the same way commercial paper is for corporations. In other words, it is a bank's promise to pay principal and interest—secured by no physical asset and backed only by the bank's good faith and credit.

2. 1. 2. 6. 2 Bankers' Acceptance

A banker's acceptance (BA) is a short-term time draft with a specified payment date drawn on a bank. Essentially, a BA is a postdated check or line of credit. The payment date of a banker's acceptance is normally between 1 and 270 days (9 months). Corporations use BAs extensively to finance international trade; that is, a banker's acceptance typically pays for goods and services in a foreign country.

2. 1. 2. 6. 3   Commercial Paper (prime paper, promissory notes)

Corporations issue short-term, unsecured commercial paper, known as promissory notes, to raise cash to finance accounts receivable and seasonal inventory gluts. Commercial paper maturities range from 1 to 270 days, although most mature within 90 days. Typically, companies with excellent credit ratings issue commercial paper.

2. 1. 2. 6. 4   U.S. Treasury Bills

U.S. Treasury bills are direct short-term debt obligations of the U.S. government. They are issued weekly with maturities of 4 weeks, 13 weeks, 26 weeks, and at times, 52 weeks.

TAKE NOTE

Though T-Notes and T-Bonds are issued with longer maturities than T- Bills, once the notes and bonds have only a year left to maturity they are considered to be money market instruments.

2. 1. 2. 6. 5   Repurchase Agreements (REPOs)

In a repurchase agreement (repo), a financial institution, such as a bank or broker-dealer, raises cash by temporarily selling some of the securities it holds with an agreement to buy back the securities at a later date at a slightly higher price. Thus, a repo is an agreement between a buyer and a seller to conduct a transaction (sale), and then to reverse that transaction (repurchase) in the future. The contract would include the repurchase price and a maturity date.

TAKE NOTE

There are also agreements known as reverse repurchase agreements. In a repo, a dealer agrees to sell its securities to a lender and buy them back at a higher price in the future. In a **reverse repurchase agreement**, or **reverse repo**, a dealer agrees to buy securities from an investor and sell them back later at a higher price.

2. 1. 2. 7   Federal Funds

The Federal Reserve Bank (FRB) mandates how much money its member banks must keep on reserve at the FRB. Any deposits in excess of the required amount are known as federal funds. These excess reserves or federal funds can be loaned from one member bank to another for the purpose of meeting the reserve requirement. These loans are very short-term and in most cases can literally occur overnight.

TEST TOPIC ALERT

In summation, why would you place money market securities in a client's portfolio?

■ Highly liquid

■ Very safe

■ A good place to invest money that will be needed soon (short-term)

In doing so, the client would be incurring the following risks.

■ Because of their many advantages, the rate of return is quite low, so these are not suitable for long-term investors.

■ Due to short-term maturities, principal is potentially being reinvested at a different rate each time the instrument matures (short intervals). In this light, not only is income minimal, but it will fluctuate with each new instrument purchased.

QUICK QUIZ 2.A

LEARNING OBJECTIVES
■ Compare the characteristics of equity and debt securities

1. Mr. Jones purchased $200,000 of ABC Corporation common stock five years ago. At one point, the value of his investment doubled. However, as a result of a recent class action law suit, the company has been ordered to pay 50% more than the company's net worth and ABC filed for bankruptcy. What is the maximum loss Mr. Jones can lose on his investment?

   A. $100,000, 50% of his original investment
   B. No more than his original investment of $200,000
   C. His original investment plus a 50% assessment for a total of $300,000
   D. $400,000, the amount his investment was once valued at

2. Rights of common stockholders include all of the following EXCEPT

   A. voting for the Board of Directors
   B. transferring ownership of the stock at any time
   C. receiving audited semi-annual reports
   D. preemptive rights

3. Zoe Smith wants to invest $100,000 in ABC common stock. Which of the following would be appropriate objectives when placing the order?

   I. A long term hedge against inflation
   II. The limited liability of ABC's common stock
   III. The stock may appreciate in value and pay a consistent cash dividend
   IV. The need for monthly dividend checks
   A. I and III
   B. I and IV
   C. II and III
   D. II and IV

4. Which two of the following preference items define preferred stock?

   I. Preferred dividends must be paid prior to paying common dividends.
   II. Preferred dividends are guaranteed, common dividends are not.
   III. Preferred stockholders are paid before common stockholders in the event of liquidation.
   IV. Preferred stockholders voting rights exceed those of common stockholders.
   A. I and III
   B. I and IV
   C. II and III
   D. II and IV

5. Match the following types of preferred stock to the definitions provided.

Callable

Convertible

Cumulative

Straight

Participating

Adjustable Rate

A. _____No special privileges, dividends not paid are not recovered

B. _____May receive a higher than stated dividend in profitable years

C. _____Dividend is tied to industry benchmarks such as the yield of Treasury bills

D. _____Is entitled to dividends in arrears

E. _____May be exchanged for shares of the corporation's common stock

F. _____Often redeemed by the issuer when interest rates fall

6. Under Rule 144, how long must a restricted security be held before it can be sold?

A. 90 days

B. 3 months

C. 6 months

D. 1 year

2. 1. 3   OPTIONS

Options are derivative securities. This means that they derive their value from that of an underlying instrument, such as a stock, stock index, interest rate, or foreign currency. Option contracts offer investors a means to hedge, or protect, an investment's value or speculate on the price movement of individual securities, markets, foreign currencies, and other instruments.

Two parties are involved in the contract; one party has the right to exercise the contract to buy or sell the underlying security, and the other is obligated to fulfill the terms of the contract. The amount paid for the contract when purchased, or received for the contract when it is sold, is called the contract premium.

The buyer who pays the premium for the contract is often referred to as the owner, holder, or party who is long the contract. The buyer has the right to exercise the contract.

The seller, who receives the premium for the contract, is referred to as the writer or party who is short the contract. The seller will be obligated to perform if the buyer chooses to exercise the contract.

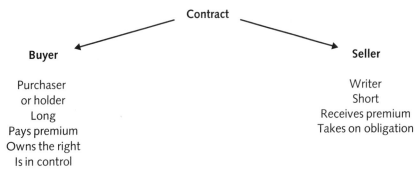

Contract

Buyer

Purchaser
or holder
Long
Pays premium
Owns the right
Is in control

Seller

Writer
Short
Receives premium
Takes on obligation

In theory, options can be created on any item with a fluctuating market value. The most familiar options are those issued on common stocks; they are called equity options. For the reminder of our discussion of options we'll focus on equity options.

There are two types of option contracts: *calls* and *puts*. Because two types of options (calls and puts) and two types of transactions (purchases and sales) exist, four basic transactions are available to an option investor:

- Buy calls
- Sell calls
- Buy puts
- Sell puts

2. 1. 3. 1   Basic Calls and Puts

As noted previously, investors can either buy or sell calls and puts. Buying and selling calls and puts are the basic option strategies. We'll look now at all four transactions.

2. 1. 3. 1. 1   Calls

An investor may buy calls (go long) or sell calls (go short). The features of each side of a call contract (long and short) are as follows:

- Long call (purchase): a call buyer owns the right to buy 100 shares of a specific stock at the strike price before the expiration if he chooses to exercise the contract. Therefore a call buyer is a bullish investor; one who anticipates the price of the underlying security will rise.

EXAMPLE

Long 1 XYZ Jan 60 call at 3

Long	The investor has bought the call and has the right to exercise the contract.
XYZ	The single contract represents 100 shares of XYZ stock.
Jan	The contract expires on the third Friday of January at 11:59 pm ET.
60	The strike price of the contract is 60.
Call	The type of option is a call, and the investor has the right to buy the stock at 60 since he is long the call.
3	The premium of the contract is $3 per share. Contracts are issued with 100 shares, so the total premium is $300. The investor paid the premium to buy the call.

Buyers of calls want the market price of the underlying stock to rise. The investor who owns this call hopes that the market price will rise above 60. He then has the right to buy the stock at the strike price of 60, even if the market price is higher (e.g., 80).

- Short call (sale): a call writer (seller) has the obligation to sell 100 shares of a specific stock at the strike price if the buyer exercises the contract. Therefore, a call writer is a bearish investor; one who anticipates the price of the underlying security will fall.

EXAMPLE

Short 1 XYZ Jan 60 call at 3

Short	The investor has sold the call and has obligations to perform if the contract is exercised.
XYZ	The single contract represents 100 shares of XYZ stock.
Jan	The contract expires on the third Friday of January at 11:59 pm ET. If expiration occurs, the writer keeps the premium without any obligation.
60	The strike price of the contract is 60.
Call	The type of option is a call, and the investor is obligated to sell the stock at 60, if exercised, because he is short the call.
3	The premium of the contract is $3 per share. Options contracts are issued with 100 shares, so the total premium is $300.

Writers of calls want the market price of the underlying stock to fall or stay the same. The investor who owns this call (the buyer) hopes that the market price will rise or go above 60. Therefore the writer hopes the market price will stay at or below 60 so that the contract would not be exercised. If the contract is unexercised by the time it expires the writer keeps the premium of $300 with no further obligation.

2. 1. 3. 1. 2   Puts

An investor may buy puts (go long) or sell puts (go short). The features of each side of a put contract (long and short) are as follows:

■ Long put (purchase): a put buyer owns the right to sell 100 shares of a specific stock at the strike price before the expiration if he chooses to exercise the contract. Therefore a put buyer is a bearish investor because he wants the price of the underlying security to fall.

EXAMPLE

Long 1 XYZ Jan 60 put at 3

Long	The investor has bought the put and has the right to exercise the contract.
XYZ	The single contract represents 100 shares of XYZ stock.
Jan	The contract expires on the third Friday of January at 11:59 pm ET.
60	The strike price of the contract is 60.
Put	The type of option is a put, and the investor has the right to sell the stock at 60 since he is long the put.
3	The premium of the contract is $3 per share. Contracts are issued with 100 shares, so the total premium is $300. The investor paid the premium to buy the put.

Buyers of puts want the market price of the underlying stock to fall. The investor who owns this put hopes that the market price will fall below 60. He then has the right to sell the stock at the strike price of 60, even if the market price is lower (e.g., 40).

■ Short put (sale): a put writer (seller) has the obligation to buy 100 shares of a specific stock at the strike price if the buyer exercises the contract. Therefore a put writer is a bullish investor because he wants the price of the underlying security to rise or remain unchanged.

Short 1 XYZ Jan 60 put at 3

Short	The investor has sold the put and has obligations to perform if the contract is exercised.
XYZ	The single contract represents 100 shares of XYZ stock.
Jan	The contract expires on the third Friday of January at 11:59 pm ET. If expiration occurs, the writer keeps the premium without any obligation.
60	The strike price of the contract is 60.
Put	The type of option is a put, and the investor is obligated to buy the stock at 60, if exercised, because he is short the put.
3	The premium of the contract is $3 per share. Options contracts are issued with 100 shares, so the total premium is $300.

2. 1. 3. 2 Market Attitude (Bullish or Bearish)

Depending on if investors are the buyers or the sellers of either a call or a put, they will have a particular market attitude about the underlying stock (bullish or bearish). Though being bullish or bearish on the underlying security was noted earlier, let's revisit and sum up market attitude.

CALLS

- A call buyer is a bullish investor because he wants the market to rise. The call is exercised only if the market price rises.
- A call writer is a bearish investor because he wants the market to fall (or remain unchanged). The contract is not exercised if the market price is below the strike price.

PUTS

- A put buyer is a bearish investor because he wants the market to fall. The put is exercised only if the market price falls below the strike price.
- A put writer is a bullish investor because he wants the market to rise or remain unchanged. The contract is not exercised if the market price is above the strike price.

Bullish and Bearish Options Positions

	Long	Short
Calls	Right to buy Bullish	Obligation to sell Bearish
Puts	Right to sell Bearish	Obligation to buy Bullish

(Buyer, Holder, Owner)   (Seller, Writer, Grantor)

2. 1. 3. 3 In-the-Money, At-the-Money, Out-of-the-Money, intrinsic value and parity

Options contracts can be described using various terms unique to the options marketplace. One way to describe a contract is being in, at, or out-of-the-money. Another would be to describe whether or not it has intrinsic value, or is trading at parity. We'll look at all of these for both calls and puts.

2. 1. 3. 3. 1   Calls (In, At, or Out-of-the-money, Intrinsic Value and Parity)

In-the-money—A call is **in-the-money** when the price of the stock exceeds the strike price of the call. A buyer will exercise calls that are in-the-money at expiration. Buyers want options to be in-the-money; sellers do not.

At-the-money—A call is **at-the-money** when the price of the stock equals the strike price of the call. A buyer will not exercise contracts that are at-the-money at expiration. Sellers want at-the-money contracts at expiration; buyers do not. Sellers then keep the premium without obligations to perform.

Out-of-the-money—A call is **out-of-the-money** when the price of the stock is lower than the strike price of the call. A buyer will not exercise calls that are out-of-the-money at expiration. Sellers want contracts to be out-of-the-money; buyers do not. Sellers then keep the premium without obligations to perform.

Intrinsic value—**Intrinsic value** is the same as the amount a contract is in-the-money. A call has intrinsic value when the market price of the stock is above the strike price of the call. Options never have negative intrinsic value; intrinsic value is always a positive amount or zero. Options that are at-the-money or out-of-the-money have an intrinsic value of zero. Buyers like calls to have intrinsic value; sellers (writers) do not. A call that has intrinsic value at expiration will be exercised by the buyer. A call that has no intrinsic value will simply be allowed to expire.

During the lifetime of an option contract, buyers want the contract to move in-the-money; sellers want the contract to move out-of-the-money.

Parity—A call option is at **parity** when the premium equals intrinsic value.

EXAMPLE

ABC stock is at 62

ABC June 60 call trading at 2

With ABC stock trading at 62, a 60 call has an intrinsic value of 2 (Stock Price 62 – Strike Price 60 = 2). Given this call contract is trading at a premium of 2, it is known to be trading at parity.

---

2. 1. 3. 3. 2   Puts (In, At, or Out-of-the-money, Intrinsic Value and Parity)

In-the-money—A put is **in-the-money** when the price of the stock is lower than the strike price of the put. A buyer will exercise puts that are in-the-money at expiration. Buyers want inthe-money contracts; sellers do not.

At-the-money—A put is **at-the-money** when the price of the stock equals the strike price of the put. A buyer will not exercise contracts that are at-the-money at expiration. Sellers want at-the-money contracts; buyers do not.

Out-of-the-money—A put is **out-of-the-money** when the price of the stock is higher than the strike price of the put A buyer will not exercise puts that are out-of-the-money at expiration. Sellers want out-of-the-money contracts; buyers do not.

Intrinsic value—**Intrinsic value** is the same as the amount a contract is in-the-money. A put has intrinsic value when the market price of the stock is below the strike price of the put. Remember that options never have negative intrinsic value; it is always a positive number or zero. Buyers like options to have intrinsic value; sellers do not. A put that has intrinsic value at expiration will be exercised. A put that has no intrinsic value at expiration will simply be allowed to expire.

Parity—A put option is at **parity** when the premium equals intrinsic value.

EXAMPLE

ABC stock is at 58

ABC June 60 put trading at 2

With ABC stock trading at 58, a 60 put has an intrinsic value of 2. (Strike Price 60 – Stock Price 58 = 2) Given this put contract is trading at a premium of 2, it is known to be trading at parity.

2. 1. 3. 4   Basic Calculations (Breakeven, Maximum Gain and Maximum Loss)

For each of the four basic options positions (long call, short call, long put short put) you will want to be comfortable with calculating the investors breakeven point, maximum potential gain and maximum potential loss. The breakeven (BE) point is the point at which the investor neither makes nor loses money. Realizing maximum gain (MG) or maximum loss (ML) has to do with the market attitude of the position (bullish or bearish) which direction the stock moves, and far it goes in that direction. Remember that in theory a stock could go as high as infinity or as low as zero.

2. 1. 3. 4. 1   Calls: BE, MG and ML

Long call—Remember that call buyers are *bullish*. By purchasing calls, an investor can profit from an increase in a stock's price.

Breakeven (BE)—For calls, the breakeven is found by adding the strike price and the premium. For the call buyer, the contract is profitable above the breakeven.

Maximum Gain (MG)—Theoretically, the potential gains available to call buyers are unlimited because there is no limit on how far a stock's price can rise. In theory it can rise to infinity and thus the potential gain is unlimited.

Maximum Loss (ML)—The most the call buyer can lose is the premium paid. This will happen if the stock price is at or below the strike price of the option at expiration.

EXAMPLE

Long 1 July 40 call at 3

BE = strike price + premium (40 + 3) = 43

Above 43 the call buyer is profitable

MG = unlimited, because the stock can rise to infinity

ML = premium paid (3 points) = $300)

Short call—Remember that call sellers (writes) are bearish. By writing calls, an investor can profit if the stock price falls.

Breakeven (BE)—Once again, for calls the breakeven is found by adding the strike price to the premium but the for the call seller, the contract is profitable below the breakeven.

Maximum Gain (MG)—A call writer's maximum gain is the premium received. The maximum gain is earned when the stock price is at or below the exercise price at expiration.

Maximum Loss (ML)—A call writer's maximum loss is unlimited because the writer could be forced to buy the stock at a potentially unlimited price, if the option is exercised by the buyer, for delivery at the strike price.

EXAMPLE

Short 1 July 40 call at 3

BE = strike price + premium (40 + 3) = 43

At or below 43 the call writer is profitable

MG = premium received (3 points) = $300

ML = unlimited, because the writer can be forced to purchase the stock at an unlimited number; infinity.

TAKE NOTE

Call Summary

BE is the same for both buyer and seller, while one investor's MG is the other's ML.

Call	Buyer	Seller
BE	Strike Price + Premium	Strike Price + Premium
Max Gain	Unlimited	Premium
Max Loss	Premium	Unlimited

2. 1. 3. 4. 2   Puts: BE, MG and ML

Long put—Remember that put buyers are *bearish*. By purchasing puts, an investor can profit from a decrease in a stock's price.

Breakeven (BE)—For puts, the breakeven is found by subtracting the premium from the strike price. For the put buyer, the contract is profitable below the breakeven at expiration.

Maximum gain (MG)—The maximum potential gain available to put owners is the option's strike price less the amount of the premium paid (same as the breakeven). A stock's price can fall no lower than zero.

Maximum loss (ML)—The most the put buyer can lose is the premium paid. This happens if the market price is at or above the strike price at the option's expiration.

EXAMPLE

Long 1 July 40 put at 3

BE = strike price – premium (40 – 3) = 37

Below 37 the put buyer is profitable

MG = from the BE down to 0. The same as BE = 37 points ($3,700)

ML = premium paid (3 points) = $300

Short put—Remember that put sellers (writers) are *bullish*. By writing puts, an investor can profit if the stock price rises.

Breakeven (BE)—Once again, for puts, the breakeven is found by subtracting the premium from the strike price. For the put seller, the contract is profitable at or above the breakeven at expiration

Maximum Gain (MG)—A put writer's maximum gain is the premium received. The maximum gain is earned when the stock price is at or above the exercise price at expiration.

Maximum Loss (ML)—A put writer's maximum loss is the put's strike price less the premium received (the same as the breakeven); it occurs when the stock price drops to zero. The investor is forced to buy the worthless stock at the option's strike price. The investor's loss is reduced by the premium received.

E X A M P L E

Short 1 July 40 put at 3

BE = strike price – premium (40 – 3) = 37

At or above 37 the put writer is profitable

MG = premium received (3 points) = $300

ML = from the BE down to 0. The same as BE = 37 points ($3,700)

T A K E   N O T E

Put Summary

BE is the same for both buyer and seller, while one investor's MG is the other's ML.

Put	Buyer	Seller
BE	Strike price – premium	Strike price – premium
Max gain	Strike price – premium	Premium
Max loss	Premium	Strike price – premium

2. 1. 3. 5   Options Clearing Corporation (OCC) and Contract Specifications

The **Options Clearing Corporation** (OCC) is the clearing agent for listed options contracts; that is those listed for trading on U.S. options exchanges. Its primary functions are to standardize, guarantee the performance of, and issue option contracts. The OCC determines when new option contracts should be offered to the market on an underlying security. It designates the contract specifications such as strike prices and expiration months for new contracts utilizing standards to maintain uniformity and liquidity. Following are some standards and characteristics of listed option contracts:

- **Trading times**—Listed options trade from 9:30 am – 4:00 pm ET.
- **Settlement**—Listed options settle on the next business day after trade date (T + 1).
- **Expiration**—Listed options expire on the third Friday of the expiration month at 11:59 pm.
- **Exercise**—Listed options can be exercised by the owner from the time of purchase until they expire. The exercise process is guaranteed by the OCC. If a holder of an option wishes to exercise his contract, his broker-dealer notifies the OCC.
- **Automatic exercise**—Any contract that is in-the-money by at least .01 will be exercised automatically at expiration for the holder unless the holder gives "do not exercise" instructions.
- **Assignment**—When the OCC receives an exercise notice they *assign* the exercise notice to a short broker-dealer; that is one who has a customer who is short the contract. The short broker-dealer assigns a short customer who is now obligated to perform (buy or sell the stock at the strike price).

The OCC assigns exercise notices to short broker-dealers on a **random** basis. Broker-dealers may then assign exercise notices to their short customers on a random basis, on a first in, first out (FIFO) basis, or any other method that is fair and reasonable.

TAKE NOTE

Options contracts are traded without a certificate. An investor's proof of ownership is the trade confirmation.

2. 1. 3. 6   Exercise and Assignment

The owner of a call (party long the contract) has the right to **buy** the stock at the strike price. To do so they must exercise the call. The writer of the call will then be assigned, meaning they must now fulfill their obligation to sell the stock at the strike price.

The owner of a put (party long the contract) has the right to sell the stock at the strike price. To do so they must exercise the put. The writer of the put will then be assigned, meaning they must now fulfill their obligation to buy the stock at the strike price.

TAKE NOTE

Only owners of options contracts, those who are long the contracts, have the right to exercise them. Writers of contracts, those who are short the contracts, will be assigned to fulfill their obligation to perform; either sell, if short a call, or buy if short a put.

2. 1. 3. 6. 1   American vs. European

Call or put buyers can exercise a contract any time before expiration if the contract is an American-style option. European-style options can be exercised on expiration day (last day of trading) only. Nearly all equity options are American style. Foreign currency options may be either American style or European style.

2. 1. 3. 7   Underlying Security or Cash Settled

When an equity option is exercised shares of stock must be delivered. This is known as being settled in the underlying security. However, index and foreign currency options are cash settled. Instead of shares of stock being delivered as a result of the exercise, cash must be delivered by the party assigned (short the contract). This is because delivering all of the components of an index would be nearly impossible and delivering foreign currency would require exchanging one currency for another, and possibly having banking relationships abroad. Settling in cash (U.S. dollars) facilitates the exercise and assignment process much easier for U.S. investors.

2. 1. 3. 8 Risks, Approvals, and Disclosures

The OCC requires that certain documents be provided to customers who wish to open options accounts. The **OCC Options Disclosure Document** (ODD) must be provided at or before the time the account approval. This document explains options strategies, risks, and rewards and is designed to provide full and fair disclosure to customers before they begin options trading.

Before any trading can take place, an options account must be approved. Initially it can be approved by a branch office manager (BOM), but then promptly thereafter it must be approved by a registered options principal (ROP) of the firm.

TEST TOPIC ALERT

All options accounts must ultimately be approved by a firms registered options principal (ROP).

Then, not later than 15 days after the account approval, the customer must return the signed **options agreement**. This document states that the customer has read the options disclosure document, understands the risks of options trading, and will honor all rules regulations regarding options trading. By signing, the customer also agrees to advise the firm if any changes occur in his financial situation, investment objectives, and so forth that would impact whether or not the account should still be approved for options trading.

If the signed options agreement is not returned within 15 days of account approval, the investor cannot open new options positions. Only closing transactions are allowed if the options agreement is not returned as required.

TAKE NOTE

Note the chronological conundrum that exists. The options account must be approved before trading can occur. However, it is possible that the account has been approved, trades have occurred, and yet the customer, having 15 days after approval to do so, still has not returned the signed options account agreement.

Options Account Diagram

2. 1. 3. 9   Covered vs. Uncovered (Naked)

Those who sell calls and puts—those who are short the contract—are known as writers. When we note an option contract as being covered or uncovered we are speaking to the writer's option position and whether or not they already own the underlying security to be delivered (or have the cash available if the contract is cash settled) in the event that the owner exercises the contract.

■ **Covered**—If the contract is covered, the writer already owns the underlying security. This ensures the writer's ability to perform (deliver), should the owner exercise the contract.

■ **Uncovered (naked)**—If the contract is uncovered (naked), the writer does not own the underlying security. If the contract is exercised by the owner the writer will need to purchase the underlying security at the current market price in order to deliver it.

TAKE NOTE

Uncovered (naked) contracts entail much more risk due to the uncertainty in price regarding purchase of the security in the current marketplace if the contract is exercised. Writers of naked calls are willing to accept that risk in return for taking in the premium when selling short (writing) the call.

EXAMPLE

Covered Call

Long 100 shares of XYZ at 40

Short 1 XYZ July 45 call

If the owner exercises the call, the writer will need to deliver the stock at the strike price (45). Already owning the stock at 40, this poses no risk.

EXAMPLE

Uncovered Call (Naked)

Short 1 XYZ July 45 call

If the owner exercises the call, the writer will need to deliver the stock at the strike price (45). Not owning the stock, the writer will need to purchase the stock in the open market in order to deliver it.

QUICK QUIZ 2.B

LEARNING OBJECTIVES

■ Recognize the basic option contract characteristics

■ Calculate premiums, breakeven points, and maximum gain and loss for simple option positions

1. An investor is long 1 XYZ May 40 call and XYZ stock has a current market value of 44. Which of the following is TRUE?

    A. The May 40 call is at-the-money.
    B. The May 40 call is in-the-money.
    C. The May 40 call is out-of-the-money.
    D. The May 40 call has no intrinsic value.

2. An investor is long 1 August XYZ 30 put and XYZ is has a current market value of 25. Which of the following is TRUE?

    A. The August 30 put is in-the-money by 5 points.
    B. The August 30 put is at-the-money.
    C. The August 30 put is out-of-the-money by 30 points.
    D. The August 30 put has no intrinsic value.

3. An investor writes (sells) a July 25 ABC call. Which of the following is a TRUE statement?

    A. The investor has the right to purchase ABC stock at 25.
    B. The investor has the right to sell ABC stock at 25.
    C. The investor will be obligated to purchase ABC stock at 25 if the call is exercised by the owner (buyer).
    D. The investor will be obligated to sell the ABC stock at 25 if the call is exercised by the owner (buyer).

4. An investor writes a September 65 ABC put. Which of the following is a TRUE statement?

    A. A.) The investor will be obligated to sell ABC stock at 65 if the put is exercised by the owner (buyer).
    B. The investor will be obligated to purchase ABC stock at 65 if the put is exercised by the owner (buyer).
    C. C.) The investor has the right to sell ABC stock at 65.
    D. D.) The investor has the right to purchase ABC stock at 65.

5. An investor is long 1 January 30 call at 2. Calculate the following:

    Breakeven _____

    Maximum Gain _____

    Maximum Loss _____

6. An investor is long 1 January 15 put at 4. Calculate the following:

    Breakeven _____

    Maximum Gain _____

    Maximum Loss _____

7. All of the following are true statements EXCEPT

    A. BE is always the same number for both buyer and seller of an option contract
    B. the maximum loss for options buyers is the premium paid
    C. the maximum gain for options buyers is always unlimited
    D. BE is calculated using the same formula for both buyer and seller

8. Listed options transactions settle regular way

    A. on the third Friday of the expiration month
    B. on the next business day after trade date (T + 1)
    C. on the third business day after trade date (T + 3)
    D. when the option finally expires

9. Regarding assignment of exercises notices, which of the following are TRUE?
   I. OCC assigns short broker-dealers randomly.
   II. OCC assigns short broker-dealers using the first in, first out (FIFO) accounting method.
   III. Short broker-dealers can assign their short customers randomly only.
   IV. Short broker-dealers can assign their short customers randomly, using the first in, first out (FIFO) accounting method or by any other fair method.
   A. I and III.
   B. I and IV.
   C. II and III.
   D. II and IV.

10. A customer of a broker-dealer is opening a new options account. The customer must return the options agreement
    A. signed before the account can be approved
    B. prior to the first transaction can occur
    C. signed and not later than 15 days after the account approval
    D. before he will be allowed to view the options disclosure document

2. 1. 4 INVESTMENT COMPANIES

An **investment company** is a corporation or trust that pools investors' money and then invests that money in securities on their behalf. Investors are able to pool their money and have the investment company invest it based on a clearly defined objective such as growth or income. By investing these pooled funds as a single large account, jointly owned by every investor in the company, the investment company is able to invest in many different securities and therefore reduce the overall risk associated with investing in only one or a few. These pooled investments can total hundreds of millions or even billions of dollars. They are very popular investment vehicles as it is common for them to allow minimum investments of perhaps only $100 or even less. While investing $100 many times might not purchase a single share of stock or one bond, the ability to pool that $100 with thousands or millions of investors gives the individual investor a great advantage—purchasing power in the marketplace.

Like corporate issuers, investment companies raise capital by selling shares to the public. Investment companies must abide by the same registration and prospectus requirements imposed by the Securities Act of 1933 on other issuers. Investment companies are subject to regulations regarding how their shares are sold to the public, and they are regulated by the **Investment Company Act of 1940**.

2. 1. 4. 1 Types of Investment Companies

The Investment Company Act of 1940 classifies investment companies into three broad types: face-amount certificate companies (FACs), unit investment trusts (UITs), and management investment companies.

Classification of Investment Companies

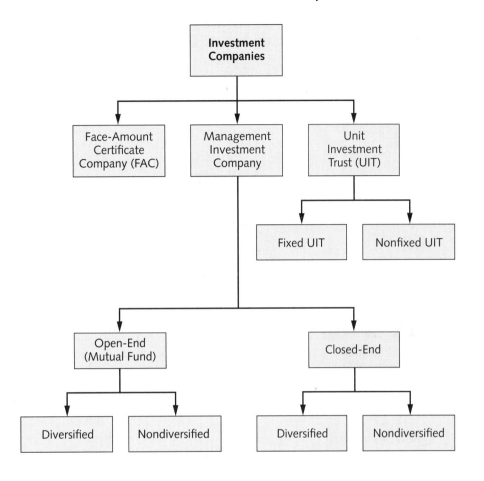

Variable annuities have subaccounts that are defined as either UITs or open-end management investment companies.

2. 1. 4. 1. 1   Face Amount Certificates

A face-amount certificate (FAC) is a contract between an investor and an issuer in which the issuer guarantees payment of a stated (face amount) sum to the investor at some set date in the future. In return for this future payment, the investor agrees to pay the issuer a set amount of money either as a lump sum or in periodic installments. If the investor pays for the certificate in a lump sum, the investment is known as a fully-paid face-amount certificate.

Issuers of these investments are face-amount certificate companies. Very few face-amount certificate companies operate today.

2. 1. 4. 1. 2   Unit Investment Trusts (UITs)

A **unit investment trust** (UIT) is an investment company organized under a trust indenture. Unit investment trusts do not have boards of directors (they have trustees).

UITs create a portfolio of debt or equity securities designed to meet the company's objectives. They then sell **redeemable interests**, also known as **units** or **shares of beneficial interest,** in their portfolio of securities. Each share is an undivided interest in the entire underlying portfolio.

A UIT may be fixed or nonfixed. A debt **fixed UIT** typically purchases a portfolio of bonds and terminates when the bonds in the portfolio mature. An equity fixed UIT purchases a portfolio of stocks and, because stocks don't have a maturity date, terminates at a pre-determined date. A **nonfixed UIT** purchases shares of an underlying mutual fund.

TAKE NOTE

- FACs and UITs are not managed; once the portfolios are composed, they do not change.

- FACs and UITs do not trade in the secondary market; they are redeemable only through the issuer.

2. 1. 4. 1. 3   Managed Investment Companies (Closed and Open-End)

The most familiar type of an investment company is the **management investment company,** which actively manages a securities portfolio to achieve a stated investment objective. A management investment company is either closed-end or open-end. Both closed- and open-end companies sell shares to the public in an initial public offering; the primary difference between them is that a closed-end company's initial offering of shares is limited (it closes after a specific authorized number of shares have been sold) and an open-end company is perpetually offering new shares to the public (it is continually open to new investors). In this section, we'll look at each.

Closed-end investment companies—A closed-end company will raise capital for its portfolio by conducting a common stock offering, much like any other publicly traded company that raises capital to invest in its business. In the initial offering, the company registers a fixed number of shares with the SEC and offers them to the public with a prospectus for a limited time through underwriters. Once all the shares have been sold, the fund is closed to new investors. Many times, a fund elects to be a closed-end company because the sector in which it intends to invest has a limited amount of securities available. Closed-end investment companies may also issue bonds and preferred stock.

Closed-end investment companies are often called **publicly traded funds**. After the stock is sold in the initial offering, anyone can buy or sell shares in the secondary market (i.e., on an exchange or OTC) in transactions between private investors. Supply and demand determine the **bid price** (price at which an investor can sell) and the **ask price** (price at which an investor can buy). Closed-end fund shares may trade above (at a premium to) or below (at a discount to) the shares' net asset value (NAV). Simply put, the fund's NAV is its assets minus its liabilities. The NAV per share is the fund's NAV divided by the number of outstanding shares.

TEST TOPIC ALERT

- Closed-end investment companies are the only investment company security that trades in the secondary market.

- Closed-end investment companies may issue common stock, preferred stock, and debt securities.

Open-end investment companies (Mutual Funds)—An open-end company only issues one class of security, which is common stock (no preferred shares or bonds). It does not specify the exact number of shares it intends to issue but registers an open offering with the SEC. In other words, mutual funds conduct a continuous primary offering of common stock. With this registration type, they can raise an unlimited amount of investment capital by continuously issuing new shares.

When investors want to sell their holdings in a mutual fund, the fund itself redeems those shares. In this respect, mutual fund shares are like FACs and UITs in that they do not trade in the secondary market. When an investor sells shares back to the fund (the fund is redeeming the shares), the fund sends the investor money for the investor's proportionate share of the fund's net assets. Therefore, a mutual fund's capital shrinks when investors redeem shares but so does the number of outstanding shares; the value of each share does not fall as a result of the redemption.

TAKE NOTE

You should understand that while mutual funds only issue common shares to their shareholders, the funds themselves can purchase common stock, preferred stock, and bonds for their investment portfolios. As noted, each fund has a stated investment objective, and which types of securities the fund portfolio purchases has largely to do with fulfilling that objective.

This table summarizes the differences between open-end and closed-end fund companies.

Comparison of Open-End and Closed-End Investment Companies

	Open-End	Closed-End
Capitalization	Unlimited; continuous offering of shares	Fixed; single offering of shares
Issues	Common stock only; no debt securities; permitted to borrow	Common and preferred stock; debt securities
Shares	Full or fractional	Full only
Offerings and Trading	Sold and redeemed by fund only; continuous primary offering; must redeem shares	Initial primary offering; secondary trading OTC or on an exchange; does not redeem shares
Pricing	NAV + sales charge; selling price determined by formula in the prospectus	CMV + commission; price determined by supply and demand
Shareholder Rights	Dividends (when declared); voting	Dividends (when declared); voting; preemptive
Ex-date	Set by BOD	Set by the exchange or FINRA

2.1.4.1.4 Variable Contracts/Annuities

An **annuity** is an insurance contract designed to provide retirement income. The term *annuity* refers to a stream of payments guaranteed for some period of time. That might be for the life of the annuitant, until the annuitant reaches a certain age, or for a specific number of years. The actual amount to be paid out may or may not be guaranteed, but the stream of payments itself is. Because an annuity can provide an income for the rest of someone's life, the contract has a **mortality guarantee**. When you think about a retiree's greatest fear, it is typically outliving their income. This product can take away that fear.

Insurance companies introduced the variable annuity as an opportunity to keep pace with inflation. For this potential advantage, the investor assumes the investment risk rather than the insurance company. Because the investor takes on this risk, the product is considered a security. Individuals who are both insurance licensed and securities licensed are eligible to sell variable insurance products.

The premium payments for variable annuities are invested in what is called the separate account. The separate account is comprised of various subaccounts that behave like the diversified portfolios of mutual funds (we just can't call them mutual funds). These accounts will have a variety of investment objectives to choose from such as growth, income, and growth and income. The returns in the separate account are not guaranteed and therefore a loss of principal is possible.

If the investment manager of an insurance company is responsible for selecting the securities to be held in the separate account, the separate account is **directly managed** and must be registered under the Investment Company Act of 1940 as an open-end management investment company. However, if the investment manager of the insurance company passes the portfolio management responsibility to another party, the separate account is **indirectly managed** and must be registered as a unit investment trust under the Investment Company Act of 1940.

TAKE NOTE

A **fixed annuity** differs from a variable annuity. Though both are insurance company products and both guarantee a stream of income for life, a fixed annuity simply promises a stated rate of return. Therefore it is the insurance company who is at risk to provide the rate of return it promised. The investor assumes no investment risk with a fixed annuity. With no investment risk for the investor to shoulder, the product is not considered to be a security.

2. 1. 4. 2   Mutual Fund (Open-End) Characteristics

Here we'll discuss the characteristics unique to mutual (open-end) funds. A mutual fund is a pool of investors' money invested in various securities as determined by the fund's stated investment objective. Mutual funds have several unique characteristics detailed in this section.

Unlike most other securities, mutual funds offer guaranteed marketability; if an investor wants to sell shares previously purchased in a mutual fund, it is the mutual fund that stands ready to buy them back. Mutual funds, therefore, are **redeemable securities**. You will recall that this means they do not trade in any secondary market.

Each investor in the mutual fund's portfolio owns an undivided interest in the portfolio. All investors in an open-end fund are mutual participants; no one investor has a preferred status over any other investor because mutual funds issue only one class of common stock. Each investor shares mutually with other investors in gains and distributions derived from the investment company portfolio.

Each investor's participation in the fund's performance is based on the number of shares owned. Mutual fund shares may be purchased in either full or fractional shares, unlike corporate stock, which may only be purchased in full shares. Because mutual fund shares can be fractional, the investor can think in terms of dollars rather than number of shares owned.

EXAMPLE

Suppose a mutual fund's shares are priced at $12.34 / share and an investor wishes to invest $$4,000. Given the share price and the amount the investor wants to invest, the purchase will be for 324.15 shares ($4,000 / $12.34 = 324.15). In other words, the investor doesn't need to specify purchasing any specific number of shares (i.e., 323, 324, or 325 shares). Instead, the investor can simply decide on how much ($) she wants to invest, and however many shares that dollar amount will purchase will be the number of shares the investor will now own.

An investment company portfolio is elastic. Money is constantly being invested or paid out when shares are purchased or redeemed. The mutual fund portfolio's value and holdings fluctuate as money is invested or redeemed and as the value of the securities in the portfolio rises and falls. The investor's account value fluctuates proportionately with the mutual fund portfolio's value.

Here are several characteristics of mutual funds:

- A professional investment adviser manages the portfolio for investors.
- Mutual funds provide diversification by investing in different companies or securities.
- Most funds allow a minimum investment, often $500 or less to open an account, and they allow additional investment for as little as $25.
- An investment company may allow investments at reduced sales charges based on the amount of the investment.
- An investor retains voting rights similar to those extended to common stockholders, such as the right to vote for changes in the BOD, approval of the investment adviser, changes in the fund's investment objective, changes in sales charges, and liquidation of the fund.
- Mutual funds must offer reinvestment of dividends and capital gains at NAV (without a sales charge).
- An investor may liquidate a portion of his holdings without disturbing the portfolio's balance or diversification.
- Tax liabilities for an investor are simplified because each year the fund distributes a Form 1099 explaining taxability of distributions.
- A fund may offer various withdrawal plans that allow different payment methods at redemption.
- Funds may offer reinstatement provisions that allow investors who withdraw funds to reinvest up to the amount withdrawn within 30 days with no new sales charge. This provision must be in the prospectus and is available one time only.

2. 1. 4. 2. 1   Share Classes

Investors can purchase the same underlying mutual fund shares in several ways. Generally, investors can purchase Class A shares, Class B shares, and Class C shares. The differences among these shares are how much and in what way investors will pay sales charges (loads) and related expenses. In essence, these sales charges are the way the distribution services that a fund's underwriter provides are paid for. Some fund companies market their shares directly to the public without the assistance of underwriters. In these instances, the companies offer what are referred to as no-load funds—a fund with no sales charges.

Class A (Front-End Load) Shares—Class A shares have front-end sales charges (loads). With A shares, the sales charges are paid at the time an investor buys shares and the sales charge is taken from the total amount invested. Front-end loads are the most common way of paying for mutual fund shares.

Suppose a fund company offers a fund with a 5% sales charge and an investor wants to invest $10,000. Because 5% of the $10,000 investment must be allocated to the sales charge, only $9,500 is actually going to purchase fund shares ($10,000 × .05 = $500 sales charge), ($10,000 invested – $500 sales charge = $9,500 available to purchase shares).

Class B (Back-End Load) Shares—Class B Shares have a back-end sales load, also called a contingent deferred charge (CDSC). A back-end sales charge is paid at the time an investor sells shares previously purchased (has them redeemed). The sales load, a declining percentage charge reduced annually (e.g., 8% the first year, 7% the second, 6% the third), is applied to the proceeds of any shares sold in that year. The back-end load is usually structured so that it drops to zero after an extended holding period usually no longer than five years. At that time, the shares are converted to Class A shares and no sales charge would be applied at the time of redemption.

With Class B shares, the full investment amount is available to purchase shares as no sales charge is applied at the time of purchase but is instead deferred to the time of redemption. If an investor wants to invest $10,000 the entire amount is available to purchase shares.

While it might seem appealing to pay sales charges later—at the time of redemption instead of at the time of purchase as with A shares—it must be considered that if the shares grow in value as one hopes they will, the sales charges will be paid on amounts that are greater than the amount initially invested. This means that if the shares aren't held long enough to have the sales charge dissipate to zero, the sales charges can be costly as redemptions take place over time.

Class C (Level Load) Shares—Class C shares typically have a one-year, 1% contingent deferred sales charge (CDSC), a .75% 12b-1 fee (fees used to promote the fund discussed later), and a .25% shareholder services fee. Because these fees never go away, C shares are commonly referred to as having a level load. Class C shares are appropriate for investors that have short time horizons because the annual charges make them expensive to own if investing for more than four to five years.

No-Load Shares—As noted earlier, some companies market their shares directly to the public eliminating the need for underwriters and thus the sales charges used to compensate them. As the name no-load implies, the fund does not charge any type of sales charge. However, not every type of fee passed on to shareholders is considered to be a sales charge. No-load funds are permitted to charge fees that are not considered sales charges, such as purchase fees, account fees, exchange fees, and redemption fees. Although a redemption fee is deducted from redemption proceeds just like a deferred sales load, it is not considered to be a sales load as it is generally much smaller and often a fixed dollar amount instead of a percentage of the redemption.

2. 1. 4. 2. 2 *Market Timing*

Market timing is short-term buying and selling of mutual fund shares to take advantage of inefficiencies in mutual fund pricing. Market timing can harm long-term mutual fund shareholders because it can dilute the value of their shares. While not illegal per se, market timing is prohibited by the vast majority of mutual funds. Consider that mutual fund investments are intended to be, best suited for investors with longer term investment time horizons, and in fact, have sales charges structured this way. They are not intended to be investments where day-trading (trading in and out of a security many times over a short period of time) or market timing should be the investment strategy of the investor purchasing mutual fund shares.

2. 1. 4. 2. 3 *Net Asset Value (NAV)*

Because mutual funds don't trade in the secondary market, the value of shares is not determined by supply and demand, but rather by formula. Everything begins with **net asset value (NAV)** per share.

To calculate the NAV of a fund share, the fund starts with its total assets and subtracts out its total liabilities: **total assets − total liabilities = total net asset value of the fund**.

The fund then divides the Total Net Assets by the number of shares outstanding. This gives the Net Asset Value (NAV) per share: **net asset value of the fund / shares outstanding = NAV per share**.

EXAMPLE   The ABC fund has total assets of $100 million and $5 million in liabilities. If it has 10 million shares outstanding, what is its NAV per share?

Net Assets: $100 million (total assets) − $5 million (total liabilities) = $95 million total NAV, and NAV per share: $95 million ÷ 10 million shares outstanding = $9.50 / share.

The NAV of a fund share is the amount the investor receives upon redemption. It must be calculated at least once per business day. A typical fund calculates its NAV at the end of each business day. The price the customer receives is the next NAV calculated after receipt of his redemption request. This practice is known as forward pricing; we always have to wait until the next available calculation to determine the value of shares redeemed or, for that matter, the number of shares purchased.

The purchase price of a fund share is called the public offering price, or POP. For the class of fund shares known as front-end loaded shares, it is simply the NAV plus the sales charge; NAV + SC = POP.

As noted earlier, the sales charge is paid as compensation to the underwriters for marketing or bringing the shares to the public. And as a reminder, sales charges can be levied at the time of purchase (front-end load), at the time of redemption (back-end load), over the course of ownership (level load), or there can simply be no sales charge (no-load), meaning that shares are both purchased and redeemed at NAV.

The NAV changes daily because of changes in the market value of the securities in a fund's portfolio. This table illustrates which events increase, decrease, or do not affect the fund's NAV.

Changes in NAV

Increases	Decreases	Does not change
Market value of securities increases	Market value of securities declines	Manager buys or sells securities
Fund receives dividends	Fund distributes dividends	Fund issues shares
Fund receives interest	Fund distributes capital gains	Fund redeems shares
Liabilities decline	Liabilities increase	

2. 1. 4. 2. 4   Mutual Fund Prospectus

Investors must be provided with specific information when purchasing and tracking mutual funds.

Prospectus—This is the full and fair disclosure document that provides a prospective investor with the material information needed to make a fully informed investment decision. If using a prospectus to solicit a sale, it must be distributed to an investor before or during the solicitation. The front of a mutual fund prospectus must contain key information to appear in plain English in a standardized order. Information in this clear and concise format includes the fund's objective, investment policies, sales charges, management expenses, and services offered. It also discloses one-, five-, and 10-year performance histories, or performance over the life of the fund, whichever is shorter.

EXAMPLE

If a fund has been in existence for eight years, it will show performance for one, five, and eight years; if it has been in existence for only four years, it will show one and four years.

The delivery of any type of sales literature is considered a solicitation of sale and therefore must be accompanied or preceded by the delivery of a prospectus.

TEST TOPIC ALERT

A prospectus may not ever be altered in any way. This means no highlighting, writing in, or taking any measure to bring attention to any specific passage or section is permitted.

Summary Prospectus—A mutual fund can provide a summary prospectus to investors that may include an application that investors can use to buy the fund's shares.

The summary prospectus is a standardized summary of key information in the fund's full or final prospectus sometimes referred to as the fund's statutory prospectus. Investors who receive the summary have the option of either purchasing fund shares using the application found therein or requesting a full (statutory) prospectus. An investor who purchases fund shares on the basis of the summary prospectus must be able to access a full prospectus no later than the confirmation of the sale. Delivery may be made online.

There are some very specific requirements for a summary prospectus. The following must be included on the cover page of the summary prospectus or at the beginning of the summary prospectus:

■ The fund's name and the class or classes of shares

■ The exchange ticker symbol for the fund's shares; and if the fund is an exchange-traded fund (ETF), identification of the principal U.S. market or markets on which the fund shares are traded

■ A legend must appear on the cover page that refers to the summary nature of the prospectus and the availability of the fund's full (statutory) prospectus. The legend must provide a toll-free number to request paper delivery of the prospectus or a Website where one may be downloaded.

Additionally the summary must provide specific information in a particular sequence such as investments, risks, and performance; fee tables; investment objectives, investment strategies, and any related risks; the portfolio holdings as well as details regarding management; shareholder information; and any financial highlights.

Statement of Additional Information (SAI)—Mutual funds (open-end) as well as closed-end funds are required to have a statement of additional information (SAI) available for delivery within three business days of an investors request without charge. Investors can obtain a copy by calling or writing to the investment company, via a company website, contacting a broker that sells the investment company shares, or contacting the Securities Exchange Commission (SEC).

While a prospectus is always sufficient for the purpose of selling shares, some investors may seek additional information not found in the prospectus. This additional information is not considered mandatory to make an informed investment decision but may be useful to the investor.

The SAI affords the fund an opportunity to have expanded discussions on matters such as the fund's history and policies. It will also typically contain the fund's consolidated financial statements, including:

■ the balance sheet;

■ statement of operations;

■ an income statement; and

■ a portfolio list at the time the SAI was compiled.

Following is a summary for mutual fund disclosure:

Mutual Fund Sale Disclosure Summary

Document	Purpose	Contains	Presented
Summary Prospectus	Rule 498: Short form that may be used to make the sale	Summary of key information in the prospectus	Prior to or with the solicitation
Prospectus (statutory)	Sale document	Full and fair disclosure of all material facts for investment decision	Prior to or with solicitation or if a summary prospectus is used, no later than confirmation of the sale
Statement of Additional Information	SAI: More data for the investor	Additional details about the fund not necessary for the prospectus	Within three business days of customer request

2. 1. 4. 2. 5 Disclosures

The SEC requires a fund company to include additional disclosures in its prospectus or annual reports. Intended to enhance and align with making full disclosure they include:

■ a discussion of factors and strategies that materially affected its performance during its most recently completed fiscal year;

■ a line graph comparing its performance to that of an appropriate broad based securities market index; and

■ the name(s) and title(s) of the person(s) primarily responsible for the fund portfolio's day-to-day management.

Financial Reports—The Investment Company Act of 1940 requires that shareholders receive financial reports at least semiannually. One of these must be an audited annual report. The reports must contain:

■ the investment company's balance sheet;

■ a valuation of all securities in the investment company's portfolio as of the date of the balance sheet (a portfolio list);

■ the investment company's income statement;

■ a complete statement of all compensation paid to the board of directors and to the advisory board; and

■ a statement of the total dollar amount of securities purchased and sold during the period.

TAKE NOTE

An investment company must send a copy of its balance sheet to any shareholder who requests one in writing between semiannual reports.

Fund Costs and Fees—The services mutual funds offer may include retirement account custodianship, investment plans, check-writing privileges, transfers by telephone or online, withdrawal plans, and a number of other services and privileges. However, an investor should always weigh the cost of services provided, as the costs are ultimately passed on to the investor, against the value of the services to the investor. Sales loads, management fees, and operating expenses reduce investor returns because they reduce the amount of money available for the fund to invest.

Sales Loads—Discussed earlier, funds can charge sales loads in different ways, front-end (A shares), back-end (B shares), or level-load (C shares) sales charges.

Though most fund companies charge far less, they are permitted to charge up to 8.5% of the money invested for A shares. B shares charge the sales charge when the money is withdrawn. In both cases, the percentage sales charge compensates the sales force—the broker-dealers and underwriters who market and sell the shares to the public.

Expenses—Like any business, fund companies incur a number of expenses to operate the business. Among them are:

Operating expenses—Typical expenses would be salaries and administrative fees.

Fund portfolio management fee—paid to those hired to manage the investments in the fund portfolio it is calculated as a percentage of assets under management.

TAKE NOTE

The management fee is every fund's single greatest expense. Charged annually, this fee is a percentage of the total assets under management.

12b-1 asset based fee—Section 12b-1 of the Investment Company Act of 1940 permits a mutual fund to collect a fee for promoting, selling, or undertaking activity in connection with the distribution of its shares. The fee is determined annually as a flat dollar amount or as a percentage of the fund's average total NAV during the year and is charged quarterly. The fee must be disclosed in the fund's prospectus.

Typically, these 12b-1 fees are associated with no-load fund companies, however, if the fee is more than .25% of the average net assets, the fund may not use the term no-load to describe itself.

Finally, as a way for investors to compare one fund's expense charges to another, a simple ratio known as the expense ratio can be used. A fund's expense ratio compares the management fees and operating expenses, including any 12b-1 fees, with the fund's net assets. All mutual funds, both load and no load, have expense ratios. The expense ratio is calculated by dividing a fund's expenses by its average net assets.

EXAMPLE   An expense ratio of 1.72% means that the fund charges $1.72 per year for every $100 invested.

Stock (equity) funds generally have expense ratios between 1 and 1.5% of a fund's average net assets. Typically, more aggressive funds, perhaps those employing more sophisticated or risky investment strategies, have higher expense ratios. For bond (debt) funds, the ratio is typically between .5 and 1%, a bit lower than stock funds.

Non-U.S. Market Securities—Some funds invest either in part or exclusively in the securities of companies that have their principal business activities outside of the United States. While there is no limit to what their objectives can be, most are structured for long-term capital appreciation.

Generally, the advantage for an investor is the ability to add worldwide diversification to one's investment portfolio, but there are risks.

Whenever investing in securities issued in non-U.S. markets, investors need to be sensitive to the different risks that might apply to foreign investments. While the funds themselves are U.S. securities and would be considered to be liquid and so on, the securities in the fund portfolio wouldn't be U.S. securities. Those securities within the portfolio could be subject to political forces, currency risk, and liquidity risk, all of which will be discussed later in this unit.

2. 1. 5   DIRECT PARTICIPATION PROGRAMS (DPPS)

Direct participation programs (DPPs) are unique forms of business that raise money to invest in real estate, oil and gas, equipment leasing, and other similar business ventures. DPPs are not taxed directly as a corporation would be; instead, the income or losses are passed directly through to the owners of the partnership—the investors. The investors are then individually responsible for satisfying any tax consequences.

There is virtually no secondary market for an investor to divest interest in a DPP, and in this regard, they are considered highly illiquid and therefore on the point of liquidity alone, not suitable for many investors.

2. 1. 5. 1 Types of DPPs

Following are the most common types of programs. Each is a unique form of business with different investment objectives and benefits.

2. 1. 5. 1. 1 Real Estate Programs

Real estate programs can invest in raw land, new construction, or existing properties. Depending on the properties held by the program, they can provide investors with the following benefit opportunities:

■ **Capital growth potential**—achieved through appreciation of property

■ **Cash flow (income)**—collected from rents

■ **Tax deductions**—from mortgage interest expense and depreciation allowances for "wearing out the building" and capital improvements

■ **Tax credits**—for government-assisted housing and historic rehabilitation (tax credits are very strong incentives as they reduce tax liability dollar for dollar)

2. 1. 5. 1. 2 Oil and Gas Programs

Oil and gas programs include speculative or exploratory (wildcatting) programs to locate new oil deposits—generally considered the riskiest developmental programs that drill near existing producing wells in the hopes of locating new deposits—and income programs that invest in producing wells—generally considered the least risky. Unique tax advantages associated with these programs include the following:

■ **Intangible drilling costs (IDCs)**—These are costs associated with drilling, such as wages, supplies, fuel, and insurance that have no salvage value when the program ends. These IDCs can be written off (deducted) in full in the first year of operation. In contrast, tangible drilling costs are associated with items that have some salvage value at the end of the program, such as drilling equipment. These types of tangible costs, instead of being immediately deductible, are instead deductible over several years. The deduction is taken as depreciation. In other words, each year the asset is worth a little less and that depreciated amount can now be deducted.

■ **Depletion allowances**—Tax deductions that compensate the program for the decreasing supply of oil or gas (or any other resource or mineral) after it is taken out of the ground and sold.

2. 1. 5. 1. 3 Leasing Programs

Equipment leasing programs are created when DPPs purchase equipment leased to other businesses. This type of equipment can be as far ranging as jetliners or railcars leased to airlines and railroads, trucks leased to shipping companies, or computers leased to any business in need of them. Investors receive income from lease payments and also a proportional share of write-offs from operating expenses, interest expense, and depreciation of the actual equipment owned by the program. The primary investment objective of these programs is tax-sheltered income; the income being sheltered by the write-offs.

2. 1. 5. 2   Limited Partnerships

The most common type of DPP in the securities industry is a limited partnership (LP). LPs are investment opportunities that permit the economic consequences of a business to flow or pass through to investors. The businesses themselves are not tax-paying entities. These programs pass through to investors a share in the income, gains, losses, deductions, and tax credits of the business entity. The investors (partners) would then have the responsibility to report individually to the IRS.

The greatest disadvantage to limited partners is the lack of liquidity in the partnership interest. The secondary market for limited partnership interests is extremely limited; investors who wish to sell their interests frequently cannot locate buyers (i.e., interest in the business is not freely transferable).

2. 1. 5. 3   Investors in a Limited Partnership (Tenants in Common)

A limited partnership involves two types of partners: the general partner (GP) and the limited partners (LPs). A limited partnership must have at least one of each. Property in these partnerships is usually held in the form of a Tenant in Common (TIC), which provides limited liability and no management responsibilities the limited partners.

2. 1. 5. 3. 1   General Partners

General partners have unlimited liability, meaning that they can be held personally liable for business losses and debts. Their role is to manage all aspects of the partnership and have a fiduciary responsibility to use the invested capital in the best interest of the investors. In managing the partnership, they make decisions that legally bind the partnership, buy and sell property for the partnership, and are compensated for fulfilling these duties. They may not compete personally with the business, borrow money from the partnership or commingle the partnership funds with their own personal assets.

2. 1. 5. 3. 2   Limited Partners

As their title implies, limited partners have limited liability, meaning that they can't lose more than they invested. They have no business management responsibilities, and in fact, should they participate in any day-to-day management of the business, they can lose their limited liability status and be considered a general partner. LPs have the right to vote on overall business objectives and the right to receive cash distributions, capital gains, and tax deductions generated by the business. They have the right to inspect all books and records and if the GP does not act in the best interest of the business, LPs have the right to sue the GP.

Limited partners enjoy several advantages:

- An investment managed by others (the general partner)
- Limited liability (can only lose the amount invested)
- Flow-through of income and certain expenses

2. 1. 5. 3. 3   Partnership Sales and Dissolutions

LPs may be sold through private placements or public offerings. If sold privately, investors receive a private placement memorandum for disclosure. Generally, such private placements involve a small group of limited partners, each contributing a large sum of money. These investors must be *accredited* investors (meeting income and net worth criteria) and must have substantial investment experience. The general public generally does not meet this description.

In a public offering, limited partnerships are sold by prospectus for disclosure. In a public offering distribution, a larger number of limited partners each making a relatively small capital contribution ($1,000 to $5,000) is more likely because they do not need to be accredited investors.

Generally, limited partnerships are liquidated on a predetermined date specified in the partnership agreement. Early shutdown may occur if the partnership sells or disposes of its assets or if a decision is made to dissolve the partnership by the limited partners holding a majority interest. When dissolution occurs, the general partner must settle accounts in the following order:

■ Secured lenders

■ Other creditors

■ Limited partners—first, for their claims to shares of profits and then for their claims to a return of contributed capital

■ General partners

2. 1. 6   REAL ESTATE INVESTMENT TRUSTS (REITS)

A real estate investment trust (REIT) is a company that manages a portfolio of real estate, mortgages, or both to earn profits for shareholders. REITs pool capital in a manner similar to an investment company bt are not investment companies, neither open or closed-end. Shareholders receive dividends from investment income or capital gains distributions. REITs normally:

■ own commercial property (equity REITs);

■ own mortgages on commercial property (mortgage REITs); or

■ do both (hybrid REITs).

REITs are organized as trusts in which investors buy shares or certificates of beneficial interest either on stock exchanges or in the over-the-counter market.

Under the guidelines of Subchapter M of the Internal Revenue Code, a REIT can avoid being taxed as a corporation by receiving 75% or more of its income from real estate and distributing 90% or more of its net investment income to its shareholders.

2. 1. 6. 1   Registered vs. Nonregistered REITs

Many REITs are registered with the SEC and therefore subject to all disclosure requirements. These are known as **public** REITs. However there are REITs that are not registered with the SEC known as **private** REITs. Nonregistered REITs are not subject to the same disclosure requirements as public REITs and therefore subject to greater risk.

2. 1. 6. 2   Listed vs. Non-listed REITs

Many REITS are traded on a stock exchange. These are known as exchange traded or **listed** REITs. For those that are not listed on an exchange and trade instead in the OTC market, unique risks exist. Not being exchange traded they can be difficult to price and possibly illiquid.

The following are five important points to remember about REITs.

■ An owner of REITs holds an undivided interest in a pool of real estate investments.

■ REITs may or may not be registered (public or private) with the SEC

■ REITs may or may not be listed (trade) on exchanges

■ REITs are *not* investment companies (open or closed-end)

■ REITs offer dividends and gains to investors but do not pass through losses like limited partnerships and, therefore, are not considered to be direct participation programs (DPPs).

2. 1. 7   HEDGE FUNDS

Many companies rely on one of the exceptions from the definition of being an investment company under the Investment Company Act of 1940. They are not classified as face amount certificate companies, unit investment trusts, or management companies (open- or closed-end). These companies are commonly known as private investment companies. Some private investment companies can be what are known as hedge funds.

Hedge funds are considered unregulated as they currently do not have to be registered with the Securities Exchange Commission.

2. 1. 7. 1   Basic structure and characteristics

Hedge funds are similar to mutual funds in that investments are pooled and professionally managed, but they differ in that the fund has more flexibility in the investment strategies employed. While hedging is the practice of attempting to limit risk, most hedge funds specify generating high returns as their primary investment objective. In attempting to achieve these returns they tend to shoulder a substantial amount of risk. Aggressively managed portfolios of investments, hedge funds utilize advanced and sometimes complicated investment strategies. In this light, these investment vehicles are generally considered suitable for sophisticated investors only; those meeting specific income and net worth criteria and those who are known as accredited investors.

While hedge funds are unregulated, U.S. laws do require that investors meet the test of being a sophisticated investor. This means they should be considered "accredited" investors, having a minimum annual income and net worth as well as considerable investment knowledge.

Some of the more common strategies employed by hedge funds are:

- highly leveraged portfolios (borrowing to purchase securities);
- the use of short positions (selling securities the portfolio does not own);
- the utilization of derivative products such as options and futures;
- currency speculation;
- commodity speculation; and
- the investment in politically unstable international markets.

Most hedge funds are organized as private investment partnerships, allowing them to limit the number of investors or require large initial or minimum investments if they so desire. Some also require that investors maintain the investment for a minimum length of time (e.g., one year) and to that extent they can be considered illiquid. These minimum holding requirements are known as lock-up provisions.

TAKE NOTE   It is not unusual for hedge fund organizers to also be investors in the fund.

2. 1. 8   EXCHANGE-TRADED PRODUCTS (ETPS)

Exchange-traded products (ETPs) are securities that trade intra-day on a national securities exchange, and are priced so the value of the product is derived from other investment instruments, such as a commodity, a currency, a share price, or an interest rate. Generally, these types of products are benchmarked to stocks, commodities, or indices. They can be actively or passively managed portfolios. Following are two common ETPs.

2. 1. 8. 1   Exchange-Traded Funds (ETFs)

This type of fund, considered an equity security, invests in a specific group of stocks and generally does so to mimic a particular index, such as the S&P 500. In this way, an ETF is similar to a mutual fund that tracks an index. The difference is that the exchange-traded fund trades like a stock on the floor of an exchange and, in regards to how it trades, is similar to a closed-end investment company rather than an open-end mutual fund. They are registered however, as either an open-end fund or as a unit investment trust (UIT), but are obviously different in many ways.

Because of the way they trade, an investor can take advantage of intraday price changes due to normal market forces, rather than just the underlying value of the stocks in the portfolio. And, unlike mutual funds, ETFs can be purchased on margin and sold short.

Expenses tend to be lower than those of mutual funds and the management fee is low as well. Consider that the portfolio is designed to track an index, and just as the securities contained in the index are unlikely to change, so are the securities in the fund portfolio. In other words, there is little trading activity required to keep the fund securities aligned with those in the index it is intended to track. This generally results in greater tax efficiency for the investor.

On the other hand, every time a person purchases or sells shares, there is a commission, and those charges can add up over a period of time.

Understanding that exchange traded fund (ETF) shares are not mutual fund shares, but are registered as open-end funds, it should be expected and is common that they are often compared to mutual fund shares. In that light, exchange-traded funds have some advantages and disadvantages to be considered when compared to open-end (mutual funds).

Following are some advantages of exchange-traded funds when compared to open-end (mutual funds).

- **Pricing and ease of trading**—since individual ETF shares are traded on exchanges, they can be bought or sold anytime during the trading day at the price they are currently trading at as opposed to mutual funds which use forward pricing and are generally priced once at the end of the trading day.

- **Margin**—ETFs can be bought and sold short on margin like other exchange-traded products. Mutual funds cannot be bought on margin nor can they be sold short.

- **Operating costs**—ETFs traditionally have operating costs and expenses that are lower than most mutual funds.

- **Tax efficiency**—ETFs can and sometimes do distribute capital gains to shareholders like mutual funds do, but this is rare. Understanding that these capital gains distributions are not likely, there are no further tax consequences with ETF shares until investors sell their shares. This may be the single greatest advantage associated with ETFs.

Following are some disadvantages of exchange-traded funds when compared to open-end (mutual funds).

- **Commissions**—the purchase or sale of ETF shares is a commissionable transaction. The commissions paid can erode the low expense advantage of ETFs. This would have the greatest impact when trading in and out of ETF shares frequently or when investing smaller sums of money.

- **Overtrading**—given the ability to trade in and out of ETFs easily, the temptation to do so is possible. Excessive trading can eliminate the advantages associated with investing in a diversified portfolio and add to overall commissions being paid by the investor, further eroding any of the other expense and operating cost advantages associated with ETFs.

- **Market influences on price**—Because ETFs trade on exchanges, share prices can be influenced by market forces such as supply and demand, like any other exchange traded product. In this light, investors need to recognize that just as they might receive less than book value per share when selling corporate shares of stock, they might also receive less than NAV per share when selling ETF shares.

2. 1. 8. 2   Exchange-Traded Notes (ETNs)

Exchange-traded notes (ETNs) are senior, unsecured debt securities issued by a bank or financial institution. Therefore they are backed only by the good faith and credit of the issuer.

The notes track the performance of a particular market index, but do not represent ownership in a pool of securities the way share ownership of a fund does.

ETNs are bond-like instruments with a stated maturity date, but they do not pay interest and offer no principal protection. Instead, ETN investors receive a cash payment linked to the performance of the underlying index minus management fees when the note matures.

While the market price of an ETN in theory depends on the performance of the underlying index or benchmark, the ETN has an additional risk compared to an ETF; if the credit of the underwriting bank should falter, the note might lose value in the same way any other senior debt of the issuer would. Additionally, there are limits to the size of ETN issues. This means, with limited availability, there are times when an ETN might trade at a premium to its inherent valuation. Investors purchasing at a premium could be subject to losses later depending on the value of the note at maturity.

QUICK QUIZ 2.C

LEARNING OBJECTIVES

■ Compare the characteristics of different investment products

1. All the following could be found in the money market EXCEPT

   A. T-bonds maturing in 12 months
   B. T-bills
   C. Commercial paper
   D. Equities such as common and preferred shares

2. The most common type of direct participation program in the securities industry is

   A. a limited partnership
   B. a REIT
   C. a CMO
   D. an investment company

3. All of the following are benefits for the limited partners in a direct participation program (DPP) EXCEPT

   A. passive losses
   B. flow through of income
   C. unlimited liability
   D. an investment managed by the GP

4. A pooled investment which is organized as a trust in which investors buy shares or certificates of beneficial interest, either on stock exchanges or in the over-the-counter market is

   A. an investment company
   B. a REIT
   C. a CMO
   D. a DPP

5. An open end management company may charge what amount annually and still advertise itself as a no-load fund?

   A. 8.5%
   B. 2.5%
   C. 1.25%
   D. .25%

6. All of the following are true for exchanged traded funds (ETFs) EXCEPT

   A. ETFs can be bought or sold throughout the trading day
   B. ETFs are not marginable securities
   C. ETF share prices are subject to market forces like supply and demand
   D. ETF transactions are commissionable trades

7. An investment established by states to provide other government entities such as cities or counties a place to invest funds short-term is an

   A. FDIC
   B. ABLE
   C. LGIP
   D. REPO

8.   Regarding annuity products offered by insurance companies which of the following is TRUE?

   A.   Variable annuities are securities, fixed annuities are not
   B.   Fixed annuities are securities, variable annuities are not
   C.   Neither variable nor fixed annuities are securities
   D.   Both variable and fixed annuities are securities

9.   A private, unregulated investment company organized in such a way so as to invest and achieve high returns utilizing debt leverage and derivative products such as options and margin is best described as a

   A.   mutual fund
   B.   direct participation program (DPP)
   C.   real estate investment trust (REIT)
   D.   hedge fund

10.   An investor has placed money in a debt like instrument issued by a financial institution and linked to the performance of the S&P 500 Index. From the investment, which has a stated maturity date but makes no interest payments, the investor anticipates receiving a cash payment minus any applicable management fees when the instrument matures. This describes which of the following investments?

   A.   Municipal bond
   B.   Direct participation program (DPP)
   C.   Exchange traded note (ETN)
   D.   Variable annuity (VA)

2. 2   INVESTMENT RISKS

LEARNING OBJECTIVES:

■   Define different investment risks

■   Evaluate risks associated with different investment products

In general terms, the greater the risk investors are willing to assume with an investment, the greater the potential reward should be. For example, safe investments tend to offer lower yields, but investments where considerable risk is attached should offer much higher potential yields.

Additionally, different types of risk can be associated with different investments and securities. In all cases, investors should be aware of the risks they shoulder with any investment, be able to afford the risk, and be comfortable with doing so.

For our part as securities industry professionals, understanding the many types of risk and ensuring our customers understand these risks lends itself to the topic of determining suitability. Just as every investment is different, so is every investor. Several types of risk must be considered in determining whether or not any investment is suitable for any investor.

Risk can generally be broken into two categories: systematic and nonsystematic risk.

2. 2. 1   SYSTEMATIC RISK

Systematic risk is the risk that changes in the overall economy will have an adverse effect on individual securities regardless of the company's circumstances. It is generally caused by factors that affect all businesses, such as war, global security threats, or inflation.

No matter how diversified a portfolio of investments is, it will still be subject to systematic risk. Said another way, one cannot diversify away systematic risk.

Following we'll discuss the most common systematic risks.

2. 2. 1. 1   Market Risk

Market risk is the risk that when the overall market declines, so too will any portfolio made of securities the market is comprised of.

EXAMPLE

If the Dow Jones Industrial Average or any other market index were to plummet substantially, so too would a portfolio of common stock. Regardless of the number of stocks and the diversity of their makeup, they could not escape a large fall in the market without being affected.

2. 2. 1. 2   Interest Rate Risk

Interest rates fluctuate in the market all the time. If market conditions or the Federal Reserve push interest rates higher, the market price of all bonds will be affected. When interest rates rise, the market price of bonds falls and that is why this is a systematic risk. This risk is sometimes referred to as the market risk for bonds.

2. 2. 1. 3   Reinvestment Risk

This is a variation of interest rate risk. When interest rates decline, it is difficult to reinvest proceeds from redemptions, securities that have been called (call risk), or investment distributions and maintain the same level of income without increasing credit or market risks.

2. 2. 1. 4   Inflation Risk (Purchasing Power Risk)

Sometimes referred to as purchasing power risk, inflation risk is the effect of continually rising prices on investment returns. If an investments yield is lower than the inflation rate, the purchasing power of the client's money diminishes over time.

EXAMPLE

An investor has purchased a 30-year bond yielding 5%. Inflation rates push upward over time to levels above 5%. The interest payments are no longer sufficient to purchase the goods and services that they had been initially. This diminished buying power would also be true for the principal amount returned in 30 years as well.

2. 2. 2   NONSYSTEMATIC RISK

Unlike systematic risk, which is nondiversifiable, these risks can be reduced through diversification. They are risks that are unique to a specific industry, business enterprise, or investment type. Following are some of the most common nonsystematic risks.

2. 2. 2. 1   Capital Risk

Capital risk is the potential for an investor to lose some or all of his money—his invested capital—under circumstances unrelated to an issuer's financial strength.

EXAMPLE

Capital risk is minimal to none when investing in securities backed by the federal government such as T-bills but could be far greater when investing in derivative products such as options or businesses such as direct participation programs.

2. 2. 2. 2   Business Risk

This is an operating risk, generally caused by poor management decisions. At best, earnings are lowered; at worst, the company goes out of business and common stockholders could lose their entire investment.

EXAMPLE

Introduction of a new product that turns out to have a very narrow market or underestimating a competitor's new product and failing to compete are both examples of poor business decisions that impact the price of a company's stock.

2. 2. 2. 3   Financial Risk

Often confused with business risk (it is similar), financial risk relates primarily to those companies that use debt financing (leverage). An inability to meet the interest and principal payments on those debt obligations could lead to bankruptcy and, once again, total loss for the stockholders. For that reason, this is sometimes called credit risk or default risk.

2. 2. 2. 4   Call Risk

Call risk is the risk that a bond might be called before maturity and an investor will be unable to reinvest the principal at a comparable rate of return. In this light, the occurrence of call risk can lead to reinvestment risk discussed earlier. When interest rates are falling, bonds with higher coupon rates are most likely to be called. Investors concerned about call risk should look for **call protection**—a period during which a bond cannot be called. Most corporate and municipal issuers generally provide some years of call protection.

EXAMPLE
An investor holds a callable bond yielding 5%. Because interest rates have fallen to 3%, the issuer of the bond calls it in and the investor receives his principal. The investor is now left to reinvest the proceeds of the called bond, on which he had been earning 5%, at the now lower current interest rate of 3%.

2. 2. 2. 5 Prepayment Risk

Prepayment risk is the risk that a borrower will repay the principal on a loan or debt instrument (bond) before its maturity and thus deprive the lender of future interest payments. This risk is often associated with call risk discussed earlier.

2. 2. 2. 6 Currency Risk

Currency risk is the possibility that an investment denominated in one currency could decline if the value of that currency declines in its exchange rate with the U.S. dollar. Fluctuating currency exchange rates become an important consideration whenever investing in a foreign security or any security denominated in a foreign currency.

2. 2. 2. 7 Liquidity Risk

The risk that an investor might not be able to sell an investment quickly at a fair market price is known as liquidity or marketability risk. The marketability of the securities a registered representative recommends must be consistent with the client's liquidity needs.

EXAMPLE
While common stocks and money market instruments are considered fairly liquid with potential buyers and markets to sell them in readily available, investments in fixed assets like real estate, fine art, or collectibles are not.

2. 2. 2. 8 Regulatory Risk

A sudden change in the regulatory climate can have a dramatic effect on the performance of a business and entire business sectors. Changes in the rules a business must comply with can devastate individual companies and industries almost overnight.

Common examples of this risk are rulings made by the Environmental Protection Agency (EPA) or the Food and Drug Administration (FDA). Rule changes for affected businesses to follow can sometimes upset their business models and their ability to be profitable.

EXAMPLE
An investor owns shares of XYZ stock, a pharmaceutical company. The Food and Drug Administration orders an immediate halt to all sales of the company's best- selling drug. Shares of XYZ stock begin to fall as a result of the news and the investor is left with a decision to either sell at the now depressed price or hold the shares in the hopes of a price correction sometime in the future.

2. 2. 2. 9   Legislative Risk

It is common to lump together regulatory and legislative risk, but there is a difference. Whereas regulatory risk comes from a change to regulations, legislative risk results from a change in the law. A governmental agency, state or federal, may pass certain regulations, but only a legislature can pass a law. Changes to the tax code are the most obvious legislative risks.

EXAMPLE

The implementation of a luxury tax on higher priced items such as automobiles and boats severely impacts those industries.

2. 2. 2. 10   Political Risk

While political risk can be interrelated with legislative risk, most attribute this risk specifically to the potential instability in the political underpinnings of the country. While this is particularly true in emerging economies, it can occur even in highly developed societies.

2. 2. 2. 10. 1   Sovereign Risk

Sovereign risk ratings capture the risk of a country defaulting on its commercial debt obligations. When a country is at risk of defaulting on its debt, the impact is felt on financial markets worldwide.

QUICK QUIZ 2.D

LEARNING OBJECTIVES
- Define different investment risks
- Evaluate risks associated with different investment products

1. One of the advantages of a security being traded on a listed stock exchange is the ready availability of buyers and sellers. This has the tendency to reduce or even eliminate

   A. inflation risk
   B. liquidity risk
   C. market risk
   D. price risk

2. Prior to making an investment, it is wise to evaluate the potential risk involved. It is safe to assume that

   I.   the greater the risk, the greater the potential reward
   II. the greater the risk, the lower the potential reward
   III. the lower the risk, the greater the potential loss
   IV. the lower the risk, the lower the potential reward

   A. I and III
   B. I and IV
   C. II and III
   D. II and IV

3. Twenty years ago, an investor purchased an AAA rated corporate bond with a coupon rate of 6%. The bond is about to mature and when searching for a new bond, it seems that the rates being paid on 20-year AAA bonds is about 4%. This would be an example of

   A. call risk
   B. liquidity risk
   C. market risk
   D. reinvestment risk

4. When the interest rate paid on a debt security is less than the current inflation rate, the investor suffers from which of the following risks?

   A. Liquidity risk
   B. Call risk
   C. Purchasing power risk
   D. Currency risk

5. A company operating in State A has just been notified that the state legislature has passed a new law on permitted emissions and several of the company's plants in that state do not comply. As a result, operations at those facilities must cease. This is an example of

   A. legislative risk
   B. market risk
   C. unexpected risk
   D. reinvestment risk

6. Which of the following are risks that are most likely to be faced by investors in domestic debt securities?

   I. Liquidity risk
   II. Currency risk
   III. Political risk
   IV. Inflation risk

   A. I and I1
   B. I and IV
   C. II and IIII
   D. II and IV

UNIT TEST/ANSWERS AND RATIONALES

QUICK QUIZ 2.A

1. **B.** Because common stock has limited liability, the maximum amount of money an investor can lose is the value of his investment; in this case, $200,000. When the investment increased to $400,000, the capital appreciation was unrealized. In other words, he would have had to sell the investment, and receive the $400,000 in order to realize the gain. If he did that, he would no longer have a position in ABC common stock.

2. **C.** Shareholders have the right to receive an audited financial statement on an annual basis, not semi-annually.

3. **A.** Investors in common stock do so for several reasons: capital appreciation (a hedge against inflation), income, or a combination of growth and income. Dividends are typically declared by the board of directors on a quarterly basis, not monthly. Limited liability is a characteristic of common stock, not an investment objective.

4. **A.** The two preference items listed that define preferred stock are dividend preference and priority at dissolution over common stock. Dividends are never guaranteed. Preferred stock has no voting rights.

5. **A.** Straight

   B. Participating

   C. Adjustable Rate

   D. Cumulative

   E. Convertible

   F. Callable

6. **C.** According to Rule 144, after holding restricted stock fully paid for six months, an affiliate may begin selling shares but is subject to volume restrictions. Unaffiliated investors (after the six-month hold) are not subject to any restrictions if they choose to sell.

QUICK QUIZ 2.B

1. **B.** Options are in-the-money by the amount of their intrinsic value. This May 40 call has intrinsic value of 4 points and is therefore in-the-money by 4 points. Calls have intrinsic value when the current market value of the stock is above the strike price.

2. **A.** Options are in-the-money by the amount of their intrinsic value. This August 30 put has intrinsic value of 5 points and is therefore in-the-money by 5 points. Puts have intrinsic value when the current market value of the stock is below the strike price.

3. **D.** Writers of options incur an obligation if the option is exercised by the other party to the contract (owner or buyer). If the owner of a call exercises his right to purchase the stock, the writer will be obligated to sell the stock. Therefore, this investor will be obligated to sell the ABC stock at the strike price (25) if the call is exercised by the owner (buyer).

4. **B.** Writers of options incur an obligation if the option is exercised by the other party to the contract (owner or buyer). If the owner of a put exercises his right to sell the stock, the writer will be obligated to purchase the stock. Therefore, this investor will be obligated to purchase ABC stock at the strike price (65) if the put is exercised by the owner (buyer).

5. Breakeven = 32 [for a call, BE = strike price (30) + premium (2)]

   Maximum Gain = unlimited (market attitude for a long call is bullish; the stock could go to infinity)

Maximum Loss = $200 (the most an investor can lose when purchasing options is the premium paid; 2 points = $200)

6.   Breakeven = 11 [for a put, BE = strike price (15) – premium (4)]

Maximum Gain = $1100 [market attitude for a long put is bearish; the stock can fall to zero leaving the investor with a gain from the BE point (11) down to 0]

Maximum Loss = $400 (the most an investor can lose when purchasing options is the premium paid; 4 points = $400)

7.   **C.**   BE is calculated using the same formula for both buyer and seller of an option contract. Therefore, BE is always the same number for both buyer and seller. The formula for calls is strike price + premium and the formula for puts is strike price – premium. The most any options buyer can lose (ML) for a call or a put is the premium paid. However, maximum gain, while unlimited for a call buyer (bullish market attitude), is limited for a put buyer. Remember that the market attitude of a put buyer is bearish and the farthest the stock could fall to is zero. Therefore the put buyers' MG is limited to amount from BE point to zero.

8.   **B.**   Options transactions settle on the next business day after trade date (T + 1).

9.   **B.**   When an exercise notice is received, OCC assigns short broker-dealers on a random basis only. In turn, a short broker-dealer may exercise its short customers in one of three ways: randomly, using the first in, first out (FIFO) accounting method, or by any other fair method.

10.   **C.**   Once the account is approved by a principal of the broker-dealer the customer has 15 days to return the signed options agreement. Remember that the customer must be given the OCC options disclosure document *before* the account can be approved. Once approved, the customer may trade immediately but still has 15 days to get the signed options agreement back to the broker-dealer.

QUICK QUIZ 2.C

1.   **D.**   Money market instruments are fixed-income (debt) securities with short-term maturities, typically one year or less. Even though T-bonds (and T-notes) have longer maturities than 12 months when they are issued, at some point they will mature. When they fall into the 12-month or less to maturity status, they too could be found trading in the money market. Equities (stock) are considered money market securities as they are not debt instruments.

2.   **A.**   The most common type of DPP in the securities industry is a limited partnership (LP).

3.   **C.**   As the name implies, a limited partner has limited liability. In other words, a limited partner can't lose more than what was initially invested. The same cannot be said, however, of the general partner (GP).

4.   **B.**   A real estate investment trust (REIT) is a company that manages a portfolio of real estate, mortgages, or both to earn profits for shareholders. A REIT pools capital in a manner similar to an investment company, but it is not classified as one. Shareholders receive dividends from investment income or capital gains distributions.

5. **D.** Section 12b-1 of the Investment Company Act of 1940 permits a mutual fund to collect this fee, which is charged annually but deducted quarterly, as a way to offset advertising and other expenses of the fund. Typically these 12b-1 fees are associated with no-load fund companies. However, if the fee is more than .25% of the average annual net assets, the fund may not use the term "no load" to describe itself.

6. **B.** Exchanged traded funds (ETFs) trade as all other exchange traded products do. Commissionable transactions can occur throughout the trading day where prices are subject to all normal market forces. Like other exchange traded products, they can be purchased on margin.

7. **C.** Local government investment pools (LGIPs) are established by states to provide other government entities such as cities, counties, school districts, or other state agencies with a short-term investment vehicle to invest funds.

8. **A.** Premiums paid into variable annuities are invested in the separate account, which is a portfolio of investments intended to keep pace with inflation. Investing the premiums this way, the returns in the separate account are not guaranteed, and therefore a loss of principal is possible for the investor. Because the investor is assuming this risk, VAs are considered securities. Fixed annuities, however, guarantee a fixed rate of return and therefore the risk is shouldered by the insurance company instead of the investor.

9. **D.** Hedge funds are unregulated investments with a goal of achieving high returns. They do this primarily utilizing strategies associated with risk, such as trading in commodities, currencies, and derivatives, and utilizing debt leverage and margin.

10. **C.** Exchange traded notes (ETNs) are debt like instruments issued by banks and other financial institutions that trade on exchanges. Their performance is generally linked to a specific market index. At maturity of the note investors receive a cash payment minus any management fees.

QUICK QUIZ 2.D

1. **B.** Liquidity risk is the uncertainty that an investor will be able to find a buyer for a security when the need to sell arises. Listed securities virtually always have ready marketability.

2. **B.** One of the primary axioms of investing is the relationship between risk and reward. Basically, when an investor takes more risk, it is in the expectation of a greater reward. Reducing the risk should result in a lower reward.

3. **D.** Reinvestment risk is the risk that occurs when an investor is unable to reinvest the proceeds from the redemption of a security at the same rate previously earned.

4. **C.** Purchasing power risk, also known as inflation risk, is the risk faced by investors in almost all debt securities. It is most prevalent in a time of rising inflation where the interest payments on the security are below the rate of inflation. This will have the effect of reducing the purchasing power of the interest payments received.

5. **A.** Legislative risk results from a change in the law. Because there is frequently a political agenda behind legislation, this risk is sometimes referred to as political risk. Unexpected risk is a term that is not found in the industry.

6. **B.** Because debt securities are rarely listed on an exchange, they tend to have greater liquidity risk than equity securities. One of the least avoidable risks encountered by investors in debt securities is inflation or purchasing power risk. With domestic issues, there is no currency risk and although possible, political risk is less of a factor than the others.

3

Understanding Trading, Customer Accounts, and Prohibited Activities

N ow that we've built a foundation consisting of different securities markets, products, and their risks, we can begin to explore some of the issues that impact broker-dealers, registered personnel, and their customers accounts on an ongoing basis.

We'll begin with transactions and how they are initiated using different order types, how these transactions settle, and ultimately, how ownership changes hands. With purchases and sales, customers establish long and short positions. Existing positions within an account can be impacted by a number of corporate actions and you will be introduced to those actions and the accompanying mechanics associated with adjusting positions.

Broker-dealers maintain customers' accounts for them to hold their customers' securities positions; account types can vary. It's important to understand their differences—what can or cannot be done in each and how best to utilize them to accomplish the customers' goals. To service these accounts, broker-dealers must maintain proper documentation, meet requirements for account statement, and trade confirmation delivery, as well as abide by standardized record keeping rules.

Finally, we will examine prohibited activities that registered personnel and firms must avoid in order to maintain high standards of commercial honor and just and equitable principles of trade. ■

When you have completed the unit you should be able to:

- **recognize** order types and their uses;

- **distinguish** between different corporate actions and their impact on trading and settlement;

- **compute** adjustments for stock dividends, stock splits, and corporate actions;

- **distinguish** between different securities trade settlements;

- **recognize** different account types and registrations;

- **list** the information required on account statements and trade confirmations;

- **contrast** anti-money laundering, privacy, and communications compliance as they relate to knowing your customer; and

- **define** and **explain** prohibited activities.

3. 1 TRADING, SETTLEMENT, AND CORPORATE ACTIONS

LEARNING OBJECTIVES:

■ recognize order types and their uses

■ distinguish between different corporate actions and their impact on trading and settlement

■ compute adjustments for stock dividends, stock splits, and corporate actions

■ distinguish between different securities trade settlements

In the following sections, we will begin to explore the trading of securities in the secondary markets. Investors buy and sell securities from one another on stock exchanges and other trading venues such as the over-the-counter (OTC) market in the hopes of realizing gains and income received while owning the securities.

Additionally, we'll look at how ownership changes hands—settlement. And we'll also look at how corporate actions such as dividend payments and stock splits might impact our securities holdings.

3. 1. 1 ORDERS AND STRATEGIES

We can begin our discussion of orders with simple order instructions taken from investors to buy or sell securities. An investor will enter an order with a broker-dealer to execute a buy or sell transaction and the order will be entered by the broker-dealer on the appropriate exchange or trading venue. Following, we will discuss the different types of orders.

3. 1. 1. 1 Types of orders

Most orders entered are either market or limit orders:

■ **Market order**—buy or sell, executed immediately at the best available market price

■ **Limit order**—buy or sell, limits the acceptable purchase or selling price paid or received for the securities

While market orders are always executed immediately at the current market price, limit orders can only be executed at the limit price designated by the customer or better. For a buy limit order, *or better* means at the limit price <u>or lower</u>. For a sell limit order, *or better* means at the limit price <u>or higher</u>.

EXAMPLE

BUY MARKET ORDER: **Buy 1000 shares XYZ at MKT**

(This order would be executed immediately to buy at the best available market price.)

SELL MARKET ORDER: **Sell 1000 shares XYZ at MKT**

(This order would be executed immediately to sell at the best available market price.)

BUY LIMIT ORDER: **Buy 1000 shares of XYZ at 32**

(This order could only be executed to purchase XYZ at 32 or better. Because this is an instruction to buy, *or better* would be lower. Therefore, it would need to be executed at 32 or lower.)

SELL LIMIT ORDER: **Sell 1000 shares of XYZ at 32**

(This order could only be executed to sell XYZ at 32 or better. Because this is an instruction to sell, *or better* would be higher. Therefore, it would need to be executed at 32 or higher.)

Limit orders to either buy or sell come with an inherent risk. The risk is that the market may never go as low as the buy limit designated on the order, or as high as the sell limit designated on the order. As a consequence, it is possible their order will never be executed. In this light, customers who enter limit orders risk missing the market—that is, the opportunity to buy or sell because of the limit they've imposed on the buy or sell order instruction.

TAKE NOTE

Limit orders stand in time priority. There may be multiple orders to buy stock at a particular price. Once the stock begins trading at that price, those limit orders that were entered first will be filled first.

In conjunction with market and limit orders, there are unique order types known as **stop** and **stop limit** orders.

Stop order—Buy or sell, a stop order does not become a "live" working order in the market place until the stock trades at or through a specified price (the stop price). Once the order is "triggered" by the stock reaching the specified stop price, the order becomes a market order, and like any other market order, it should be executed immediately at the best available market price.

EXAMPLE

XYZ CMV = 12

Order: Buy 2000 shares XYZ at 15 stop

As soon as XYZ trades at or through the stop price of 15, this order will become a live working market order and like all market orders, it will be executed immediately at the next available price.

Stop limit order—Buy or sell, this order type also has a stop price and does not become a "live" working order until the stock trades at or through the stop price. However, it also has a limit price, so once the order is "triggered" by the sock reaching the specified stop price, the order becomes a limit order to buy or sell at the specified limit. Like any other limit order, it may or may not be executed depending on where the price of the stock is.

Finally, in addition to an order being either a market, limit stop order, there are a number of designations that can be applied to an order. In other words, there are additional instructions attached to the order that a customer would like adhered to. Though not all of these designations are accepted on every exchange or trading venue, the following are the most common.

- **Day order**—Unless marked to the contrary, an order is assumed to be a day order, valid only until the close of trading on the day it is entered. If the order has not been filled (executed in full), it is canceled at the close of the day's trading. Keep in mind that while market orders should be filled immediately, this is of more importance with limit orders.

- **Good-til-cancelled (GTC) order**—GTC orders are valid until executed or cancelled. However, all GTC orders are automatically cancelled if unexecuted on the last business day of April and the last business day of October. If the customer wishes to have the order remain working beyond those specific days, the customer must reenter the order.

- **Market-at-open or market-on-close order**—These are market orders designated to be executed at the opening of the day or at the close of the day. Depending on the market (exchange or OTC) the order is being sent to, the customer is not guaranteed the exact opening or closing price but instead a price at, or close to the first or last price of the day.

- **Fill-or-kill (FOK) order**—Applicable to limit orders, this is an instruction to fill (execute in its entirety) the order immediately or kill (cancel) the order completely. In this light, there can't ever be a partial execution.

- **Immediate-or-cancel (IOC) order**—IOC orders are like FOK orders except that a partial execution is acceptable. In other words, if only a portion of the order can be filled, it is, and the remaining unexecuted portion is canceled.

- **All-or-none (AON) order**—AON orders must be executed in their entirety or not at all. AON orders can be day or GTC orders. They differ from the FOKs in that they do not have to be filled immediately. In other words, they can be held until the end of the day (for day orders) or beyond (for GTC orders) until they can be filled in their entirety.

3. 1. 1. 1. 1 Quotations (Bid-Ask)

Often in the securities industry you will hear expressions like "the current quote is" or the "stock is being quoted at". What do these mean? What is a **quote**?

All quotes are two sided, consisting of both a **bid** price and **ask** (offer) price. The current bid price for a security is the highest price anyone is willing to pay for the securities at that moment in time. The current ask (offer) price is the lowest price anyone is willing to accept to sell the securities at that moment in time.

TAKE NOTE

All quotes maintained in active markets like a stock exchange are dynamic and change constantly throughout the trading day.

A typical quote might be expressed as 63 bid – ask (offer) 63.07. The highest price anyone is willing to pay to purchase the securities is 63, and the lowest price anyone is willing to accept to sell the securities is 63.07. The difference between the bid and ask is known as the spread. In this example the spread is .07, the difference between 63 and 63.07.

EXAMPLE

XYZ quote; **24 bid – ask 24.25**

Using this quote, an investor who enters a market order to buy (Buy 100 shares XYZ at MKT) would have to pay the best available price anyone else is willing to sell at. In this case, the investor would have to pay 24.25, as this is currently the best ask (offer). Conversely if an investor wanted to sell at the market (Sell 100 shares XYZ at MKT), they would have to sell at the best available price anyone else is willing to pay. In this case, the investor would have to sell at 24 as this is currently the best bid.

3. 1. 1. 1. 2 Trade Capacity (Principal or Agency)

All firms can act in one of two capacities in a customer transaction, agent or principal.

Agent—If the firm acts as an agent, it is a broker acting on behalf of its customer to buy or sell securities in the market. The firm is paid a commission when acting as an agent.

AGENT = BROKER = COMMISSION

Principal—If the firm is acting as a principal, the firm is buying into, or selling out of its own inventory to accommodate its customer. In this capacity the firm is a dealer and will markup the securities it is selling out of its inventory or mark down the securities it is buying into its inventory, rather than charge the customer a commission.

PRINCIPAL = DEALER = MARKUP or MARKDOWN

3. 1. 1. 1. 3 Long (Bullish) and Short (Bearish)

An investor's position in a security can be either long or short. Let's look at both.

Long—When an investor buys a security, they are known to have taken a position in that security. Owning a security is also known as being long or having a long position in the security. When someone is long a security they have taken an ownership position in the hopes that the security will rise in value and they will be able to sell it later for a profit. This is known as being bullish (anticipating the security will rise in value).

The risk associated with a long position is that the price of the security falls. Maximum loss for the investor occurs if the security becomes worthless.

Investors can open a position by buying a security and then later close the position by selling the security, hopefully at a higher price for a profit,

---

TEST TOPIC ALERT

Buy to open a position = Long = Bullish

EXAMPLE

Three customer accounts are as follows:

Bill Smith: Long 3000 shares of XYZ

Sarah Mills: Long 30 XYZ Warrants

Jill Burns: Long 20 XYZ call options

Someone who owns shares of stock (Bill Smith) is considered bullish. Owning securities convertible into the shares of stock such as rights, warrants (Sarah Mills), or long call options (Jill Burns), would also be a considered a bullish market attitude.

Short—An investor can also sell a security to open a position. To do this, an investor is actually selling a security they do not own. This is done by borrowing stock from a stock lender and selling (shorting) the borrowed shares. Selling a security one does not own is known as being short or having a short position in the security. Just the opposite of being long, a short customer is taking the view that the stock will decline in price, enabling them to buy the shares back later at a lower price. Buying back the shares enables the investor to return them to the party they were initially borrowed from. In this scenario, the customer profits by the difference between the short sale price and the price at which the shares are bought back. This is known as being bearish (anticipating the security will fall in value).

The risk to a short seller is that the price of the borrowed shares increases, forcing the seller to buy back at a higher price instead of a lower price as anticipated. Because there is no limit on how high a security's price may rise, a short seller has unlimited loss potential.

Just as investors can open a position by buying a security, so too can they open a position (a short position) by selling a security. Later, to close the position, hopefully at a lower price for a profit, they would buy back the security.

TEST TOPIC ALERT

Sell to open a position = Short = Bearish

EXAMPLE

Two customer accounts are as follows:

John Jones: Short 3000 shares of XYZ

Jane Smith: Long XYZ put options

Someone who sells shares of stock short (John Jones) is considered bearish. Owning contracts that allow one to sell the underlying security such as being long put options (Jane Smith) would also be considered a bearish market attitude.

Finally, remember that both buys and sells can be opening or closing transactions. Whichever transaction occurs first is the opening transaction and the latter transaction is the closing transaction—the one that closes the position.

EXAMPLE

Buy 1000 shares of ABC (opening transaction)

Sell 1000 shares of ABC (closing transaction)

or

Sell short 1000 shares of ABC (opening transaction)

Buy back 1000 shares of ABC (closing transaction)

3. 1. 1. 1. 4   Naked and Covered

Remember that to sell short, one must borrow the securities to be sold. Selling a stock short without first borrowing the shares or confirming a location where the shares can be borrowed from is known as **naked** short selling. Naked short selling is a violation. By contrast, if the shares have been properly borrowed or they have been located, and therefore it is known they can be borrowed, the short seller can now move forward and sell short. These shares, because they have already been borrowed or located to be borrowed, are known to be **covered**.

It should be noted here that locating and borrowing shares to be sold short is not something investors undertake themselves but instead is considered a back office function of a broker-dealer. Meeting the location requirements and the borrowing of the securities is done by the BD on behalf of the short selling customer.

3. 1. 1. 2   Discretionary vs. Non-Discretionary Orders

An account set up with preapproved authority for a registered representative to make transactions without having to ask for specific approval is a discretionary account. Discretion is defined as the authority to decide:

- what security;
- the number of shares or units; or
- whether to buy or sell.

Discretion does not apply to decisions regarding the timing of an investment or the price at which it is acquired only.

An order from a customer worded, "Buy 100 shares of ABC for my account whenever you think the price is right," is not a discretionary order and would not need to be executed in a discretionary account. Why? Because the customer chose the security (ABC) and the number of shares (100).

A customer can give discretionary power over his account(s) only by filing a **trading authorization** or a limited power of attorney with the broker-dealer. No transactions of a discretionary nature can take place without this document on file. Once authorization has been given, the customer is legally bound to accept the decision made by the person holding discretionary authority, although the customer may continue to enter orders on his own.

In addition to requiring the proper documentation, discretionary accounts are subject to the following rules.

■ Each discretionary order must be identified as such at the time it is entered for execution.

■ An officer or a partner of the brokerage house must approve each order promptly and in writing, but not necessarily before order entry.

■ A record must be kept of all transactions.

■ No excessive trading, or **churning** (trading for the sole purpose of generating commissions), may occur in the account relative to the size of the account and the customer's investment objectives.

■ To safeguard against the possibility of churning, a designated supervisor or manager must review all trading activity frequently and systematically.

3. 1. 1. 3   Solicited vs. Unsolicited Orders

A transaction initiated by an agent or registered representative is known as a **solicited** transaction. Unsolicited transactions are those initiated by the customer. Order tickets should be marked solicited or **unsolicited**.

3. 1. 2   INVESTMENT RETURNS AND TAX CONSEQUENCES

There are a number of ways investors can realize returns from their investments. But first, let's separate earned income from investment income. Earned income includes salary bonuses and income that is derived from active participation in a trade or business. Investment income is that which is earned from one's investments. Sometimes referred to as portfolio income, it would include dividends, interest, and capital gains derived from the sale of securities.

It should be noted here that income, depending on its source and type, can have different tax consequences. An important consideration is the amount of investment return an investor will be able to realize after taxes are taken. For tax purposes, income will generally be taxed at one of two rates: **ordinary income tax** rate or **capital gains tax** rate. These tax rates differ significantly and can have a big impact on the after tax returns.

■ **Ordinary income**—Ordinary income can be defined as the income earned from interest, wages, rents, royalties, and similar income streams. Ordinary income is taxed at different rates depending on the amount of income received by a taxpayer in a given tax year. The IRS divides ordinary income into tax brackets.

■ **Capital gains**—Capital gains are usually associated with the sale or exchange of property, including securities. The category of capital gain taxation is further broken down into long and short-term capital gains. If an asset is sold within one year (12 months or less) of its purchase, the gain is considered to be a short-term gain and it will be taxed at the same rate as the taxpayer's other ordinary income. Therefore, for short term capital gains, the tax rates are the same as the taxpayer's ordinary income. However, if the asset is held for more than one year, the gain is considered to be a long-term capital gain and is taxed at a favorable long-term rate.

3. 1. 2. 1   Dividends

Dividends are distributions of a company's profits to its shareholders. Investors who buy stock or mutual funds for example are entitled to dividends if and when the board of directors votes to make such distributions. Shareholders are automatically sent any dividends to which their shares entitle them. Dividends are typically paid in one of two ways:

■ **Cash dividends**—Cash dividends are normally distributed by check if an investor holds the stock certificate, or they are automatically deposited to a brokerage account if the shares are held in **street name** (held in a brokerage account in the firm's name to facilitate payments and delivery). When declared, cash dividends are typically paid quarterly and are taxed in the year they are distributed.

■ **Stock dividends**—If a company wishes to reinvest its profits for business purposes rather than to pay cash dividends, its board of directors may declare a stock dividend. This is typical of many growth companies that invest their cash resources in research and development. Under these circumstances, the company issues additional shares of its common stock as a dividend to its current stockholders instead of cash. The net result is that the shareholder now owns more shares after the distribution but the cost per share is adjusted downward. The stock dividend itself is not taxable, but the adjusted cost per share (new cost basis) will impact the tax consequences when the shares are sold.

EXAMPLE   An investor buys 200 shares of XYZ at $60 per share for a total cost of $12,000. If XYZ were to declare and pay a 20% stock dividend, the investor would now have a total of 240 shares (200 shares × 20% = 40 additional shares). Dividing $12,000 by 240 shares results in a new cost basis of $50 per share. In this light, when the shares are later sold, the investor will list $50 per share as the cost. The difference between the cost and sale price will be the investors gain or loss per share.

Finally, cash dividends may be taxed as either nonqualified (ordinary-taxed at the investor's ordinary income tax rate) or as qualified. The maximum tax rate on qualified dividends is specified by current IRS tax code and will depend on the investor's income tax bracket. The higher the investor's income tax bracket, the higher the tax on qualified dividends will be, up to the specified maximum. However, it will always be lower than the investor's ordinary income tax rate.

3. 1. 2. 1. 1   Dividend Disbursement Dates

There are four dates to remember that are associated with the dividend disbursing process: declaration, ex-dividend, record, and payable.

- **Declaration date**—When a company's board of directors (BOD) approves a dividend payment it is recognized as the date the dividend was declared. At this time the BOD would also designates the payment date and the dividend record date discussed following.

- **Ex-dividend date**—On the basis of the dividend record date, FINRA or the exchange (if the stock is listed) posts an ex-date. The **ex-date** is one business day before the record date. Because most trades settle the regular way—two business days after the trade date—a customer must purchase the stock two business days before the record date to qualify for the dividend. Or said another way, to receive the dividend, the stock must be purchased before the ex-dividend date.

- Conversely, if the stock is purchased on or after the ex-date, the new owner has purchased the stock "ex" without the dividend and is therefore not entitled to receive it.

- **Record date**—The stockholders of record (those who own the stock) on the record date receive the dividend distribution.

- **Payable date**—On the payable date the dividend disbursing agent sends dividend checks to all stockholders whose names appear on the books as owners as of the record date.

TAKE NOTE

DERP will help you remember the order in which the dates involving dividend distributions occur. The order of dates is Declaration, Ex, Record, and Payable.

TEST TOPIC ALERT

Declaration, record, and payment are determined by the board of directors (BOD), and FINRA(the exchange) determines ex-dividend date.

3. 1. 2. 2   Interest

Interest is the income paid to those who purchase debt securities—bond holders. It is generally stated as a percentage of face (also known as PAR) value on an annual basis. Interest is taxed as ordinary income.

EXAMPLE

A corporate bond has a face (PAR) value of $1,000 and it pays 6% interest. 6% × $1,000 = $60 annual interest. Under normal circumstances the annual interest is paid on a semiannual basis. In this case the $60 annual interest would be paid in two $30 semiannual payments.

3. 1. 2. 3   Capital Gains and Loses

The sale of securities can result in a capital gain or a capital loss. A **capital gain** occurs when a security is sold for a price higher than the cost basis. If the selling price is lower than the cost basis, a **capital loss** occurs.

Upon liquidation, cost basis represents a return of capital. The cost basis is not taxed as a gain but any sales proceeds above cost basis would be.

3. 1. 2. 4   Benchmarks and Indices

Regarding investment returns, investors must set reasonable expectations. A return on one's investments that could be considered strong in one market environment might be considered weak in another. While there's no single unwavering standard or benchmark, there are performance standards one can monitor. Therefore, while an investment should be judged within the context of the chosen portfolio strategy, it can also be judged against the appropriate standard or benchmark.

For example, when we refer to the stock market's performance in general, we are most likely referring to the performance of an index or average that tracks stocks or bonds. These benchmarks can serve as an indicator of the overall direction of the market as a whole, or of individual market sectors. They can be used by investors to see how one's own particular investments or combinations of investments are performing relative to that market as a whole. Following are a few of the more frequently cited indexes and averages.

Dow Jones Industrial Average—The most widely cited measure of the market, the DJIA tracks the performance of 30 stocks of large, well-known companies.

S&P 500 Index—Standard and Poor's index tracks 500 stocks of large-company U.S. companies and is the basis for several index mutual funds and exchange-traded funds.

Russell 2000—This index tracks 2,000 small-company stocks and serves as the benchmark for that component of the overall market.

Dow Jones Wilshire 5000—Tracking over 5,000 stocks, the Wilshire covers all the companies listed on the major stock markets, including companies of all sizes across all industries.

Lipper Fund Indexes—Lipper calculates several indexes tracking different categories of mutual funds, such as Growth, Core, or Value funds.

Barclays Capital Aggregate Bond Index—This is a composite index that combines several bond indexes to give a picture of the entire bond market.

3. 1. 3   TRADE SETTLEMENT

The date a transaction occurs is known as the trade date. Settlement date, on the other hand, is the date on which ownership actually changes between the buyer and seller. It is the date on which broker-dealers are required to exchange the securities and funds involved in a transaction and customers are requested to pay for securities bought and to deliver securities sold.

3. 1. 3. 1   Regular Way Settlement

In the securities industry, it is the Financial Industry Regulatory Authority's (FINRA) Uniform Practice Code (UPC) that standardizes the dates and times for each type of settlement. "Regular way", as its name suggests, is the regular way that securities transactions settle after the securities trade. Regular way settlement for most corporate securities (equity and debt) transactions is the second business day following the trade date, known as T + 2.

If a trade occurs on a Tuesday (trade date), it will settle regular way two business days later on Thursday. If a trade takes place on a Thursday, it will settle two business days later on the following Monday.

It is important to know that while corporate securities generally settle regular way T + 2, others have different regular way settlement dates. Briefly:

- T + 2—corporate securities, municipal bonds and government agency securities (Ginnie
- Mae, Fannie Mae and Freddie Mac debt securities)
- T + 1—federal government securities (T-bills, notes and bonds) and options
- Same day as trade date—Money market securities

3. 1. 3. 1. 1   Cash Settlement

Cash settlement, or same-day settlement, requires delivery of securities from the seller and payment from the buyer on the same day a trade is executed. Stocks or bonds sold for cash settlement must be available on the spot for delivery to the buyer. Both parties to the transaction would have to agree for cash settlement to occur.

3. 1. 3. 1. 2   Seller's Option

This form of settlement is available to customers who want to sell securities but cannot deliver the physical securities in time for regular way settlement. A **seller's option** contract lets a customer lock in a selling price for securities without having to make delivery on the second business day. Instead, the seller can settle the trade as specified in the contract. Or, if the seller elects to settle earlier than originally specified, the trade can be settled on any date from the fourth business day through the contract date, provided the buyer is given a one-day written notice. A buyer's option contract works the same way, with the buyer specifying when settlement will take place.

T A K E   N O T E   Seller's or buyer's settlement option cannot take place any sooner than the trade date plus three business days (T + 3). Consider that regular way settlement would be T + 2 and that a seller's or buyer's option settlement is allowing settlement to occur after regular way. Therefore, it couldn't occur any sooner than the day after regular way.

3. 1. 3. 2   Physical vs. Book Entry

When securities are issued with physical paper certificates (bonds or shares) it is those certificates that would be required for physical delivery. However, some securities are sold without a physical certificate. In those instances, evidence of ownership is kept on record at a central agency. For example, earlier we noted that government securities issued by the U.S. Treasury are all issued in book-entry form, meaning that no physical securities (paper certificates) exist. Transfer of ownership is recorded by entering the change on the books or electronic files.

3. 1. 4 CORPORATE ACTIONS

Earlier in this unit we addressed adjusting cost basis for one type of corporate action, the payment of stock dividends. There are other corporate actions that require cost basis be adjusted as well.

3. 1. 4. 1 Types of Corporate Actions

Different corporate actions require different rules to adjust cost basis. Aside from the payment of stock dividends, the two most common corporate actions utilizing standard adjustments would be stock splits, both forward and reverse.

3. 1. 4. 1. 1 Stock Splits (Forward and Reverse)

Forward Split—Although investors and corporate executives are generally delighted to see a company's stock price rise, a high market price may inhibit trading of the stock. To make the stock price attractive to a wider base of investors the company can declare a forward stock split. A forward stock split increases the number of shares and reduces the price without affecting the total market value of shares outstanding; an investor will receive more shares, but the value of each share is reduced. The total market value of the ownership interest is the same before and after the split.

TAKE NOTE More shares, reduced value per share = same total ownership interest before and after the adjustment.

A forward split can be characterized as either an even split or an uneven split. In an even split, the investor will always be given a certain number of shares for each share owned; 2 for 1, or 3 for 1, for example. In an uneven split, the split can be designated in any ratio: 3 for 2, or 5 for 4 for example. Let's look at the math involved in both an even and uneven split in the following two examples. Keep in mind that the total position value for the investor is always the same before and after the split.

EXAMPLE EVEN SPLIT

An investor owns 100 shares at $60 per share. Therefore, the total position value is $6,000 [100 × $60 = $6,000].

Assume a 2:1 split. To find the new number of shares, multiply the original number by 2 (the first number of the split) and then divide by 1 (the second number of the split) (100 × 2 = 200; 200 ÷ 1 = 200). We now know the investor has 200 shares. Because the total position value of the shares is the same before and after the split, determine the new per share value as follows:

200 × ? = 6,000 (6,000 ÷ 200 = 30). The new per share value is $30.

After the adjustment for the 2:1 corporate split action the investor now owns 200 shares at $30 per share.

EXAMPLE

UNEVEN SPLIT

An investor owns 100 shares at $60 per share. Therefore the total position value is $6,000 (100 × $60 = $6,000).

Assume a 5:4 split. To find the new number of shares, multiply the original number by 5 (the first number of the split) and then divide by 4 (the second number of the split) (100 × 5 = 500; 500 ÷ 4 = 125). Determine the new per share value as follows:

125 × ? = 6,000 (6,000 ÷ 125 = 48). The new per share value is $48.

After the adjustment for the 5:4 corporate split action the investor now owns 125 shares at $48 per share.

Reverse Split—Sometimes a stock price becomes so low that it attains an undesirable aura about it. In some cases, a low stock price might not meet the listing criteria of a stock exchange that it is listed on and delisting can occur. To combat these issues, one corporate action that can be taken, strictly related to the price of the stock, is a reverse stock split. Unlike a forward split where the number of shares is increased and the price per share is decreased, a reverse split has the opposite effect on the number and price of shares. After a reverse split, investors own fewer shares worth more per share.

TAKE NOTE

Fewer shares, increased value per share = same total ownership interest before and after the adjustment.

A reverse split can also be characterized as either an even split or an uneven split. In an even split, the investor will always be given one share for a certain number of shares owned: 1 for 2, or 1 for 3, for example. In an uneven split, the split can be designated in any ratio: 2 for 3, or 4 for 5, for example. Let's look at the math involved for an even reverse split. As with forward splits, always keep in mind that the total position value for the investor is always the same before and after the split.

EXAMPLE

REVERSE EVEN SPLIT

An investor owns 100 shares at $5. Therefore, the total position value is $500 (100 × $5 = $500).

Assume a 1:4 reverse split, what is the new number and value of shares?

100 × 1 = 100; 100 ÷ 4 = 25. The new number of shares is 25.

25 × ? = $500 ($500 ÷ 25 = $20). The new per share value is $20.

After the adjustment for the 1:4 corporate split action the investor now owns 25 shares at $20 per share.

Not all questions on splits involve calculations. If you remember that there are more or fewer shares at lower or greater value as a result of the corporate action (split) depending on if it is a forward or reverse split, you might be able to answer the question without using math.

3. 1. 4. 1. 2   Stock Rights and Stock Warrants

Rights—Rights, sometimes known as **preemptive rights**, entitle existing common stockholders to maintain their proportionate ownership shares in a company by buying newly issued shares before the company offers them to the general public.

A rights offering allows stockholders to purchase common stock below the current market price. The rights are valued separately from the stock and trade in the secondary market during the subscription period which is typically 30 to 45 days.

A stockholder who receives rights may:

- exercise the rights to buy stock by sending the rights certificates and a check for the required amount to the rights agent;

- sell the rights and profit from their market value (rights certificates are negotiable securities); or

- let the rights expire and lose their value (not a likely scenario).

Stock Warrants—A warrant is a certificate granting its owner the right to purchase securities from the issuer at a specified price, normally higher than the current market price at the time the warrants are issued, and at some time in the future. Unlike a right, a warrant is usually a long-term instrument that gives the investor the option of buying shares at a later date at the specified (exercise) price. Note that while the exercise price is higher than the current market value when the warrants are issued, it is hopeful that the exercise price will be below current market value when the warrants are eventually exercised.

Warrants are usually offered to the public as sweeteners in connection with other securities, such as debt instruments (bonds) or preferred stock, to make those securities more attractive. Such offerings are often bundled as units. For example, an investor might buy a corporate bond and with it receive 10 warrants allowing them to purchase 10 shares of common stock at a specified price on a later date.

It pays to remember by comparison:

- **Rights**—short term, given to existing shareholders, allows one to purchase shares below current market value.

- **Warrants**—long term, bundled with other securities, allows someone to purchase shares at a price that is above the current market value at the time the warrants were issued.

3. 1. 4. 1. 3   Unique (Nonstandard) Corporate Actions

Up to this point we've discussed the most common corporate actions: dividend declarations (both cash and stock), stock splits (both forward and reverse) and the issuance of rights and warrants. In the case of making any adjustments to cost basis the adjustments are standardized. There are, however, corporate actions that are always unique, and thus standardized adjustments would not be applicable. These would include but not be limited to mergers and acquisitions (M&A), takeovers, spin-offs, tender offers, buybacks, or any of the previous where options contracts are traded on the issuer's securities. Adjustments made for these events will vary from situation to situation and each is made to fit the circumstances and terms of the specific action.

Mergers and Acquisitions (M&A)—These are transactions in which the ownership of companies or their operating units are transferred as in the case of an acquisition, or combined as in the case of a merger. M&A can allow enterprises to grow, shrink, or change the nature of their business.

Takeover—A takeover is the purchase of one company, known as the target company, by another company known as the bidder or buyer. A hostile takeover is accomplished when the buyer goes directly to the target company's shareholders bypassing the board of directors or management.

Spin-Off—A type of divestiture where a parent company sells all of the shares of a subsidiary or distributes new shares of a company or division it owns to create a new company.

Tender Offer—An offer to buy securities for cash or for cash plus securities.

Buyback—A buyback, sometimes referred to as a repurchase, is when a company buys its own outstanding shares in the open market from existing shareholders. Companies might buy back shares for a number of reasons. For example, doing so reduces the number of shares available (supply) and therefore can increase the value of shares still available (demand). Sometimes by removing available shares from the market a company might be trying to eliminate any threats of takeover.

3. 1. 4. 2   Delivery of Notices and Corporate Action Deadlines

Issuers are required by the Securities Exchange Commission (SEC) to give notice of corporate actions to shareholders for such actions as cash dividends, stock dividends, a forward or reverse split, or a rights or warrants offering.

TAKE NOTE

A notice is not required for an ordinary interest payment on a corporate debt (bond) security.

The following should be included in the notice:

- Title of the security
- Date of declaration
- Date of record for determining holders entitled to receive the distribution or to participate in the split
- Date of payment or distribution
- For a cash dividend—the amount to be paid
- For a stock dividend—the rate of the dividend; example 10%
- For a split (forward or reverse) the rate of the distribution; example 2:1, 3:2

Notice should be given no later than 10 days prior to the record involved or, in case of a rights subscription or other offering if giving 10 days advance notice is not practical, on or before the record date and in no event later than the effective date.

3. 1. 4. 3   Proxies and Proxy Voting

Every publicly traded company must have an annual general shareholder meeting where management presents any decisions that would require shareholder approval. The approval (or disapproval) is given by means of voting for each decision. Shareholders may attend the meeting in person to vote or they may vote by proxy either electronically or by mail.

Rather than attend meetings in person, most corporate stockholders usually vote by means of a proxy, which is like an absentee ballot. A proxy is a limited power of attorney that a stockholder gives to another person, transferring the right to vote on the stockholder's behalf.

A proxy is automatically revoked if the stockholder attends the shareholder meeting or, if the proxy is replaced by another proxy, the stockholder executes at a later date.

3. 1. 4. 3. 1   Proxy Solicitation

Stockholders can receive multiple proxy solicitations for controversial company proposals. If proxies are solicited, the SEC requires a company to give stockholders information about the items to be voted on and allow the SEC to review this information before it sends the proxies to stockholders. In a proxy contest, everyone who participates must register with the SEC. Also, anyone who is not a direct participant but who provides stockholders with unsolicited advice must register as a participant.

3. 1. 4. 3. 2   Forwarding Proxies and Related Material

Member broker-dealer firms must cooperate with issuers by ensuring that customers whose stock is held in the broker-dealer's name (street name) are alerted to all financial matters concerning issuers (e.g., quarterly reports and proxy statements). To do so, members act as forwarding agents for all proxies and other corporate materials received from an issuer for street name stock.

Member firms that are nominal owners of record (the stock is held in street name) must vote street name stock in accordance with the wishes of the beneficial owners (the broker-dealers' customers who purchased the shares). If a customer signs and returns a proxy statement and fails to indicate how the shares are to be voted, the member must vote the shares as recommended by management.

If a customer does not return the proxy by the 10th day before the annual shareholders' meeting, the member may vote the shares as it sees fit as long as the matters to be voted on are of minor importance. If the matters to be voted on are of major importance (e.g., merger or issuance of additional securities), the member may never vote the shares as it sees fit. In this case, if the proxy is not returned, the shares are not voted.

TAKE NOTE

Member broker-dealer firms are reimbursed by issuers for all costs relating to the forwarding of proxy materials. Such costs include postage and related clerical expenses.

QUICK QUIZ 3.A

LEARNING OBJECTIVES

■ Recognize order types and their uses

■ Distinguish between different corporate actions and their impact on trading and settlement

■ Compute adjustments for stock dividends, stock splits and corporate actions

■ Distinguish between different securities trade settlements

1. ABC stock is currently trading at $63. Mr. Jones would like to purchase ABC stock but not at $63. If the price of ABC stock were to fall to $58 or less, then Mr. Jones wants to buy the stock. Which type of order should Mr. Jones place considering his objective?

   A. Market order
   B. Buy Limit
   C. Buy stop
   D. Buy stop limit

2. The current quote for DEF stock is 49.50 bid – ask 49.75. If an investor wanted to buy or sell DEF stock, we can conclude which of the following?

   I. The best price anyone in the secondary market is willing to sell at is 49.50.
   II. The best price anyone in the secondary market is willing to sell at is 49.75.
   III. The best price anyone in the secondary market is willing to buy at is 49.50.
   IV. The best price anyone in the secondary market is willing to buy at is 49.75.
   A. I and III
   B. I and IV
   C. II and III
   D. II and IV

3. When an investor is long a stock

   A. the investor is bearish
   B. buying the stock in the secondary market will close the position
   C. there is limited gain potential
   D. the investor is bullish

4. All of the following is true about an investor that sells a stock short EXCEPT

   A. the investor will close his position by purchasing the stock
   B. the price of the stock must go down in order to profit
   C. loss is limited to the amount of the investment
   D. the investor is bearish

5. Which of the following is a taxable event for an investor when it occurs?

   A. Stock dividend distribution
   B. Cash dividend distribution
   C. Forward split
   D. Reverse split

6. A stock is purchased on June 10 of this year and sold on January 10 of next year for a profit of $200. How will the $200 be taxed?

    A. As a short term capital gain, taxed at the ordinary income tax rate
    B. As a short term capital gain, taxed at the lower capital gain rate
    C. As a long term capital gain, taxed at the ordinary income tax rate
    D. As a long term capital gain, taxed at the lower capital gain rate

7. A customer has returned a signed proxy statement for stock held in street name by a member firm. He did not indicate how he wanted to vote for any issues listed on his ballot. What action, if any, is required of the member firm?

    A. No action is required and no votes are cast.
    B. The firm must contact the beneficial owner of the stock and ask for direction on how to vote on the proposals listed.
    C. The firm may vote on the ballot as it sees fit for the benefit of the customer.
    D. The firm must vote in accordance with the recommendations made by the issuer of the stock.

8. Which of the following securities will settle regular way, T+1?

    A. Corporate bond
    B. Revenue bond
    C. Treasury bond
    D. GNMA

3. 2 CUSTOMER ACCOUNTS AND COMPLIANCE CONSIDERATIONS

LEARNING OBJECTIVES:

- Recognize different account types and registrations

- List the information required on account statements and trade confirmations

- Contrast anti-money laundering, privacy, and communications compliance as they relate to knowing your customer.

In this section, you will be introduced to different account types and numerous ways an account can be registered (titled) at a broker-dealer. We'll conclude with a comprehensive accounting of the many compliance issues confronting broker-dealers when new accounts are established.

3. 2. 1 ACCOUNT TYPES

Accounts can be largely broken down into two types: cash accounts and margin accounts. By simple comparison, in a cash account, payment is expected to be made in full at the time securities are purchased, but in a margin account, payment can be partially made at the time of purchase.

3. 2. 1. 1   Cash Account

A **cash account** is the basic type of investment account. Anyone eligible to open an investment account can open a cash account. In a cash account, a customer pays in full for any securities purchased. Payment in full as defined by the Securities Exchange Commission (SEC) under Regulation T must occur not later than two business days after the standard settlement period.

EXAMPLE   Corporate stock is purchased in a cash account and it will settle regular way T + 2. In a cash account full payment would be required no later than two business days after T + 2—in other words, T + 4.

Certain accounts must be opened as cash accounts, such as individual retirement accounts (IRAs), corporate retirement accounts, and custodial accounts. We'll discuss these different account registrations later in this unit.

3. 2. 1. 2   Margin Account

Trading **on margin** is a common practice in the securities industry. It allows customers to increase their trading capital by borrowing either cash or securities via their broker-dealers.

There are two types of margin accounts: long and short. In a long margin account, customers purchase securities and pay interest on the money borrowed until the loan is repaid. In a short margin account, stock is borrowed and then sold short, enabling the customer to profit if its value declines. All short sales must be executed through, and accounted for in a margin account.

Stock can be borrowed from several sources for short sales in a margin account: the member firm executing a short sale on behalf of the customer, margin customers of that member firm, other member firms, specialized companies known as stock lending firms, and institutional investors. The most common source is another customer's margin account, but permission must be given by signing a loan consent agreement, which we'll speak to later in this unit.

TAKE NOTE   In long margin accounts, customers borrow money; in short margin accounts, customers borrow securities.

Margin accounts offer some advantages for customers. Consider that in a margin account a customer can:

- purchase more securities with a lower initial cash outlay; and
- leverage the investment by borrowing a portion of the purchase price.

Leveraging magnifies the customer's rate of return or rate of loss in adverse market conditions. The table following demonstrates this but does not account for trading costs (commissions) or for interest costs applied for the funds borrowed.

Cash/Margin Purchase

	Cash Purchase	Margin Purchase
Purchase of 1,000 shares of ABC for $20	Customer pays $20,000 for purchase	Customer borrows 50% ($10,000) from broker-dealer, deposits equity of $10,000
Return after increase from $20 to $30 per share	Customer experiences 50% return (gain/initial investment: $10,000 ÷ $20,000 = 50%)	Customer experiences 100% return (gain/initial investment: $10,000 ÷ $10,000 = 100%)
Return after decrease from $20 to $15 per share	Customer experiences 25% loss (loss/initial investment: – $5,000 ÷ $20,000 = – 25%)	Customer experiences 50% loss (loss/initial investment: – $5,000 ÷ $10,000 = – 50%)

The advantages of margin accounts for broker-dealers are:

■ margin account loans generate interest income for the firm; and

■ margin customers typically trade larger positions because of increased trading capital, generating higher commissions for the firm.

3. 2. 1. 2. 1 Hypothecation and Re-Hypothecation

Hypothecation is the pledging of customer securities as collateral for margin loans. A hypothecation agreement must be signed by a customer who wants to open a margin account. This agreement is generally contained within the margin agreement, and thus, customers are giving permission for this process to occur when they sign the margin agreement.

After customers pledge their securities to the broker-dealer by signing the margin agreement, the broker-dealer **re-hypothecates** (repledges) them as collateral for a loan from a bank. In this light, you can see that a broker-dealer is not lending its own funds to customers purchasing securities on margin but instead is borrowing money from a bank for that purpose. Regulation U oversees the process of a bank lending money to broker-dealers based on customer securities having been pledged as collateral for the loan.

Firms cannot commingle customer securities with securities owned by the firm. However firms can commingle one customer's securities with another customer's securities for hypothecation if customers have given specific permission by signing the hypothecation agreement.

3. 2. 1. 2. 2 Types of Accounts Permitted to Trade on Margin

Later in this unit we'll outline different account types or registrations. For now, it is important to understand that not all account types will be able to utilize margin, be set up as margin accounts, and trade on margin. The breakdown is as follows:

■ **Individual and joint accounts** (those with more than one party to the account) can utilize margin.

■ **Corporate accounts** may utilize margin only if it is not restricted in the corporation's charter or by-laws. In other words, trading on margin may be listed as being prohibited, and if so, would not be allowed.

■ **Partnership accounts** may utilize margin only if it is not restricted in the partnership resolution. Like a corporate account, a partnership agreement might list trading on margin as being prohibited, and if so would not be allowed.

- **Fiduciary (trust and custodial) accounts** could only utilize margin if it is specifically permitted within the trust or custodial agreement. Note the difference here. In this instance, margin must be specifically listed as being permitted.
- **Individual retirement accounts** (IRAs) and other qualified plans prohibit the use of margin.

3. 2. 1. 2. 3   Account Approvals

Like all accounts, margin accounts would need to be approved by a principal of the firm prior to the first trade. The approval would need to be in accordance with whether or not margin is permissible for the type of account being set up as outlined in the previous section.

3. 2. 1. 2. 4   Eligible and Ineligible Securities

Regulation T also identifies which securities are eligible for purchase on margin and which may be used as collateral for loans for other purchases.

TEST TOPIC ALERT

Differentiate between the use of the terms margin and marginable.

- Margin is the amount of equity that must be deposited to buy securities in a margin account.

- Marginable refers to securities that can be used as collateral in a margin account.

The following may be purchased on margin and used as collateral:

- Exchange-listed stocks, bonds
- Nasdaq stocks
- Non-National Market Securities (NMS) OTC issues approved by the FRB
- Warrants

The following cannot be purchased on margin and cannot be used as collateral for a margin loan:

- Options (both calls and puts)
- Rights
- Non-National Market Securities (NMS) OTC issues not approved by the FRB
- Insurance contracts

The following cannot be bought on margin but can be used as collateral after being held for 30 days:

- Mutual funds
- New issues

Lastly, certain securities are exempt from the Federal Reserve Board's Regulation T margin requirements.

Securities exempt from Regulation T include:

- U.S. Treasury bills, notes, and bonds;
- government agency issues; and
- municipal securities.

If these exempt securities are bought or sold in a margin account, they are subject to the firm's determination of an initial deposit requirement. Firms may impose stricter requirements but at a minimum must follow maintenance requirements established by FINRA.

TAKE NOTE

The Federal Reserve Board (FRB) can change Regulation T at any time, but the current requirement (50%) has been in place since 1974. Assume Regulation T equals 50% in test questions unless it is specified differently.

3. 2. 1. 2. 5   Required Disclosures

Customers who open margin accounts must sign a margin agreement before trading can begin. The agreement consists of three parts: the credit agreement, the hypothecation agreement, and the loan consent form.

Credit agreement—The credit agreement discloses the terms of the credit extended by the broker-dealer, including the method of interest computation and situations under which interest rates may change.

Hypothecation agreement—As noted earlier in this unit, the hypothecation agreement allows the securities to be pledged for the loan and gives permission to the broker-dealer to repledge customer margin securities as collateral. The firm re-hypothecates customer securities to the bank, and the bank loans money to the broker-dealer on the basis of the loan value of these securities. All customer securities must be held in street name (registered in the name of the broker-dealer) to facilitate this process. When customer securities are held in street name, the broker-dealer is known as the nominal, or named, owner. The customer is the beneficial owner because he retains all rights of ownership.

Loan consent form—If signed, the loan consent form gives permission to the firm to loan the customers margin securities to other customers or broker-dealers, usually to facilitate short sales where securities need to be borrowed.

TEST TOPIC ALERT

To open a margin account, it is mandatory that the customer signs the credit agreement and hypothecation agreement. The loan consent form is optional.

Additionally, before opening a margin account, you must provide customers with a risk disclosure document. This information must also be provided to margin customers on an annual basis. The document discusses the risks associated with margin trading, some of which are shown in the following.

- Customers are not entitled to choose which securities can be sold if a maintenance call is not met.
- Customers can lose more money than initially deposited.
- Customers are not entitled to an extension of time to meet a margin call.
- Firms can increase their in-house margin requirements without advance notice.

3. 2. 1. 2. 6   Federal and FINRA Margin Requirements

Customers are required to deposit a minimum amount of equity for their first purchase in a margin account. Although Regulation T states that a deposit of 50% of the market value of the purchase is required, FINRA rules require that this initial deposit cannot be less than $2,000.

The customer is required to deposit the greater of the Regulation T requirement (50%) or the FINRA minimum. The exception occurs when the customer's initial purchase is less than $2,000; the customer is not required to deposit $2,000—only the full purchase price. The following table depicts the required deposit.

Initial Requirements Example

Customer Purchase	Regulation T Requirement	FINRA Minimum Rule	Customer Deposit Required
100 shares at $50/share	$2,500	$2,000	$2,500
100 shares at $30/share	$1,500	$2,000	$2,000
100 shares at $15/share	$750	$1,500	$1,500

There is another way to look at this: if the customer's first purchase in a margin account is;

■ greater than $4,000, deposit 50%.

■ between $2,000 and $4,000, deposit $2,000.
less than $2,000, deposit 100% of the purchase price.

3. 2. 1. 2. 7   Margins calls

As previously discussed, Regulation T requires margin account customers to meet initial margin deposit requirements no more than four business days after the trade date, T + 2 plus two additional business days. The deposit may be made in cash or in fully paid for marginable securities. If made using fully paid for marginable securities remember that they are only marginable to the extent of 50% of their value. Therefore, the securities must be valued at twice the amount of the Regulation T margin call.

If payment is late, the broker-dealer may apply to its designated examining authority (DEA) for an extension.

TAKE NOTE

A firms' designated examining authority (DEA) could be a U.S. exchange or FINRA. This would be the designated authority tasked with monitoring and auditing the firm for industry rule compliance.

For introducing broker-dealers who do not clear their own trades, the extension request is made by the clearing firm. For an amount less than $1,000, the broker-dealer can choose to take no action.

If no extension is requested, or one is requested but not granted, on the morning of the sixth business day, the firm must sell out the securities purchased and freeze the account for 90 days.

If the customer wants to purchase securities in a frozen account, the customer must have adequate funds in the account before order entry. In other words, the customer must have the funds available in the account to pay for the securities in full.

3. 2. 1. 3 Discretionary vs. Nondiscretionary Accounts

Earlier we learned about discretionary orders, those that can be entered by the registered representative without the orders being approved first by the customer. It should be noted that accounts can be set up as being either discretionary or nondiscretionary. In a nondiscretionary account, no order can be entered without the customer's prior approval.

3. 2. 1. 4 Commission vs. Fee-Based Accounts

Accounts can be set up as commission-based, where a commission is billed for each transaction, or as fee-based. Firms can offer investors fee-based accounts that charge a single fee (either fixed or a percentage of assets in the account) instead of commission-based charges for brokerage services.

Fee-based accounts are appropriate only for investors who engage in at least a moderate level of trading activity. Accounts with a low level of trading activity may be better off with commission-based charges. Rules require that, before opening a fee-based account, investors be given a disclosure document describing the services to be provided and the cost.

3. 2. 1. 4. 1 Wrap Accounts

Wrap accounts are accounts for which firms provide a group of services, such as asset allocation, portfolio management, executions, and administration, for a single fee. Wrap accounts are generally investment advisory accounts.

3. 2. 1. 5 Educational Accounts

Just as tax-advantaged accounts are available to save for retirement, tax-advantaged accounts exist to save for education as well.

3. 2. 1. 5. 1 Section 529 plans

In Unit 2, under municipal securities we covered section 529 plans. Remember that they are a specific type of education savings account available to investors.

3. 2. 1. 5. 2 Coverdell (Education IRA)

Coverdell Education IRAs allow after-tax contributions of up to $2,000 per student per year for children younger than age 18. Contribution limits may be reduced or eliminated for higher-income tax payers. Distributions are tax free as long as the funds are used for qualified education expenses. These expenses include those for college, secondary, or elementary school. If a student's account is not depleted by age 30, the funds must be distributed to the individual subject to income tax and 10% penalty or rolled into an education IRA for another family member beneficiary.

3. 2. 2 CUSTOMER ACCOUNT REGISTRATIONS

When an account is opened, it is registered in the name(s) of one or more persons. These persons are the account owners and the only individuals allowed access and control of the investments in the account.

3. 2. 2. 1 Individual/Single Accounts

A **single** account has one beneficial owner. The account holder is the only person who can control the investments within the account and request distributions of cash or securities from the account.

TAKE NOTE

If a person not named on an account will have any authority over the account, the customer must file written authorization with the broker-dealer giving that person access to the account. This trading authorization usually takes the form of a power of attorney. Two basic types of trading authorizations are full and limited powers of attorney. Both would be cancelled upon the death of either party.

Full power of attorney—A full power of attorney allows someone who is not the owner of an account to deposit or withdraw cash or securities and make investment decisions for the account owner. Custodians, trustees, guardians, and other people filling similar legal duties are often given full powers of attorney.

Limited power of attorney—A limited power of attorney allows an individual to have some, but not total, control over an account. The document specifies the level of access the person may exercise. Limited power of attorney, also called limited trading authorization, allows the entering of buy and sell orders but no withdrawal of assets. Entry of orders and withdrawal of assets is allowed if full power of attorney is granted.

3. 2. 2. 1. 1 Transfer on Death (TOD)

Transfer on death (TOD) is a type of individual account that allows the registered owner of the account to pass all or a portion of it, upon death, to a named beneficiary or beneficiaries. This account avoids probate (i.e., having the decedent's will declared genuine by a court of law) because the estate is bypassed. However, the assets in the account do not avoid estate tax, if applicable.

3. 2. 2. 2 Joint Accounts

In a **joint** account, two or more adults are named on the account as co-owners, with each allowed some form of control over the account. The account forms for joint accounts require the signatures of all owners.

Joint account agreements provide that any or all tenants may transact business in the account. Checks must be made payable to the names in which the account is registered and endorsed for deposit by all tenants, although mail only needs to be sent to a single address.

In addition to the new account form, a joint account must be designated as either tenants in common (TIC) or joint tenants with right of survivorship (JTWROS). These designations determine how the account ownership will be handled if any party to the account dies.

3. 2. 2. 2. 1 Tenants in Common (TIC)

Tenants in common (TIC) ownership provides that a deceased tenant's fractional interest in the account is retained by that tenant's estate and is not passed to the surviving tenant(s).

3. 2. 2. 2. 2 *Joint Tenants With Right of Survivorship (JTWROS)*

Joint tenants with right of survivorship (JTWROS) ownership stipulates that a deceased tenant's interest in the account passes to the surviving tenant(s).

TEST TOPIC ALERT

JTWROS—all parties have an undivided interest in the account.

TIC—each party must specify a percentage interest in the account.

3. 2. 2. 3   Corporate Accounts

Corporations, like individuals, will invest in securities. When opening an account for a corporation, a firm must obtain a copy of the corporate charter as well as a corporate resolution. The charter is proof that the corporation does exist and the resolution authorizes both the opening of the account and the officers designated to enter orders.

A broker-dealer who opens an account for a corporate must establish:

- the business's legal right to open an investment account;
- an indication of any limitations that the owners, stockholders, a court, or any other entity has placed on the securities in which the business can invest; and
- the individual who will represent the business in transactions involving the account.

3. 2. 2. 4   Partnership Accounts

A partnership is an unincorporated association of two or more individuals. Partnerships frequently open accounts necessary for business purposes.

The partnership must complete a partnership agreement stating which of the partners can make transactions for the account. If the partnership opens a margin account, the partnership must disclose any investment limitations.

An amended partnership agreement (similar to a corporate resolution) must be obtained each year if any changes have been made.

3. 2. 2. 5   Fiduciary Accounts

When securities are placed in a **fiduciary account**, a person other than the owner initiates trades. The most familiar example of a fiduciary account is a trust account. Money or securities are placed in trust for one person, often a minor, but someone else manages the account. The manager or trustee is a fiduciary.

In a fiduciary account, the investments exist for the owner's beneficial interest, yet the owner has little or no legal control over them. The fiduciary makes all of the investment, management, and distribution decisions and must manage the account in the owner's best interests. The fiduciary may not use the account for his own benefit, although he may be reimbursed for reasonable expenses incurred in managing the account.

The beneficial owner's Social Security number is used on the account.

A fiduciary is any person legally appointed and authorized to represent another person, act on his behalf, and make whatever decisions are necessary to the prudent management of his account. Fiduciaries include a(n):

- trustee designated to administer a trust;

- executor designated in a decedent's will to manage the affairs of the estate;
- administrator appointed by the courts to liquidate the estate of a person who died intestate (without a will);
- guardian designated by the courts to handle a minor's affairs until the minor reaches the age of majority or to handle an incompetent person's affairs;
- custodian for a minor;
- receiver in a bankruptcy; and
- conservator for an incompetent person.

Any trades the fiduciary enters must be compatible with the investment objectives of the underlying entity.

Opening a fiduciary account may require a court certification of the individual's appointment and authority. An account for a trustee must include a trust agreement detailing the limitations placed on the fiduciary.

The registered representative for a fiduciary account must be aware of the following rules.

- Proper authorization must be given—the necessary court documents must be filed with and verified by the broker-dealer.
- Speculative transactions are generally not permitted.
- Margin accounts are only permitted if authorized by the legal documents establishing the fiduciary accounts.
- The prudent investor rule requires fiduciaries to make wise and safe investments.
- Many states publish a legal list of securities approved for fiduciary accounts.
- A fiduciary may not share in an account's profits but may charge a reasonable fee for services.

3. 2. 2. 6   Custodial Accounts for Minors

Accounts set up for minors can be established under either the **Uniform Gift to Minors Act** (UGMA) or the Uniform Transfers to Minors Act (UTMA). These accounts require an adult to act as **custodian** for a minor (the beneficial owner). Any kind of security or cash may be given to the account without limitation.

Under UGMA, when the minor reaches the age of majority, the property in the account is transferred into the name of the new adult. Under UTMA, the custodian can withhold transfer of property in the account until the new adult reaches age 25 (or 21 in some states).

Any securities given to a minor through an UGMA or UTMA account are managed by a custodian until the minor reaches the age of majority.

TAKE NOTE

When a person makes a gift of securities to a minor under the UGMA or UTMA laws, that person is the donor of the securities. A gift under these acts conveys an indefeasible title; that is, the donor may not take back the gift, nor may the minor return the gift. Once the gift is donated, the donor gives up all rights to the property.

The custodian has full control over the minor's account and can:

- buy or sell securities;
- exercise rights or warrants; or
- liquidate, trade, or hold securities.

The custodian may also use the property in the account in any way deemed proper for the minor's support, education, maintenance, general use, or benefit. However, the account is not normally used to pay expenses associated with raising a child because the parents can incur negative tax consequences.

Registered representatives must know the following rules of custodial accounts.

■ An account may have only one custodian and one minor or beneficial owner.

■ Only an individual can be a custodian for a minor's account.

■ A minor can be the beneficiary of more than one account, and a person may serve as custodian for more than one account as long as each account benefits only one minor.

■ The donor of securities can act as custodian or can appoint someone else to do so.

■ Unless they are acting as custodians, parents have no legal control over a custodial account or the securities in it.

3. 2. 2. 6. 1   Opening and Managing Custodial Accounts

When opening a custodial account, a representative must ensure that the account application contains the custodian's name, the minor's name and Social Security number, and the state in which the account is registered. Unlike opening a trust account where documentation of the trustee's authority is required, no documentation of custodial rights or court certification is required for an individual acting as the custodian for a minor.

Any securities in a custodial account are registered in the custodian's name for the benefit of the minor. For UGMAs, the securities cannot be registered in street name (the name of the broker-dealer), but for UTMAs they can. Securities bought in a custodial account must be registered in such a way that the custodial relationship is evident.

 EXAMPLE   Marilyn Johnson, the donor, has appointed her daughter's aunt, Barbara Wood, as custodian for the account of her minor daughter, Alexis. The account and the certificates would read "Barbara Wood as custodian for Alexis Johnson."

Because the minor is the **beneficial owner** (the account contains the minor's Social Security number), any tax liability is that of the minor. Though the minor is responsible for any and all taxes on the account, it is the parent's or legal guardian's responsibility to see that the taxes are paid.

Remember that a custodial account is a type of fiduciary account, and as such, the fiduciary is charged with fiduciary responsibilities in managing the minor's account. Certain restrictions have been placed on what is deemed to be proper handling of the investments in these accounts. The most important limitations follow.

■ Custodial accounts may be opened and managed as cash accounts only.

■ A custodian may not purchase securities in an account on margin or pledge them as collateral for a loan.

■ A custodian must reinvest all cash proceeds, dividends, and interest within a reasonable time. Cash proceeds from sales or dividends may be held in a non-interest-bearing custodial account for a reasonable period but should not remain idle for long.

■ Investment decisions must take into account a minor's age and the custodial relationship. Commodities futures, naked options, and other high-risk securities are examples of inappropriate investments. Options may not be bought in a custodial account because no evidence of ownership is issued to an options buyer. Covered call writing is normally allowed.

■ Stock subscription rights or warrants must be either exercised or sold.

■ A custodian cannot delegate away fiduciary responsibility but can grant trading authority and investment decisions to a qualified third party.

■ A custodian may loan money to an account but cannot borrow from it.

A custodian may be reimbursed for any reasonable expenses incurred in managing the account as well as compensation for doing so. However, if the custodian is also the donor, only reimbursement of expenses is permitted and not compensation.

3. 2. 2. 6. 2   Death of the Minor or Custodian

If the beneficiary of a custodial account (minor) dies, the securities in the account pass to the minor's estate, not to the parents' or custodian's estate.

In the event of the custodian's death or resignation, either a court of law or the donor of the securities in the account must appoint a new custodian.

3. 2. 2. 7   Individual Retirement Accounts (IRAs)

Individual retirement accounts (IRAs) were created as a way of encouraging people to save for retirement. These are known as "traditional" IRAs. All employed individuals, regardless of whether they are covered by a qualified corporate retirement plan, may open and contribute to an IRA. IRAs are considered qualified plans by the IRS.

Qualified plans allow the earnings in the account to grow tax deferred. Additionally, individuals making a contribution to an IRA can take a tax deduction for the amount of the contribution if certain criteria are met. If an individual is not actively participating in other qualified plans like an employer's 401(k) plan for instance, the full amount of the contribution to the IRA is deductible. For an individual covered by another qualified plan, the portion deductible is determined by that person's income level. The tax deduction gradually phases out as the taxpayer's adjusted gross income climbs. The exact income levels above which tax deductible contributions are prohibited is not critical for testing purposes because these levels are, by law, raised each year. However, contributions may still be made because the earnings on these amounts are still tax deferred.

3. 2. 2. 7. 1   Traditional IRA Terms; Contributions, Funding, Rollovers and Transfers, and Distributions

Contributions—An eligible individual may make contributions up to a maximum dollar amount that can change from year to year (as determined by the IRS tax code), provided that the contribution does not exceed earned income (normally compensation and income from self-employment) for the year. The dollar cap is increased by a catch-up amount for individuals age 50 and older.

TEST TOPIC ALERT   Current IRA contribution limits and catch-up contribution limits for those age 50 and older may be tested. These limits may change, sometimes annually. Current contribution limits can be found on **www.irs.gov/retirement-plans**.

Funding—Within an IRA, investments can be made in stocks, bonds, investment company securities, U.S.-minted gold and silver coins, and many other securities.

There are however, certain investments that are considered ineligible for use in an IRA. Collectibles (e.g., antiques, gems, rare coins, works of art, stamps) are not acceptable IRA investments. Life insurance contracts may not be purchased in an IRA.

TAKE NOTE

Although life insurance is not allowed within IRAs, other life insurance company products (like annuities) are. Annuities are frequently used as funding vehicles for IRAs.

Following is a partial list of investments appropriate for IRAs:

- Stocks
- Bonds
- Mutual funds
- UITs
- Government securities
- U.S. government-issued gold and silver coins
- Annuities

Certain investment practices are also considered inappropriate. No short sales of stock, speculative option strategies, tax-exempt municipal securities, or margin account trading are permitted within IRAs or any other retirement plan. However, covered call writing is permissible because it does not increase risk.

Ineligible Investments and Ineligible Investment Practices

Ineligible Investments	Ineligible Investment Practices
Collectibles	Short sales of stock
Life insurance	Speculative option strategies
	Margin account trading

Rollovers and transfers—Individuals may take possession of the funds and investments in a qualified plan to move them to another qualified plan but may do so no more than once every 12 months. This is known as a rollover and it must be completed within 60 calendar days of withdrawal.

EXAMPLE

If an individual changes employers, the amount in his pension plan may be distributed to him in a lump-sum payment. He may then deposit the distribution in an IRA rollover account, where the amount deposited retains its tax-deferred status.

By contrast, a transfer of funds between qualified retirement accounts differs from a rollover in that the account owner never actually takes physical possession of the funds; the money or investments are sent directly from one IRA custodian to another. There is no limit to the number of times per year a person can transfer investments between custodians, provided the assets in the accounts do not pass through the hands of the taxpayer.

Distributions/withdrawals—Distributions may begin without penalty after age 59½ and must begin by April 1 of the year after the individual turns 70½. Distributions before age 59½ are subject to a 10% penalty as well as regular income tax, except in the event of:

■ death;

■ disability;

■ first-time homebuyer for purchase of a principal residence;

■ education expenses for the taxpayer, spouse, child, or grandchild;

■ medical premiums for unemployed individuals; and

■ medical expenses in excess of defined adjusted gross income (AGI) limits.

If distributions do not begin by April 1 of the year after the individual turns 70½, a 50% insufficient distribution penalty applies. It is applicable to the amount that should have been withdrawn on the basis of IRS life expectancy tables. These are known as the IRA holder's annual **required minimum distribution** (RMD) and **required beginning date** (RBD). Ordinary income taxes also apply to the full amount.

3. 2. 2. 7. 2   Roth IRAs

Up until this point we have been discussing "traditional" IRA accounts. Let's take a brief look at another type of qualified IRA known as a **Roth IRA**. Roth IRAs allow after-tax contributions up to a maximum annual allowable limit per individual per year. Contributions to other (traditional) IRAs when combined with contributions to a Roth may not exceed the maximum annual allowable limit.

Contributions to Roth IRAs are not deductible on one's tax return. Note the difference here between a traditional IRA and a Roth. Therefore, there is no phase-out schedule regarding a contribution being deductible as there is with a traditional IRA. However, there is a phase-out schedule regarding the contribution that can be made to a Roth IRA, and again the schedule is tied to an individual's AGI. The contribution limit is phased out from the low end of the phase-out scale until the high end, above which no contribution to a Roth IRA would be allowed.

Earnings are not taxed as they accrue or when they are distributed from an account as long as the money has been in an account for five taxable years and the IRA owner has reached age 59½.

TAKE NOTE

Required minimum distributions at age 70½ do not apply to Roth IRAs. The 10% penalty for distributions before age 59½ is waived for first-time homebuyers if they use the funds to purchase a principal residence.

3. 2. 2. 8   401(k) and 403(b) Qualified Plans

Besides individual retirement accounts (IRA) there are a number of IRS **qualified plans** that allow individuals to save for retirement. Here we'll look at two commonly available: 401(k) and 403(b) plans.

3. 2. 2. 8. 1   401(k) Plans

401(k) plans are a type of retirement contribution plan that allows an employee to elect to contribute a percentage of salary up to a maximum dollar limit to a retirement account each year (a defined contribution). Just like with IRAs, catch-up contributions for those age 50 and older are also allowed. Contributions are excluded from the employee's gross income and accumulate tax deferred as do any earnings in the account. Employers are permitted to make matching contributions up to a specified percentage of the employee's contributions. In addition, 401(k) plans permit hardship withdrawals for situations such as unemployment or first time home buyers and can also allow loans against any vested balance.

3. 2. 2. 8. 2 403(b) Plans

A **403(b) plan** is type of qualified retirement plan available to employees of public educational institutions. In general, employees of colleges, universities, elementary and secondary schools are eligible to participate if they are at least 21 years old and have completed one year of service.

Generally set up as tax-sheltered annuities these plans are funded by elective employee salary deferrals. The deferred amount is excluded from the employee's gross income, and earnings accumulate tax deferred until distribution. For these plans, a written salary reduction agreement must be executed between the employer and the employee.

As with other qualified plans, distributions are 100% taxable, and a 10% penalty is applied to distributions before age 59½.

TAKE NOTE

Besides 403(b) plans for employees of educational institutions, tax sheltered annuities are also available for employees of tax-exempt organizations (501(c)(3) and religious organizations.

3. 2. 3 ANTI-MONEY LAUNDERING (AML)

The **Bank Secrecy Act** establishes the U.S. Treasury Department as the lead agency for developing regulations in connection with **anti-money laundering** (AML) programs. Before September 11, 2001, money laundering rules were concerned mostly with the origin of the cash. Money laundering was defined as the process of creating the appearance that money originally obtained from criminal activity, such as drug trafficking or terrorist activity, came from a legitimate source.

Under the act, regulators became much more focused and concerned with where the funds are going. The idea is to prevent "clean" money (money that has been laundered) from being used for "dirty" purposes (such as funding terrorist activities).

3. 2. 3. 1 Three Stages of Money Laundering

The three basic stages of money laundering are as follows:

1. **Placement**—This first stage of laundering is when funds or assets are moved into the laundering system. This stage is recognized as the time when illegal funds are the most susceptible to detection.

2. **Layering**—The goal of money launderers during this stage is to conceal the source of the funds or assets. This is done through a series of layers of transactions that are generally numerous and can vary in form and complexity.

3. **Integration**—In the final stage, illegal funds are commingled with legitimate funds in what appear to be viable legitimate business concerns. This can be accomplished using front companies operating on a cash basis, import and export companies, and many other types of businesses.

3. 2. 3. 2 AML Compliance Program

Broker-dealers are required to establish internal compliance procedures to detect abuses. There are signs or red flags that might suggest the possibility of money laundering. If a red flag is detected, it should be reported to the principal designated to receive such reports immediately. Examples of red flags include:

- a customer exhibiting a lack of concern regarding risks, commissions, or other transaction costs;
- a customer attempting to make frequent or large deposits of currency or cashier's checks;
- a customer making a large number of wire transfers to unrelated third parties;
- a customer engaging in excessive journal entries between unrelated accounts; and
- a customer who designs currency deposits or withdrawals to fall under the $10,000 cash transaction report (CTR) filing threshold, a practice known as structuring.

3. 2. 3. 3 Suspicious Activity Report (SAR)

The USA PATRIOT Act requires firms to report to **Financial Crimes Enforcement Network** (FinCEN) when there is an event, transaction, or series of events or transactions that appear to be questionable.

TEST TOPIC ALERT

Financial Crimes Enforcement Network (FinCEN) is a bureau of the United States Department of the Treasury that collects and analyzes information about financial transactions in order to combat money laundering, domestic and international terrorist financing, and other financial crimes.

The act requires firms to report to FinCEN any transaction that alone or in the aggregate involves at least $5,000 in funds or other assets if the firm suspects that it falls within one of the following four classes.

- The transaction involves funds derived from illegal activity.
- The transaction is designed to evade the requirements of the Bank Secrecy Act.
- The transaction appears to serve no business or lawful purpose.
- The transaction involves the use of the firm to facilitate criminal activity.

Firms must file a SAR within 30 days of becoming aware of the suspicious transaction(s). Copies of each SAR filing and the related documentation must be retained for five years from the date of the filing.

The act also requires that the filing of a SAR must remain confidential. The person involved in the transaction that is the subject of the report must not be notified. If subpoenaed, the firm must refuse to provide the information and must notify FinCEN of the request unless the disclosure is required by FinCEN, the SEC, an industry self-regulatory organization (SRO), or other law enforcement authority.

In addition, the USA PATRIOT Act requires firms to make and retain records relating to wire transfers of $3,000 or more. Information to be collected includes the name and address of both sender and recipient, the amount of the transfer, the name of the recipient's financial institution, and the account number of the recipient.

EXAMPLE   A pattern of cash deposits over time could trigger a suspicious activity report (SAR) filing. For example, if a customer were to deposit $1,000 each week for many weeks in a row, this might constitute suspicious activity and the filing of a SAR would be appropriate.

3. 2. 3. 4   Currency Transaction Report (CTR)

The Bank Secrecy Act requires broker-dealers to report, any currency received in the amount of more than $10,000 on a single day. Though paying for purchased securities with currency is not prohibited—many firms do not permit this. Failure to report can result in fines of up to $500,000, 10 years in prison, or both. Records relating to filed reports must be retained for five years.

The report must be filed within 15 days of receipt of the currency. This rule is part of the regulatory effort to deal with money laundering. The two federal agencies empowered to deal with this abuse are the Federal Reserve and the Department of the Treasury.

If anyone designs deposits to fall under the $10,000 radar, this is a prohibited activity known as structuring. Financial institutions should have systems in place to monitor for and recognize such attempts.

EXAMPLE   A customer makes 25 $500 deposits to pay for a $12,500 transaction. This should be recognized at an attempt to structure payments to fall under the $10,000 radar to avoid the filing of a CTR.

3. 2. 3. 5   Customer Identification Program

The **USA PATRIOT Act** requires financial institutions to maintain Customer Identification Programs (CIPs) to prevent financing of terrorist operations and money laundering. Financial institutions, such as banks and broker-dealers, must keep records of identification information and check customer names against the Specially Designated Nationals (SDN) list maintained by the Office of Foreign Asset Control (OFAC).

3. 2. 3. 5. 1   Office of Foreign Asset Control (OFAC) and the Specially Designated Nationals and Blocked Persons (SDNs) List

The **Office of Foreign Assets Control** (OFAC) publishes and maintains a list of individuals and companies owned or controlled by, or who are acting for, or on behalf of, targeted countries and individuals, groups, or entities that are designated under programs that are not country specific, such as terrorists and those trafficking in narcotics. When individuals or groups appear on the Specially Designated Nationals (SDN) list, their assets are blocked, and

U.S. persons and businesses, which include registered representatives and broker-dealers, are generally prohibited from dealing with or conducting business with them.

New customers must be advised, before the account is opened, that the firm is requesting information to verify their identities. This notification may be placed on the firm's website, delivered verbally, or placed on the new account form.

3. 2. 4 BOOKS AND RECORDS AND PRIVACY REQUIREMENTS

In the following sections you will learn about the most common records needed to be maintained by broker-dealers, how long they need to be kept (retention requirements), and the privacy requirements to protect customer information.

3. 2. 4. 1 Books and Records Retention Requirements

SEC rules mandate which records must be prepared by members, when those records must be prepared, and for how long the records must be retained. In lieu of maintaining paper records, firms may use digital storage media. Such storage media must have the capability to maintain records in non-rewriteable and non-erasable format.

For retention purposes, records are generally either lifetime records, six-year records, or three-year records.

Lifetime records—Records that must be kept for the life of the firm are partnership articles if a partnership, articles of incorporation if a corporation, minute books (records of directors' or partners' meetings), stock certificate books, and organizational documents such as Form BD and amendments.

Six-year records—There are five primary records that must be retained for six years.

■ **Blotters**—A blotter is a record of original entry. A member generally maintains blotters relating to the purchase and sale of securities, the receipt and delivery of securities, and the receipt and disbursement of cash. Blotters must reflect transactions as of trade date (or event date) and must be prepared no later than the following business day.

■ **General ledger**—The general ledger contains accounting records of the firm's assets, liabilities, and net worth accounts. From the general ledger, a firm prepares its financial statements. The general ledger must be prepared as frequently as necessary to determine compliance with the net capital rule, but in no event less frequently than monthly.

■ **Stock record**—The stock record shows all securities held by the firm, the ownership of those securities, and where the securities are held. The stock record must be posted no later than the business day after settlement date.

■ **Customer ledgers**—Customer ledgers are customer statements. Cash accounts and margin accounts are shown on separate ledgers. These ledgers must be posted no later than settlement date.

■ **Customer account records**—Customer account records might include the new account form and margin agreement, if appropriate.

In addition, a record of when someone attained a principal designation must be retained for six years.

Three-year records—Most other records are three-year records. Examples of these records include the following:

■ Advertising

■ Trial balances

■ Form U-4, U-5, and fingerprint cards for terminated personnel

- Customer confirmations
- Order tickets
- Subsidiary ledgers such as securities borrowed and securities loaned, monies borrowed and monies loaned, and dividends and interest received
- A list of every office where each associated person regularly conducts business
- Associated persons' compensation records
- The firm's Compliance and Procedures Manual

Whether a record retention requirement is six years or three years, the most recent two years must be in a readily accessible location.

TEST TOPIC ALERT
One exception to the lifetime, six-year and three-year retention is the requirement for written customer complaints. Customer complaint records must be retained for four years.

3. 2. 4. 2 Account Statements and Trade Confirmations

Broker-dealers communicate and verify activity in a customer's account via account statements and trade confirmations. While they may appear differently from one broker-dealer to the next, there is uniformity required regarding the information provided and the time frames for delivery.

3. 2. 4. 2. 1 Electronic Delivery

FINRA allows members to electronically send documents, such as confirmations and account statements, to customers as long as certain conditions are met. To do so, the firm must have procedures in place to show that the information sent has been delivered as intended and that the confidentiality and security of personal information are protected. Furthermore, customers must provide written consent to electronic delivery.

In addition, a customer who consents to receive information and documents electronically must be provided with the information in paper form, upon request.

3. 2. 4. 2. 2 Updating Customer Account Records

To ensure that the information obtained from each new customer is accurate, firms must furnish to each customer, within 30 days of opening the account, a copy of the account record. The firm must include a statement that the customer should mark any corrections on the record and return it along with a statement that the customer should notify the firm of any future changes to information in the account record so that accurate and current records can be maintained.

If the customer should ever contact the firm with any changes, the firm must furnish the customer with an updated account record within 30 days of receipt of the notice of change. Furthermore, this account updating must occur at least every 36 months thereafter.

EXAMPLE
Changes in employment and financial status are two common amendments needed to be made to an account record. Changes in investment objective should also be expected and are likely over time.

3. 2. 4. 2. 3   Account Statements and Delivery Requirements

Account statements provided to customers give a general accounting of securities and cash held in the account.

A statement shows:

■ all activity in the account since the previous statement;

■ securities positions, long or short; and

■ account balances, debit or credit.

If a customer's account has a cash balance (known as a free credit balance) the firm may hold it in the account. However, the statement must advise the customer that these funds are available on request.

Under FINRA rules, members are required to send statements to customers at least quarterly. If there is activity in the account in any given month, or penny stocks are held in the account, a statement must be sent that month.

TAKE NOTE

> Activity is defined as purchases, sales, interest, or dividends received, or any funds flowing in or out of the account. Penny stocks are defined as those priced under $5 per share.

Finally, account statements must include a statement advising customers to promptly report any discrepancy or inaccuracy to their brokerage firms and clearing firms.

3. 2. 4. 2. 4   Trade Confirmations and Delivery Requirements

A **trade confirmation** is a printed document that confirms a trade, its settlement date, and the amount of money due from or owed to the customer. For each transaction, a customer must be sent or given a written confirmation of the trade at or before the completion of the transaction—the settlement date.

The trade confirmation includes the following information:

■ Trade date—day on which the transaction is executed (the settlement date is usually the second business day after the trade date)

■ Account number—branch office number followed by an account number

■ Registered representative internal ID number (or AE number)— account executive's identification number

■ BOT (bought) or SLD (sold)—indicates a customer's role in a trade

■ Number (or quantity)—number of shares of stock or the par value of bonds bought or sold for the customer

■ Description—specific security bought or sold for the customer

■ Yield—indicates that the yield for callable bonds may be affected by the exercise of a call provision

■ CUSIP number—applicable Committee on Uniform Securities Identification Procedures (CUSIP) number, if any

■ Price—price per share for stock or bonds before a charge or deduction

■ Amount—price paid or received before commissions and other charges; also referred to as extended principal for municipal securities transactions

- Commission—added to buy transactions; subtracted from sell transactions completed on an agency basis; a commission will not appear on the confirmation if a markup (or markdown) has been charged in a principal transaction

- Net amount—obtained on purchases by adding expenses (commissions and postage) to the principal amount (whether the transaction is a purchase or sale, interest is always added whenever bonds are traded with accrued interest—interest that hasn't been paid yet but will be owed to the seller up the settlement date).

Finally, the confirmation must also show the capacity in which the broker-dealer acts (agency or principal) and the commission in cases where the broker-dealer acts as an agent.

3. 2. 4. 2. 5   Non-Trade Confirmations/Third Party Activity Notices

Firms are required to send confirmations of activity in accounts even when the activity is not trade related or initiated by a third party. Following are three examples of such instances where a confirmation of third party activity would be generated.

EXAMPLE   Customers with a foreign bank account may from time to time wire money from the foreign country back to a brokerage account in the United States (or the reverse). When the funds are credited (or debited) to/from the account, a confirmation of the deposit/withdrawal is sent.

EXAMPLE   When a deposit (or withdrawal) of a stock certificate is made, this is an activity that is non trade related. The customer receives a confirmation of the activity.

EXAMPLE   A customer with an outside money manager handling some of the customer's money may execute through a broker-dealer where the customer has an account and the manager withdraws his fee quarterly in advance. Each time a fee is taken, a confirmation is sent from the broker-dealer indicating that specific "third-party activity" occurred and was logged.

3. 2. 4. 3   Holding of Customer Mail

Your firm is permitted to hold mail for a customer (e.g., statements and confirmations) who will not be receiving mail, provided that:

- the member firm receives written instructions that include the time period the request is being made for up to three months (requests may be granted for periods longer than three months for an acceptable reason such as safety or security concerns but not merely for the sake of convenience);

- the member firm informs the customer of any alternate methods that the customer may use to receive or monitor account activity such as email or through the member firm's website (the member must obtain customer confirmation that this information regarding alternate methods was received); and

- the member verifies at reasonable intervals that the customer's instructions still apply.

Additionally, during the time that a member firm is holding mail for a customer, the firm must be able to communicate with the customer in a timely manner to provide important account information. The firm must take actions reasonably designed to ensure that a customer's mail is not tampered with or used in a manner that would violate FINRA rules or federal securities laws.

While holding mail is a courtesy that firms are permitted to extend to customers, the rule does not require them to. If extending the courtesy is consistent with the broker-dealer's in-house rules, the written request by the customer to do so implies that the customer is also giving the broker-dealer permission to do so.

3. 2. 4. 4 Business Continuity Plans (BCP)

FINRA requires member firms to create and maintain a business continuity plan to deal with the possibility of a significant business disruption. The plan must address certain points having to do with the consequences of the event, including but not limited to the following:

- Data backup and recovery (hardcopy and electronic)
- Alternate communications between the firm and its customers
- Alternate communications between the firm and its employees
- Alternate physical location of employees
- Communications with regulators
- Prompt customer access to funds and securities in the event the firm is unable to continue its business

Firms must designate a member of senior management who is also a principal to approve, update, and conduct an annual review of the plan. Additionally, FINRA requires firms to provide them with the names of two emergency contact persons who may be contacted by FINRA in the event of a significant business disruption. Each contact person must be a principal and a member of senior management, and firms must update this contact information promptly, in no case later than 30 days following any change.

Regarding communicating this information to customers, a firm must disclose to its customers how it will respond to significant events of varying scope. This disclosure must be made, in writing, to customers at the time of account opening, posted on the firm's website, and mailed to customers on request.

3. 2. 4. 5 Privacy Requirements—Regulation S-P

This regulation was enacted by the SEC to protect the privacy of customer information. In particular, the regulation deals with nonpublic personal information.

3. 2. 4. 5. 1 Nonpublic Personal Information

The SEC, in Regulation S-P notes examples of nonpublic personal information. This type of information would include a customer's Social Security number, account balances, transaction history, and any information collected through an internet cookie.

3. 2. 4. 5. 2 Confidentiality of Information

If your firm reserves the right to disclose to unaffiliated third parties nonpublic personal information, the notice must provide customers a reasonable means to opt out of this disclosure. Reasonable opt-out means include providing customers with a form with check-off boxes along with a prepaid return envelope, providing an electronic means to opt out for customers who have agreed to the electronic delivery of information, and providing a toll-free telephone number. Asking customers to write a letter to express their disclosure preferences or to opt-out would not be considered reasonable under Regulation S-P.

3. 2. 4. 5. 3   Privacy Notifications

Your firm must provide a privacy notice describing its privacy policies to customers whenever a new account is opened and annually thereafter.

3. 2. 4. 5. 4   Safeguard Requirements

In addition, the regulation embodies the obligation of financial institutions to safeguard customer information as related to all forms of existing and developing technology. For example, this would include, but not be limited to, securing desktop and laptop computers and encrypting email.

3. 2. 5   COMMUNICATIONS WITH THE PUBLIC AND GENERAL SUITABILITY REQUIREMENTS

FINRA holds broker-dealers to certain general standards regarding all member firm communications. All member communications must be based on principles of fair dealing and good faith. Statements must be clear and not misleading within the context that they are made and must be fair and balanced regarding potential risks and benefits. Omission of material facts is not permitted, nor is making false, exaggerated, or misleading statements or claims. No communication should ever imply that past performance will be repeated. Finally, FINRA mandates that members must consider the nature of the audience to which the communication will be directed and should provide details and explanations appropriate to the audience.

3. 2. 5. 1   Classifications and General Requirements

In accordance with FINRA, there are three categories of communications:

- Retail communications
- Correspondence
- Institutional communications

Retail communication means any written (including electronic) communication that is distributed or made available to more than 25 retail investors within any 30-calendar-day period. A retail investor is any person other than an institutional investor, regardless of whether the person has an account with the member.

Correspondence means any written (including electronic) communication that is distributed or made available to 25 or fewer retail investors within any 30-calendar-day period.

Institutional communication means any written (including electronic) communication that is distributed or made available only to institutional investors, but does not include a member's internal communications (e.g., internal memos). Examples of institutional investors are:

- another member firm or registered representative;
- a bank;
- a savings and loan (S&L);
- an insurance company;

- a registered investment company (mutual fund);
- an employee benefit plan;
- a governmental entity or subdivision;
- a person acting solely on behalf of an institutional investor; and
- any entity with $50 million or more of total assets.

FINRA mandates that no member may treat a communication as having been distributed to an institutional investor if the member firm has reason to believe that the communication or any part of it will be forwarded or made available to any retail investor.

TAKE NOTE

If an entity does not fall under any of the designated categories for institutional investor then they must be considered and treated as a retail customer.

3. 2. 5. 2   Communications With the Public and Telemarketing

The Telephone Consumer Protection Act of 1991 (TCPA), administered by the Federal Communications Commission (FCC), was enacted to protect consumers from unwanted telephone solicitations (telemarketing).

A telephone solicitation is defined as a telephone call initiated for the purpose of encouraging the purchase of or investment in property, goods, or services. The act governs commercial calls, recorded solicitations from autodialers, and solicitations and advertisements to fax machines and modems.

3. 2. 5. 2. 1   Do-Not-Call List

The Telephone Consumer Protection Act of 1991 (TCPA) requires an organization that does telemarketing (cold calling in particular) to:

- maintain a do-not-call list of prospects who do not want to be called, and keep a prospect's
- name on the list until they request it be removed;
- institute a written policy on maintenance procedures for the do-not-call list;
- train representatives on using the list;
- ensure that representatives acknowledge and immediately record the names and telephone
- numbers of prospects who ask not to be called again;
- ensure that anyone making cold calls for the firm informs prospects of their name, the
- firm's name, and the firm's telephone number or address;
- ensure that telemarketers do not call a prospect from the time of their do-not-call
- request; and
- ensure that solicitation occurs only between the hours of 8:00 am and 9:00 pm of the time
- zone where the prospect lives.

The act exempts calls:

- made to parties with whom the caller has an established business relationship or from
- whom the caller has prior express permission or invitation;
- made on behalf of a tax-exempt nonprofit organization;
- not made for a commercial purpose; and
- made for legitimate debt collection purposes.

Asking a particular broker-dealer to add your name to that broker-dealer's do-not-call list is not the same as adding your name to the National Do Not Call Registry. These types of requests, known as "broker specific requests" are subject to the industry's five-year record retention requirements.

3. 2. 5. 3 Suitability Requirements

Whether or not an investment strategy, or security is suitable for a customer is a determination made by a registered representative as to whether the strategy or security matches the customer's investment objectives and financial capability. The representative must have enough information about the customer to make this judgment.

3. 2. 5. 3. 1 Know-Your-Customer (KYC)

FINRA and other SROs require brokers to know their customers. This implies understanding a customer's financial status (net worth and net income), investment objectives, and all facts essential in making suitable recommendations. It is a registered representative's responsibility to perform due diligence to determine the validity of a customer's information.

Based on that information, registered representatives must have a reasonable basis to believe that a recommended transaction or investment strategy involving a security or securities is suitable for the customer.

Recommendations can be advice to invest in, or employ investment strategies to hold, or sell specific securities as well as suggestions pertaining to market sectors, day trading, or divesting of an asset or other investments to make funds available to purchase securities.

Regarding the term "customer," FINRA defines it to exclude other brokers and certain potential investors (someone who is not your client at the time the advice is given). Therefore, the rule would not apply if the recipient of the advice is not currently a client and neither the representative nor the firm receives direct or indirect compensation as a result of giving the advice.

3. 2. 5. 3. 2 Nonfinancial Considerations

A customer's nonfinancial considerations are often as important as his financial concerns. Therefore, a registered representative or an investment adviser should know the:

■ customer's age;

■ customer's marital status;

■ number and ages of customer's dependents;

■ customer's employment status;

■ employment of customer's immediate family members; and

■ customer's current and future financial needs.

3. 2. 5. 3. 3   Risk Tolerance and Investment Goals

A customer's risk tolerance and investment goals are other important considerations that will shape his portfolio. To understand a customer's attitude about investment alternatives, the representative or adviser should ask the customer the following questions in order to complete the customer profile and know the customer.

- What kind of risks can you afford to take?
- How liquid must your investments be?
- How important are tax considerations?
- Are you seeking long-term or short-term investments (investment time horizon)?
- What is your investment experience?
- What types of investments do you currently hold?

QUICK QUIZ 3.B

LEARNING OBJECTIVES

- Recognize different account types and registrations
- List the information required on account statements and trade confirmations
- Contrast Ant-Money Laundering, Privacy and Communications compliance as they relate to knowing your customer.

1. An individual opens an account with your firm. She tells you that upon her death, she wants any assets in the account to be divided equally among her three children. She also wants the ability to change the allocation in the event that conditions change and one of the children is in greater need than the others, but she does not want to incur any significant legal expense. You would suggest that the account be opened

   A. as a joint account with right of survivorship
   B. as a joint account with tenants in common
   C. as an individual TOD account
   D. under a discretionary power

2. If three individuals have a tenants in common account with your firm and one individual dies, then

   A. the two survivors continue as co-tenants with the decedent's estate
   B. the account must be liquidated and the proceeds split evenly between the two survivors and the decedent's estate
   C. trading is discontinued until the executor names a replacement for the deceased
   D. the account is converted to joint tenants with rights of survivorship

3. A wealthy individual has established a trust and wishes to establish an account with your broker-dealer that permits the trust to engage in margin transactions. Which of the following statements regarding margin trading in trust accounts is TRUE?

   A. It is not permitted.
   B. It is permitted if the trustee observes the prudent investor rule.
   C. It is permitted with the written approval of the beneficiary of the trust.
   D. It is permitted if provided for in the trust's documentation.

4. A client of a brokerage firm opened an UTMA account for her granddaughter five years ago, naming the child's father as the custodian. Through appreciation as well as additional contributions, the account value has grown to $50,000 and generates interest and dividend income in excess of $3,000. Who bears the liability for the taxes on this income?

   A. The donor
   B. The custodian
   C. The granddaughter
   D. No one, because there are no taxes on an UTMA account until the beneficiary takes possession of the account

5. All of the following would be legal investments in an IRA EXCEPT

   A. annuities issued by the ABC Life Insurance Company
   B. whole life insurance issued by the ABC Life Insurance Company
   C. mutual funds
   D. gold coins made by the U.S. Treasury

6. Which of the following is NOT true for trade confirmations?

   A. Commissions are added to the sales proceeds to arrive at the amount the seller is to receive.
   B. Commissions are not shown when a markup or markdown is charged.
   C. The firms acting capacity as agent or principal is shown.
   D. They are received by both parties at or before the the settlement date.

7. One of the concerns of a registered representative is complying with the anti-money laundering (AML) rules promulgated under the Bank Secrecy Act. There are several stages to money laundering and it is generally agreed that the one where money laundering is most easily detected is

   A. integration
   B. layering
   C. segregation
   D. placement

8. How long must a broker-dealer hold the record of a complaint?

   A. 3 years
   B. 4 years
   C. 6 years
   D. Lifetime

9. Account statements provided to customers would reflect

   I. year to date activity in the account
   II. long positions, short positions, or both
   III. whether the account was discretionary or nondiscretionary
   IV. debit or credit balances

   A. I and II
   B. I and III
   C. II and IV
   D. III and IV

10. Customer account statements are required to be sent quarterly unless the account contains

    A. bonds
    B. NYSE listed stocks
    C. options
    D. penny stocks

11. When a client makes a trade, industry rules require that a confirmation be delivered no later than completion of the trade. Included on that confirmation would be all of the following information EXCEPT

    A. the number of bonds in the transaction
    B. the number of shares of stock in the transaction
    C. the CUSIP number
    D. the capacity in which the broker-dealer executing the trade acted

12. Many years ago, a client purchased 100 shares of ABC common stock. Due to stock splits, the customer's account now holds 500 shares of ABC. If the customer had the broker-dealer send out certificates for 200 of those shares in the mail,

    A. that would be unethical because any activity would have to involve all 500 shares
    B. that would be unethical because only the transfer agent can deliver share certificates
    C. a non-trade confirmation would have to be generated
    D. the customer would incur a tax liability

13. Which of the following statements regarding electronic delivery of customer confirmations and statements are true EXCEPT

    A. the firm must have procedures in place to show that the information sent has been delivered as intended
    B. once customers agreed to electronic delivery, they can no longer receive paper copies
    C. customers must provide written consent to electronic delivery
    D. the firm must have procedures in place to show that the confidentiality and security of personal information are protected

3. 3   PROHIBITED ACTIVITIES

LEARNING OBJECTIVES:
- Define and explain prohibited activities

In the following sections, we will outline some of the activities that are prohibited and considered harmful not only to investors but the integrity of the over-all market place. Most of the provisions discussed here fall under the Securities Act of 1934.

3. 3. 1   MARKET MANIPULATION

No security is exempt from the industry's anti-fraud provisions. This means that fraud or **market manipulation** cannot be involved in the trading of any security. Following are a number of prohibited trading practices, as they are all meant to manipulate the markets and deceive market participants.

3. 3. 1. 1   Market Rumors

Misleading information or rumors can be employed for the sole purpose of manipulating the price of a stock up or down. The spreading of false information and market rumors by industry personnel is expressly prohibited.

Additionally, regulators have issued alerts to warn investors about fraudsters who may or may not be securities industry persons, attempting to manipulate share prices by spreading false or misleading information about stocks. For example, while social media can provide many benefits for investors who want to research potential investments, it also presents opportunities for fraudsters. Through social media, fraudsters can spread false or misleading information about a stock to large numbers of people with minimum effort and at a relatively low cost. They can also conceal their identities or even impersonate credible sources of market information. Social media platforms that might be used in this way would include online bulletin boards, email blasts, and Internet chat rooms.

3. 3. 1. 2   Pump and Dump

A form of securities fraud commonly known as **pump and dump** is the act of inflating (pump) the price of an owned stock by perpetrating false and misleading positive rumors, in order to sell the stock at a higher price later. Generally the shares owned are first accumulated at lower prices before the misleading information is doled out to the investing public. After the stock price rises due to the frenzied buying caused by the rumors, the operators of the scheme then sell (dump) their overvalued shares in the open market. The fraudsters profit while the selling pressure associated with dumping drives the price downward, causing investors who purchased based on the rumors to lose their money.

3. 3. 1. 3   Front Running

Front running is the act of placing orders for one's own account ahead of other orders that are known to be entering the market in an attempt to gain from the price movement that is likely to occur.

EXAMPLE   A mutual fund company enters an order to purchase 300,000 shares of AABB stock with your firm for execution at the market. Prior to entering the order to be executed in the open market a registered representative aware of the large pending order to buy places an order for his own personal account to buy 500 shares. This is front running.

3. 3. 1. 4   Excessive Trading (Churning)

Excessive trading in a customer's account to generate commissions rather than to help achieve the customer's stated investment objectives is an abuse of fiduciary responsibility known as **churning**. Excessive frequency or excessive size of transactions not in keeping with the client's trading history or financial ability are often signs that churning might be occurring.

To prevent such abuses, self-regulatory organizations require that a principal of the member firm review all accounts, especially those for which a registered representative or an investment adviser has discretionary authority.

EXAMPLE   A principal, while reviewing transactions done by the firm, notices that a client who had previously done a trade or two per quarter recently has been doing one or two per week. At a minimum, this should generate a red flag for churning. A discussion with the registered representative assigned to the account should occur to determine if any further monitoring or actions should take place.

3. 3. 1. 5   Marking the Close and Marking the Open

Entering trades before the opening, or at or near the close, solely to manipulate the reported price of where a stock will open or close is prohibited.

■ **Marking the open**—Entering orders before the opening for a stock or falsely reporting trades that never occurred to influence the opening price of a stock is called marking the open.

■ **Marking the close**—Effecting trades at or near the close of the trading day or falsely reporting trades that never occurred to influence the closing price of a stock is called marking the close. For example, putting in buy orders at the close for the purpose of pushing up the price of a stock so that it is valued higher in one's portfolio or account at the end of the day is marking the close.

3. 3. 1. 6   Backing Away

A market maker can revise a firm quote in response to market conditions and trading activity, but a market maker that refuses to do business at the price(s) quoted is **backing away** from the quote. Backing away is a violation of trading rules.

3. 3. 1. 7   Freeriding

Freeriding is a term used when securities are purchased and then sold before making payment for the purchase. Freeriding is generally prohibited in both cash and margin accounts. As a penalty, the account will be frozen for 90 days and no new transactions can occur unless there is cash or marginable securities in the account before the purchase is made.

3. 3. 1. 8   Capping

Capping is usually associated with those who are short option call contracts. This is the act of entering sell orders in a stock for the purpose of keeping it from rising above the strike price of calls someone is short; this is done so the calls won't be in-the-money and thus likely to be exercised.

3. 3. 1. 9   Supporting

Supporting is usually associated with those who are short put option contracts.
This is the act of entering purchase orders in a stock for the purpose of keeping the price from falling below the strike price of puts someone is short; this is done so the puts won't be in-the-money and thus likely to be exercised.

3. 3. 1. 10 Pegging

Pegging is a generic term that applies to any activity intended to keep the price of a stock from moving. This can involve entering either buy or sell orders or both.

3. 3. 1. 11 Wash Sales

Consider that an investor can use capital loses to offset capital gains. A **wash sale** violation is an attempt to create a loss for tax purposes (sell at a loss) when one's intent is to still maintain ownership of the securities. Any repurchase of the same within 30 days before or after the date establishing the loss, would be recognized as one's intent to maintain ownership. If this occurs, the loss established at the time of the sale is disallowed.

EXAMPLE

October 21, 2013 Buy 1,000 XYZ at 30
November 17, 2014 Sell 1,000 XYZ at 28
Note that a loss has been established

November 23, 2014 Buy 1,000 XYZ at 27
Note that the long position in XYZ stock has been reestablished a few days after the sale that had created the loss. The sale is now considered a prohibited wash sale and the loss is disallowed for tax purposes.

Two additional points on wash sale rules should be noted. First, the rule applies to recreating long positions, as in the previous example, and also to recreating short positions. Second, the rule applies for attempts to recreate the same position using not only the exact same security but also substantially identical securities. For instance, a long stock position in XYZ stock is closed with a sale for a loss. Not only do the wash sale rules prohibit reestablishing the position by repurchasing XYZ stock, but it would also recognize the purchase of XYZ call options or rights that can be exercised to purchase shares of XYZ stock as a way of reestablishing the position if the options or rights are exercised. In this light, the XYZ call options or rights would be considered substantially identical to the XYZ stock.

TAKE NOTE

The rules on wash sales do not prohibit the initial sale (for a loss) or the recreation of the position. These are permissible actions. The rule does, however, prohibit taking the loss on one's tax return if the position was recreated within the 30 days before or after the sale window.

3. 3. 1. 12 Matched Orders

Matching orders is a manipulation that involves one party selling stock to another with the understanding that the stock will be repurchased later (usually the same day) at virtually the same price. The intent of such transactions is to make it appear that far more activity in a stock (share volume) exists than actually does. This is sometimes referred to as painting the tape.

3. 3. 1. 13 Breakpoint Sales

To understand a breakpoint sale, one must first know what a breakpoint is.

Breakpoints are quantity discounts on open end management company shares (mutual funds)—the greater the dollar amount of a purchase, the lower the sales charge. There is no industry standardized breakpoint schedule so they can vary across mutual fund families. Breakpoint sales, on the other hand, is a term used in the securities industry that means sales just below the breakpoint. Allowing a sale to occur in an amount just below a breakpoint can be viewed as an effort by representatives to share in the higher sales charges. This is inconsistent with just and equitable principles of trade. FINRA does not define near or just below a breakpoint or how close a purchase can be to a breakpoint triggering a violation. Therefore, members must make certain that customers are advised of a fund's breakpoint schedule. The rule is in place because members, and indirectly, registered representatives, could earn more concession dollars on a smaller customer investment (with a higher sales charge) than on a larger customer investment (with a smaller sales charge).

EXAMPLE

Purchase	Sales Charge
$1 to $9,999	8.5%
$10,000 to $24,999	6.5%
$25,000 to $49,999	4%
$50,000 +	2%

Using this sample breakpoint table, assume a customer had $23,000 to invest. At that level of investment, the sales charge would be 6.5%. Being close to the $25,000 breakpoint, a registered representative would be required to inform the customer that for $2,000 more, the investment amount would qualify for the next breakpoint reducing the sales charge to 4%.

3. 3. 2 INSIDER TRADING AND THE SECURITIES FRAUD ENFORCEMENT ACT OF 1988

Although the Securities Act of 1934 prohibited the use of insider information in making trades, the Insider Trading and Securities Fraud Enforcement Act of 1988 amended its provisions and specified penalties for insider trading and securities fraud.

All broker-dealers must establish written supervisory procedures specifically prohibiting the misuse of inside information. Additionally, they must establish policies that restrict the passing of potentially material nonpublic information between a firm's departments. This barrier against the free flow of sensitive information is known as a firewall or an information barrier.

3. 3. 2. 1 Insider and Insider Trading

The Insider Trading and Securities Fraud Enforcement Act defines an insider as any person who has access to nonpublic information about a company that would most likely influence the price of the company's stock. Utilizing that information for the purpose of gain, or to avoid a loss constitutes insider trading

3. 3. 2. 2   Material Nonpublic Information

Inside information by definition is any material nonpublic information. That is, any information that has not been disseminated to, or is not readily available to, the general public.

3. 3. 2. 3   Identifying Involved Parties

The act prohibits insiders from trading on or communicating nonpublic information. Both the **tipper** (the person who relays the information) and the **tippee** (the person who receives the information) are liable, as is anyone who trades on information that they know or should know is not public or who has control over the misuse of this information.

The key elements of tipper and tippee liability under insider trading rules are as follows.

- Is the information material and nonpublic?
- Does the tipper owe a fiduciary duty to a company or its stockholders? Has he breached it?
- Does the tipper meet the personal benefits test (even something as simple as enhancing a friendship or reputation)?
- Does the tippee know or should the tippee have known that the information was inside or confidential?

3. 3. 2. 4   Insider Trading Penalties

The SEC can investigate any person suspected of violating any of the provisions of the Insider Trading Act. If the SEC determines that a violation has occurred, civil penalties of up to three times profits made or losses avoided may be levied. A controlling person such as a registered representative or broker-dealer could be fined $1 million or three times the profit made or loss avoided, whichever is greater.

Violators may also face criminal penalties of up to $5 million and up to 20 years in jail. If the violator is an employee of a broker-dealer, a firm (which is supposed to have procedures in place to prevent this) could be fined up to three times damages or $25 million, whichever is greater.

TAKE NOTE   Persons who enter trades at or near the same time in the same security as a person who has inside information are known as **contemporaneous traders**. Contemporaneous traders may sue persons that have violated insider trading regulations, and suits may be initiated up to five years after the violation has occurred.

3. 3. 2. 4. 1   Informer Bounties

The Insider Trading Act specifically allowed for payment to informers. However, amended under the Dodd-Frank legislation, awards may now be paid in connection with original information concerning any violation of securities law, including insider trading. The information bounty or award can range from 10% to 30% of amounts recovered based on the information received.

3. 3. 3   OTHER PROHIBITED ACTIVITIES

In addition to the prohibitions on different types of trading activity discussed in the previous section, you will need to be familiar with other prohibited activities.

3. 3. 3. 1   Use of Manipulative, Deceptive, or Fraudulent Devices

FINRA member firms are strictly prohibited from using manipulative, deceptive, or other fraudulent tactics or methods to induce a security's sale or purchase. The statute of limitations under the Securities Act of 1934 is three years from the alleged manipulation and within one year of discovering it. No dollar limit is placed on damages in lawsuits based on allegations of manipulation.

EXAMPLE   A registered representative shows a customer a brochure indicating that premiums taken in when selling naked call options can represent substantial percentage gains when the options expire worthless. But nowhere in the brochure does it state that naked call selling has unlimited loss potential. This is deceptive and would be considered a manipulative tactic to entice someone to sell naked call options with no knowledge or regard for the risk the strategy entails.

3. 3. 3. 2   Improper Use of Customers' Securities or Funds

Any time funds or securities of a customer are used in any way other than was intended by the customer, improper use has occurred. All such uses are prohibited.

FINRA expects member firms to detect or investigate "red flags" that alert the firm to improper use of customer funds. Exception reports may be generated to indicate red flags, such as conflicting information in new account applications and suspicious transfers of funds between unrelated accounts. The broker-dealer is expected to implement reasonable systems and controls regarding the supervisory review of customer accounts to thwart, among other things, the falsification of new account applications and other records to take advantage of vulnerable customers.

There is no end to the number of red flags and combinations of red flags, but just a very small sampling might include:

■ suspicious activity involving transfers and disbursements in customer accounts;

■ activity in the account of a deceased person;

■ excessive customer complaints; and

■ exception reports showing discrepancies regarding more than one address or a street address not matching a city or zip code provided or a telephone area code not matching an address provided.

3. 3. 3. 2. 1   Borrowing and Lending

The most common examples of misuse might be in the form of borrowing r lending without consent. Taking (borrowing) a customer's funds for either the firm's or representative's own use is prohibited. Lending a customer's securities for the purpose of short sales when no loan consent agreement has been signed by the customer is another way in which improper use might occur.

However, borrowing and lending arrangements can be permitted under certain circumstances. Firms that permit lending arrangements between representatives and customers must have written procedures in place to monitor such activity. Registered persons who wish to borrow from or lend money to customers are, in most cases, required to provide prior written notice of the proposed arrangement to the firm, and the firm must approve the arrangement in writing.

The Conduct rules permit the following five types of lending arrangements:

- There is an immediate family relationship between the representative and the customer (no notice or approval is needed).
- The customer is in the business of lending money (e.g., a bank; no approval is needed).
- The customer and the representatives are both registered persons with the same firm.
- The customer and the representative have a personal relationship outside the broker-customer relationship.
- The customer and the representative have a business relationship outside the broker-customer relationship.

TAKE NOTE

Generally, before borrowing from or lending to a customer, a representative must advise his firm in writing and receive written permission. However, notice and approval are not needed if the loan is between immediate family members, and approval is not needed if the customer is a lending institution and the loan is on standard commercial terms.

3. 3. 3. 2. 2   Guarantees and Sharing in Customer Accounts

Broker-dealers, investment advisers, and registered representatives may not guarantee any customer against a loss or guarantee a gain. All such guarantees or anything intended to convey a guarantee is prohibited.

Member firms and representatives are also prohibited from sharing in profits or losses in a customer's account. An exception is made if a joint account has received the member firm's prior written approval and the registered representative shares in the profits and losses only to the extent of his proportionate financial contribution to the joint account. Contribution to the account cannot be measured in knowledge or expertise but only in dollars. The firm, however, may share in a loss if the loss was due to an error made by the firm.

Exceptions to the proportion rule are made when sharing in a joint account with immediate family members. In these instances, directly proportionate sharing of profits and losses is not mandatory. Immediate family members include parents, mother-in-law or father-in-law, spouses, children, and any relative to whom the officer or employee in question contributes financial support. Financial support is broadly defined to include anyone who is living in the same residence.

TAKE NOTE

Firms cannot have joint accounts with customers. Representatives may have joint accounts with customers only if the arrangement has been approved by the principal and account proceeds are shared in proportion to each party's contribution.

3. 3. 3. 3   Financial Exploitation of Seniors

FINRA, along with other regulators specifically addresses the financial exploitation of seniors and other specified adult customers. FINRA defines the impacted accounts as those for individuals

■ age 65 and older, or

■ age 18 and older who the member reasonably believes has a mental or physical impairment that renders the individual unable to protect his or her own interests.

■ FINRA notes financial exploitation to be as follows:

■ The wrongful or unauthorized taking, withholding, appropriation, or use of funds or securities; or

■ any act or omission of an act taken by a person to obtain control, through deception, intimidation or undue influence, over the specified adult's money, assets or property; or convert the specified adult's money, assets, or property.

This includes any act aligning with the previous, done through the use of a power of attorney, guardianship, or any other authority.

Essentially, to prevent potential exploitation the rules regarding the accounts of seniors and other specified adult customers do two things:

1. Member firms and associated persons must make "reasonable efforts" to obtain the name and contact information for a trusted contact person.

2. Member firms will be permitted to, but not required to place temporary holds on customer accounts when there is a reasonable belief of financial exploitation.

3. 3. 3. 3. 1   Trusted Contact Person

A reasonable effort to obtain the name and contact information for a trusted contact person must be made when

■ opening a customer's account, or

■ updating the account information for an existing account.

Importantly, it should be noted that the member firm is not prohibited from opening an account when the customer fails or refuses to provide the information, so long as the member firm took "reasonable efforts" to obtain such information. Asking the customer to provide the name and contact information for a trusted contact person constitutes a "reasonable effort."

When the customer has provided the name and contact information for a trusted contact person, the member firm must disclose in writing to the customer that the member or an associated person is authorized to contact the trusted contact person and disclose certain information about the customer's account.

FINRA notes that the trusted contact person is intended to be a resource for the member firm in administering the customer's account, protecting assets, and responding to possible financial exploitation.

EXAMPLE   A member unable to contact a customer after multiple attempts. The member could contact a trusted contact person to inquire about the customer's current contact information.

EXAMPLE

A member firm suspects that the customer may be suffering from Alzheimer's disease, dementia, or other forms of diminished capacity. The member could reach out to the trusted contact person.

EXAMPLE

A member believes possible financial exploitation of the customer is occurring. Before placing a temporary hold on a disbursement, the member could contact a trusted contact person to discuss the facts.

3. 3. 3. 3. 2   *Temporary Holds on Disbursements and Review*

If the member firm reasonably believes that financial exploitation has occurred, is occurring, has been attempted or will be attempted, it can place a temporary hold on disbursements of funds or securities. Note that the rule does not require the member firm to take this action, but allows it to do so at its discretion.

The hold can be no longer than 15 business days under the rule. A state regulator or agency of jurisdiction however, can terminate the hold sooner, or extend the hold longer.

If a member firm places a temporary hold on disbursements, it must immediately initiate an internal review of the facts and circumstances that caused the member to initiate the temporary hold on the disbursements. In addition, the rule requires the member to provide notification of the hold and the reason for the hold to the trusted contact person and all parties authorized to transact business in the account, no later than two business days after the date the hold was initiated.

However, a member firm is not required to provide notification to the trusted contact person or a party authorized to transact business in the account, if the trusted contact person or party is unavailable or the member reasonably believes that the trusted contact person or party is the perpetrator of the financial exploitation.

3. 3. 3. 4   Activities of Unregistered Persons

Unregistered persons may not conduct certain activities. Following we will discuss the two most common prohibited activities for anyone who is not registered.

3. 3. 3. 4. 1   *Solicitation and Taking Orders*

Unregistered persons are prohibited against soliciting customers and taking orders to buy or sell securities.

3. 3. 3. 4. 2   *Paying Commissions to Unregistered Persons*

Only registered persons can be paid commissions. Similarly, member firms can only grant commissions or other allowances such as discounts or concessions (when selling new issues) to other members. In general, nonmembers are treated as the general public would be treated. In that light, nonmember firms, including suspended members, always buy at the public offering price and sell at the public bid price, never at a discount.

However, there are exceptions.

- Foreign nonmember firms—These firms, ineligible for FINRA membership, may be granted commissions, or other allowances provided they agree to abide by FINRA rules, regulations and standards.

■ Continuing commissions—A registered person who leaves a member firm (e.g., upon retirement) may continue to receive commissions on business placed while employed. While there is no requirement for members to pay **continuing commissions**, there must be a contract to this effect before the representative leaves the firm in order to do so. Heirs of a deceased representative may receive continuing commissions if this is part of the written contract.

TAKE NOTE

Continuing commissions may never be paid on business referred or introduced by an employee after that person ceases to be registered with the member.

3. 3. 3. 5 Falsifying or Withholding Documents

FINRA requires that "A member, in the conduct of his business, shall observe high standards of commercial honor and just and equitable principles of trade." It is well established that forgery and falsification of documents, including all books and records, is not consistent with the high standards of commercial honor and just, and equitable principles of trade required of registered representatives. Someone found in violation of the rule may be sanctioned.

3. 3. 3. 5. 1 Sanctions

Sanctions against a member or associated person, if found guilty of falsifying or withholding documents, are included with the written decision. Under FINRA's Code of Procedure, sanctions could include:

■ censure (generally meant to mean public disclosure);

■ fine;

■ suspension of the membership of a member or suspension of the registration of an associated person for a definite period;

■ expulsion of the member, canceling the membership of the member;

■ the barring of an associated person from association with all members; and

■ imposition of any other fitting sanction.

3. 3. 3. 5. 2 Signatures of Convenience

Altering documents previously signed by the customer or reusing or forging a customer's signature even if for the convenience of a customer is prohibited.

EXAMPLE

A customer has signed an account agreement to open an account. After some time has passed the registered representative suggests that the account be made a discretionary account. The customer agrees and to expedite the new account the RR reuses (by copy or forgery) the customer's signature on the new discretionary account form. This is strictly prohibited.

3. 3. 3. 5. 3   Responding to Regulatory Requests

FINRA grants its staff and adjudicators the authority to inspect and copy the books, records and accounts of member firms, associated persons and other persons over whom FINRA has jurisdiction. These records include documents relating to compliance with just and equitable principles of trade, other FINRA rules, SEC rules, MSRB rules and the federal securities laws.

All requests for books and records should be met promptly and as noted earlier the most two recent years should be in a readily accessible location. This would apply to hard copy (physically maintained) records or those maintained electronically.

QUICK QUIZ 3.C

LEARNING OBJECTIVES

■   Define and explain prohibited activities

1.   Match the following types of prohibited activities to the definitions provided.

Marking the close
Matched orders
Front running
Capping
Supporting
Pegging

A.   _____Entering orders designed to keep a stock from rising

B.   _____Any activity intended to keep a stock price stable

C.   _____Placing orders to buy or sell stock ahead of orders that could move the market

D.   _____Perpetrating rumors to push up the price of stock owned so as to profit later when selling

E.   _____Falsely reporting trades that never occurred or entering orders to influence the closing price of a stock

F.   _____Transactions designed to give the illusion of increased activity or volume in a stock

2.   An investor sells put options and, just prior to their expiration, buys the underlying stock. The intent is to keep the price from falling below the strike price of the options. Such an action is called

A.   supporting
B.   matched sales
C.   pegging
D.   marking the close

3.   An investor sells ABC stock at a loss in order to offset a capital gain. However, the following week the investor buys call options on ABC stock. This activity can be defined as

A.   a matched purchase
B.   front running
C.   a wash sale
D.   supporting

4. Which of the following is NOT true regarding continuing commissions to a registered representative that has retired?

   A. The agreement must be in writing.
   B. The commissions may continue to be paid to the reps heirs after death.
   C. The retired rep may receive commissions for new business if there is direct involvement in the sale.
   D. The agreement is based on business placed by the registered rep while employed by the broker-dealer.

5. A joint trading account can be created and profits and losses shared between which of the following parties?

   A. Broker-dealer (firm) and retail customer, but only if sharing is in proportion to the investment.
   B. Broker-dealer (firm) and institutional client, but only if sharing is in proportion to the investment.
   C. Registered representative and neighbor with principal approval, and only the customer has contributed to the account.
   D. Registered representative and mother-in-law, and only the mother-in-law has contributed to the account.

QUICK QUIZ ANSWERS AND RATIONALES

QUICK QUIZ 3.A

1. **B.** While market orders are always executed immediately at the current market price, limit orders can only be executed at the limit price designated by the customer or better. For a buy limit order, *or better* means at the limit price <u>or lower</u>. Mr. Jones should place a buy limit order at $58.

2. **C.** Customers always buy at the ask price. In order to buy, someone must be willing to sell and in this case the best price available from all the sellers in the secondary market is 49.75. Customers sell at the bid price. In order to sell, someone must be willing to buy, and in this case, the best price available from all the buyers in the secondary market is 47.50.

3. **D.** When an investor is long stock, the stock was purchased and the stock is owned. When an investor owns stock, he is bullish— anticipating the stock will rise in value. If the stock rises in value, the position can be closed by selling it in the secondary market for a profit. Since there is no limit to how high the price can go, profit is unlimited.

4. **C.** Short sellers are bearish. They borrow stock and sell it, hoping the price goes down so they can close their position by purchasing the stock at a price that is lower than what they sold it for. The risk to a short seller is that the price of the borrowed shares that were sold short increases, forcing them to buy back at a higher price instead of a lower price as they had anticipated. Because there is no limit on how high a security's price may rise, a short seller has unlimited loss potential.

5. **B.** There is no economic benefit for investors when a stock splits or when a stock dividend occurs. In each of these cases, the investors' cost basis in the investment is adjusted based on the resulting stock the investors own after the split or additional stock received from a stock dividend. Only cash dividends are taxable (in the year they are distributed).

6. **A.** The holding period is less than one year; June 10 of this year to January 10 of the next year, and therefore, the gain is short term and is taxed at the same rate as the taxpayer's other ordinary income. If the stock was held longer than one year before being sold, the gain would be defined as long term, taxed at a more favorable long-term capital gain rate.

7. **D.** If a customer signs and returns a proxy statement for shares held in street name and fails to indicate how the shares are to be voted, the member must vote the shares as recommended by management.

8. **C.** Regular way settlement for federal government securities (T-bills, notes, and bonds) and options is T+1.

QUICK QUIZ 3.B

1. **C.** TOD, the term used for transfer on death, will allow this client to fulfill her wishes, and there are no legal expenses involved in setting up the account in this manner.

2. **A.** Under a TIC account, the decedent's estate (via the executor or administrator) becomes a tenant in common with the survivors. Assets belonging to the deceased are ultimately disposed of as provided for in the will (or the state).

3. **D.** Although not a common practice, margin trading in a trust account is permitted only if it is specifically provided for in the trust agreement.

4. **C.** If there is taxable income in an UTMA (or UGMA) account, the tax liability is that of the beneficiary of the account (the minor). In reality, the parents are responsible for making sure their child files the proper tax return; the legal obligation is that of the minor.

5. **B.** Any form of life insurance is a prohibited investment in an IRA. However, another insurance company product, an annuity, is permitted.

6. **A.** When a commission is charged (firm acting as agent) it is added to cost to arrive at the buyers net amount due and subtracted from the sales proceeds to arrive at the net amount the seller is to receive.

7. **D.** This first stage of laundering is when funds or assets are moved into the laundering system. This stage is recognized as the time when illegal funds are the most susceptible to detection.

8. **B.** One exception to the lifetime, six-year and three-year retention is the requirement for written customer complaints. Customer complaint records must be retained for four years.

9. **C.** Customer account statements will always show the long and short positions in the account as well as any debit or credit balances. Activity since the last statement will be shown, but not year-to-date.

10. **D.** The minimum frequency for sending customer statements is once per quarter. If there is any activity in the account, then a statement must be sent following the month in which that activity took place. However, if the account contains any securities meeting the SEC's definition of *penny stock*, statements must be sent monthly.

11. **A.** When a securities transaction involves bonds, the par value is indicated, not the number of bonds.

12. **C.** Not every confirmation is trade related. When there is non-trade related or third party activity in a client's account, that activity will require a confirmation.

13. **B.** Customers are always permitted to ask for paper copies of their account activity, even when they have signed an agreement to have confirmations and statements delivered electronically.

QUICK QUIZ 3.C

1. **A.** Capping

   B. Pegging

C. Front running

D. Pump and dump

E. Marking the close

F. Matched orders

2. **A.** Writers of put options will benefit if the price of underlying stock doesn't fall below the strike price. They might try to accomplish this by supporting the stock (entering sell orders to prevent the price from falling below a certain level). Supporting is considered a manipulative activity and is prohibited activity.

3. **C.** A wash sale is an attempt to create a loss for tax purposes (sell at a loss) when one's intent is to still maintain ownership of the securities. Any repurchase of the same security or substantially same security within 30 days before or after the date establishing the loss, would be recognized as one's intent to maintain ownership. Call options are substantially the same as they give the investor the right to buy the stock, in this case, ABC stock.

4. **D.** Continuing commissions may never be paid on business referred or introduced by an employee after that person ceases to be registered with the member.

5. **D.** Firms cannot have joint accounts with customers. Representatives may have joint accounts with customers only if the arrangement has been approved by the principal and account proceeds are shared in proportion to each party's contribution. Exceptions to the proportion rule are made when sharing in a joint account with immediate family members (including in-laws).

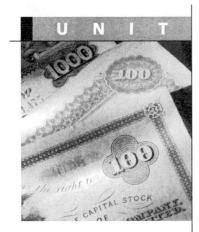

Overview of the Regulatory Framework

In this unit, you will be introduced to the registration requirements for both broker-dealers and associated persons and the ongoing continued education requirements registered persons must fulfill. Equally important are the issues that may disqualify applicants from registering.

We'll explore the Conduct Rules and those most likely to impact registered individuals in the securities industry—among them, outside business activities, private securities transactions, influencing the employees of others, political contributions, misleading or omitting information, and handling of customer complaints as well as the reporting requirements that accompany some of these events. ■

When you have completed the unit you should be able to:

- **contrast** the different SRO registration requirements;

- **state** the continuing education requirements;

- **distinguish** between acceptable and unacceptable employee conduct; and

- **identify** reportable events for employees and broker-dealers.

4. 1 SELF-REGULATORY ORGANIZATION (SRO) AND REGULATORY REQUIREMENTS FOR ASSOCIATED PERSONS

LEARNING OBJECTIVES:
- Contrast the different SRO registration requirements
- State the continuing education requirements

All SROs require members and their associated persons to register. In this section, we will examine those requirements for FINRA member firms and associates.

4. 1. 1 REGISTRATION

The **National Adjudicatory Council** (NAC) establishes rules, regulations, and membership eligibility standards. At present, the following membership standards and registration requirements are in place.

4. 1. 1. 1 Broker-Dealer Registration

Any broker-dealer registered with the SEC is eligible and may apply for membership to FINRA. Any person who affects transactions in securities as a broker, a dealer, or an investment banker also may register with FINRA, as may municipal bond firms. Application for FINRA membership carries the applying firm's specific agreement to:
- comply with the association's rules and regulations;
- comply with federal securities laws; and
- pay dues, assessments, and other charges in the manner and amounts fixed by the association.

A membership application is made to the FINRA district office in the district which the applying firm has its home office. If a district committee passes on the firm's qualifications, the firm can be accepted into membership.

4. 1. 1. 2 Associated Persons

Any person associated with a member firm who intends to engage in the investment banking or securities business must be registered with FINRA as an associated person. Anyone applying for registration with FINRA as an associated person must be sponsored by a member firm.

Before submitting an application to enroll any person with FINRA as a registered representative, a member firm must ascertain the person's business reputation, character, education, qualifications, and experience. As part of the application process, the member firm must certify that it has made an investigation (background check) and that the candidate's credentials are in order.

TEST TOPIC ALERT   A member firm's failure to register an employee who performs any of the functions of a registered representative may lead to disciplinary action by FINRA.

An associated person may also be disciplined for violating SEC rules and regulations. If the SEC bars an associated person, no broker-dealer may allow that person to associate with it without the Commission's express permission. If a member firm suspends an associated person, the firm must report the suspension to the exchanges where the firm is a member.

To become a registered representative or principal, an individual must pass the appropriate licensing examination(s).

4. 1. 1. 2. 1 Fingerprint Records

Registered broker-dealers must have **fingerprint records** made for most of their employees, and all directors, officers, and partners must submit those fingerprint cards to the U.S. attorney general for identification and processing. Persons who must be fingerprinted are those involved in sales and those who handle cash or customer securities. Clerical persons (sometimes called ministerial persons) need not be fingerprinted. However, any associated person put in a position that would have them handle cash or securities would be required to be fingerprinted.

EXAMPLE

A receptionist who handles incoming mail would need to be fingerprinted due to the likelihood of having access to cash or securities. A receptionist who does not handle incoming mail and therefore would not be in a position to have access to cash or securities would not need to be fingerprinted.

TAKE NOTE

Those selling only mutual funds, variable annuities, or direct participation programs are exempt from fingerprinting. Certain broker-dealer employees (typically clerical) are exempt from the fingerprinting requirement as well, if they:

- are not involved in securities sales;

- do not handle or have access to cash or securities or to the books and records of original entry relating to money and securities; and

- do not supervise other employees engaged in these activities.

4. 1. 1. 3 Registered Representative (RR)

All associated persons engaged in the investment banking and securities business are considered **registered representatives**, including any:

- assistant officer who does not function as a principal;
- individual who supervises, solicits, or conducts business in securities; and
- individual who trains people to supervise, solicit, or conduct business in securities.

4. 1. 1. 4 Registered Principal

Anyone who manages or supervises any part of a member's investment banking or securities business must be registered as a **principal** with FINRA (including people involved solely in training associated persons). Unless the member firm is a sole proprietorship, it must employ at least two registered principals.

4. 1. 1. 5   Ineligibility and Disqualification

A person may not act as a registered representative or principal unless FINRA's eligibility standards regarding training, experience, and competence are met.

Statutory disqualification—Disciplinary sanctions by the SEC, another SRO, a foreign financial regulator, or a foreign equivalent of an SRO may be cause for statutory disqualification of FINRA membership.

An individual applying for registration as an associated person will be rejected if he:

- has been or is expelled or suspended from membership or participation in any other SRO or from the foreign equivalent of an SRO;
- is under an SEC order or an order of a foreign financial regulator denying, suspending, or revoking his registration or barring him from association with a broker-dealer; or
- has been found to be the cause of another broker-dealer or associated person being expelled or suspended by another SRO, the SEC, or a foreign equivalent of an SRO.

The following also can automatically disqualify an applicant for registration:

- Misstatements willfully made in an application for membership or registration as an associated person
- A felony conviction, either domestic or foreign, or a misdemeanor conviction involving securities or money within the past 10 years
- Court injunctions prohibiting the individual from acting as an investment adviser, an underwriter, or a broker-dealer or in other capacities aligned with the securities and financial services industry

---

EXAMPLE   An applicant applying for registration lists a conviction for a Ponzi scheme whereby he accepted investments from individuals promising high returns. Returns paid to them subsequently came from investments received from new investors. It should be recognized that this conviction would statutorily disqualify the individual from registering as an associated person in the securities industry as the conviction involves money and fraud.

TAKE NOTE   The Central Registration Depository (CRD) maintains information on the disciplinary history of all persons currently registered. A customer can access this information toll free through the CRD's **BrokerCheck**. A hyperlink to BrokerCheck is required on all FINRA member firm websites.

The firm will be denied membership if the applicant or any associated person:

- has been expelled or suspended by another SRO or from the foreign equivalent of an SRO;
- is subject to an SEC order denying, suspending, or revoking registration as a broker-dealer; or
- has willfully filed a false or misleading application or has failed to disclose material facts.

TAKE NOTE

While a bankruptcy or unsatisfied lien does not disqualify one from registering, failure to disclose the facts would.

4. 1. 1. 6   Continuing Education (CE) Requirement

Registered persons are required to participate in **continuing education** (CE) programs. The CE requirement has two components: a firm element and a regulatory element.

4. 1. 1. 6. 1   Firm Element

The **firm element** requires member firms to prepare an annual training plan taking into account such factors as recent regulatory developments, the scope of the member's business activities, the performance of its personnel in the regulatory element, and its supervisory needs. This annual in-house training must be given to all registered persons who have direct contact with the public.

4. 1. 1. 6. 2   Regulatory Element

The **regulatory element** requires that all registered persons complete a computer-based training session within 120 days of the person's second registration anniversary and every three years thereafter (i.e., within 120 days of the person's fifth, eighth, 11th registration anniversary, and so on). The content of the regulatory element is determined by FINRA and is appropriate to either the registered representative or principal status of the person.

If a person fails to complete the regulatory element within the prescribed period, FINRA will deactivate that person's registration until the requirements of the program are met.

4. 1. 1. 7   Home Offices

It is not unusual for a broker-dealer to allow registered representatives to operate out of a home or residence, commonly referred to as working from a **home office**. In these instances, approval of the member firm's self-regulatory organization (SRO) is required as it would be for any office associated with the broker-dealer. All normal business activities including taking customer orders for the purchase and sale of securities would be permitted. Given all normal business activities are permitted at a home office, it would be subject to a premise visit and review by principals of the firm and FINRA examiners as any broker-dealer office would be. Additionally, the home office address and telephone number may be advertised in any normal manner such as on business cards or through various public media venues like newspapers and websites.

QUICK QUIZ 4.A

LEARNING OBJECTIVES

■ Contrast the different SRO registration requirements

■ State the continuing education requirements

1. FINRA membership eligibility standards are determined by the

   A. MSRB
   B. NAC
   C. SEC
   D. USA

2. An individual applying for registration as an associated person will be rejected if he

   A. submitted an application for registration which omitted mention of a minor traffic violation that occurred two years ago
   B. failed to include the zip+4 code on his home address
   C. is under a court injunction regarding a domestic issue
   D. is under an order of a foreign financial regulator denying, suspending, or revoking his registration or barring him from association with a broker-dealer

3. As a means of protecting the integrity of the industry and protection of the investing public, associated persons of FINRA member firms must submit finger-print records to the

   A. U.S. attorney general
   B. attorney general for the state in which they reside
   C. SEC
   D. FBI

4. If a registered representative has been barred from the securities industry while working for the ABC broker-dealer, which of the following is TRUE?

   A. The registered representative must refrain from engaging with the public on any securities-related activity for one year.
   B. The registered representative may apply for and obtain a principal's registration but may not engage any direct sales of securities until the bar has expired.
   C. The registered representative can be an advisor to a broker-dealer but may not be registered with a broker-dealer
   D. The registered representative may not associate with any broker-dealer.

5. The receptionist at a broker-dealer opens all incoming mail and forwards to various departments and people of the firm. Which of the following statements are TRUE?

   I. The receptionist must be fingerprinted.
   II. The receptionist need not be fingerprinted.
   III. The receptionist must be registered with FINRA.
   IV. The receptionist need not be registered with FINRA.

   A. I and III
   B. I and IV
   C. II and III
   D. II and IV

6. Which of the following states the continuing education regulatory element requirements correctly?

   A. Training must be completed within 120 days of the person's second registration anniversary and every five years thereafter.

   B. Training must be completed within 120 days of the person's first registration anniversary and then annually thereafter.

   C. Training must be completed within 120 days of the person's second registration anniversary and every three years thereafter.

   D. Training must be completed annually.

7. The continuing education firm element requires member firms to prepare in-house training for all registered persons

   A. annually

   B. bi-annually

   C. semi-annually

   D. on an as needed basis determined by the member firm

4. 2 EMPLOYEE CONDUCT AND REPORTABLE EVENTS

LEARNING OBJECTIVES:

■ Distinguish between acceptable and unacceptable employee conduct

■ Identify reportable events for employees and broker / dealers

FINRA describes four sets of rules and codes in its manual:

Conduct Rules—The **Conduct Rules** set out fair and ethical trade practices that member firms and their representatives must follow when dealing with the public. Included are events that must be reported.

Uniform Practice Code (UPC)—The **UPC** established the uniform trade practices, including settlement, good delivery, ex-dates, confirmations, don't know (DK) procedures, and other guidelines for broker-dealers to follow when they do business with other member firms.

Code of Procedure (COP)—The Code of Procedure describes how member violations of the Conduct Rules will be heard and handled.

Code of Arbitration Procedure—The Code of Arbitration Procedure governs the resolution of disagreements and claims between members, registered representatives, and the public; it addresses monetary claims.

4. 2. 1 EMPLOYEE CONDUCT

In the following sections you will learn about some of the rules governing employee conduct within the securities industry.

4. 2. 1. 1 Form U-4 and Form U-5

Representatives and principals must be registered with FINRA. Part of the registration process requires that sponsoring member firms file Form U-4 when hiring an individual and file Form U-5 when an individual terminates.

4. 2. 1. 1. 1   Form U-4

To register an associated person of a member firm with FINRA, the member fills out and submits **Form U-4**, but registration is not effective until the person passes the appropriate qualification exam(s). If a person fails the exam, 30 days must elapse before a second attempt can be made. If a person fails an exam three straight times, the person must wait six months (180 days) before making a fourth attempt.

Information required on Form U-4 is extensive and includes:

- name, address, and any aliases;
- five-year residency history;
- 10-year employment history; and
- information on any charges, arrests, or convictions relating to the investment business.

An affirmative answer (Yes) to any of the questions regarding charges, arrests, or convictions requires a detailed explanation. This information must be provided on the Disclosure Reporting Pages (DRP) on Form U-4.

Any changes to this information require filing an amended form with the **Central Registration Depository** (CRD) no later than 30 days after the member becomes aware of these changes. If the amendment involved a statutory disqualification, an amended form must be filed within 10 business days.

In addition to registering with FINRA, a representative must satisfy the registration requirements of each state he does business in. The Form U-4 must be check marked for each state and the accompanying fee and qualification exam if any must be satisfied. If a representative's firm is also a member of an exchange, such as the NYSE or the CBOE, this must be noted on the Form U-4, and once again, applicable fees must be paid and qualification exams passed if required.

TAKE NOTE
Information on marital status or educational background (degrees obtained, etc.) is not required on Form U-4. However, within the 10-year employment history required on Form U-4 full-time education would be included.

4. 2. 1. 1. 2   Form U-5

Should a person registered with a member resign or be terminated, the member must file Form U-5 with the Central Registration Depository (CRD) within 30 days of termination date. Members must also provide a copy of the form to their former employee within the same time frame. Failure to do so within 30 days will result in a late filing fee being assessed against the member. The form requires the member to indicate the reason for termination and provide an explanation where appropriate. Failure to provide accurate information could lead to severe disciplinary action.

If the member checks the Discharged or Permitted to Resign box, all of the details surrounding the termination must be disclosed.

In the event that the member, after filing the form, learns of facts or circumstances that would cause the information filed to be inaccurate or incomplete, the member must file an amended Form U-5 within 30 days of learning of facts giving rise to the amendment. A copy of the amended filing must be sent to the former employee. There is no time limit on how long after termination an amended Form U-5 is required.

If a registered person leaves one member to join another, the new employer, in addition to filing Form U-4, must get a copy of Form U-5 filed by the former employer within 60 days of the U-4 filing. A copy is obtained either from the new employee or the Central Registration Depository (CRD).

4. 2. 1. 1. 3   License and Jurisdictional Retention

If a registered person leaves the industry and reaffiliates with a member firm within two years, that person's license remains valid. If reaffiliation occurs after two years, that person must requalify by passing the appropriate exam.

Similarly, when a registered person leaves the business, FINRA retains jurisdiction over that person for two years. If that person becomes subject to a customer complaint or charges are brought against that person by FINRA, that person is still subject to FINRA rules for the two-year period following termination.

To avoid having a securities registration lapse, it may be tempting for former registered representatives to **park** their registrations with a member firm as the end of the two-year period nears. However, parking a securities license will subject the registered representative and the member firm to FINRA sanctions.

EXAMPLE

A registered individual leaves his position to begin a new business outside of the securities industry. About 20 months later, he is still unsure if his new business can turn the corner and become fully sustainable. To keep his options open, he contacts a broker dealer asking to become associated with the member firm to avoid having his securities licenses lapse at the two year anniversary of his leaving the industry. He feels that in another six to eight months he should be able to make the decision as to whether to continue with his business or reenter the securities industry. He feels having his registration already associated with the member firm would be advantageous as he would not have to retest and could hit the ground running if need be.

This would NOT be allowed. Both the registered representative and the member firm would be subject to sanctions for allowing the associated person to park their license.

4. 2. 1. 2   Misleading or Omitting Information

Broker-dealers and associated persons must not promote or disseminate false or misleading information. FINRA holds broker-dealers to certain general standards regarding all member firm communications. All member communications must be based on principles of fair dealing and good faith. Statements must be clear and not misleading within the context that they are made and must be fair and balanced regarding potential risks and benefits. Omission of material facts is not permitted, nor is making false, exaggerated, or misleading statements or claims.

The following are examples of statements or claims that might be considered misleading or omitting statements:

Recruitment advertising—A BD advertises for new registered representatives and includes this statement; "RRs with our firm make more than RRs with any other firm in the securities industry in both commissions and advisory fees". (Potential commission or fee claims may never be exaggerated.)

Brochures—A chart within a brochure shows that long call option contracts have unlimited maximum gain potential but neglects to reflect in any way that maximum loss can be the entire premium paid. (Graphs, charts, and other tools may never show opportunity for gain without also showing loss potential.)

Professional or educational designations—A RR implies in a recommendation to clients that his Bachelor of Science degree makes him uniquely qualified to recommend a certain tech stock. (Use of degrees or designations may never be used in a misleading fashion nor can reference to nonexistent designations be made.)

Finally, FINRA mandates that members must consider the nature of the audience to which the communication will be directed and should provide details and explanations appropriate to the audience.

4. 2. 1. 3 Customer Complaints

Whenever a customer complaint is received or a potential red flag for a customer or account is identified, it is essential that the proper personnel are notified. Persons who should be notified may include the account's representative, the account's principal, the branch manager, or a member of the compliance department. Generally, a principal will need to address these concerns.

A complaint is defined as a written statement by a customer (or a person acting on behalf of a customer) alleging a grievance arising out of, or in connection with, a securities transaction.

If a complaint is resolved to the satisfaction of both the member firm and the customer, no further action is needed.

If it cannot be resolved, it must be referred to FINRA's director of arbitration if it is between a member and an associated person. If it is between a client and a member, the dispute would go to arbitration only if an arbitration agreement has been signed. This is outlined in FINRA's Code of Arbitration Procedure.

TAKE NOTE

It is a common industry practice for new account forms to have an arbitration agreement which binds the client to submitting all disputes to arbitration if they cannot be resolved. Without such an agreement, disputes between members and public customers can only go to arbitration at the insistence of the customer.

EXAMPLE

A customer opens a new account and as part of the new account form signs an arbitration agreement. A few months later, the customer disputes a price paid for securities saying that his order was a limit order and the price paid went beyond the limit designated. The firm contends that the order given was a market order, not a limit order, and therefore, the purchase was made at the best available price at that time.

If the complaint between the member firm and the customer cannot be resolved to the satisfaction of each, it must be directed to FINRA's director of arbitration because the arbitration agreement was signed when the account was opened.

If the complaint involves allegations of theft, misappropriation of funds or securities, or forgery, the member must immediately report this to FINRA within 10 business days.

Finally, excessive customer complaints could be a red flag indicating that improper use of customer funds, securities, or both is occurring.

4. 2. 1. 4   Recordkeeping for Customer Complaints

Copies of all customer complaints must be maintained in a file at the office of supervisory jurisdiction (OSJ). Each complaint in the file must be accompanied by a statement of its resolution and be endorsed by a principal. Member firms must electronically file information on all customer complaints with FINRA. These filings must be made within 15 days of the end of each calendar quarter.

4. 2. 2   REPORTABLE EVENTS

The conduct rules also outline certain events as being reportable. The following sections discuss those that are most commonly run a fowl of.

4. 2. 2. 1   Outside Business Activities

An associated person cannot work for any business other than his member firm (independent activity) without his employing broker-dealer's knowledge. If a registered person wants to be employed by or accept compensation from an entity other than the member firm, that person must provide prior written notice to the member. Note that the employing member's permission is not required. The firm, however, does have the right to reject or restrict any outside affiliation if it feels a conflict of interest exists. These affiliations would also include serving as an officer or director of a company or owning any interest in another financial services company.

A **passive investment**, such as the purchase of a limited partnership unit, is not considered an outside business activity. An associated person may make a passive investment for his own account without providing written notice to the employing broker-dealer.

EXAMPLE

A registered representative currently working full time with a broker dealer wants to teach night classes in business and finance at a local community college to earn extra income while building her securities practice. Under the rules governing outside business activity, prior written notice to the employing member broker-dealer would need to be made.

The same registered representative wants to volunteer for her son's little league association serving in any way she can be of help (coaching, committees etc.). Notice to the employing member would not need to be made for participation in this activity.

4.2.2.2   Private Securities Transactions

The Conduct Rules define a **private securities transaction** as any sale of securities outside an associated person's regular business and his employing member. Private securities transactions are also known as **selling away**.

EXAMPLE   A registered representative's firm does not allow options transactions but the RR has a client who wants to do an option trade. The RR can accommodate the clients new option account and transaction but it will have to be through another broker-dealer. This is a private securities transaction and known as selling away. The RR is selling away from his employing member because options transactions are not part of its normal business.

If an associated person wishes to enter into a private securities transaction, that person must:

- provide prior written notice to his employer;
- describe in detail the proposed transaction;
- describe in detail his proposed role in the transaction; and
- disclose whether he has or may receive compensation for the transaction.

With compensation—If the transaction involves compensation, the employing member may approve or disapprove the associated person's participation. If the member approves the participation, it must treat the transaction as if it is being done on its own behalf by entering the transaction on its own books and supervising the associated person during the transaction. If the member disapproves the transaction, the associated person may not participate in it.

TAKE NOTE   Supervision, and thus the responsibility of all that is associated with the transaction, is that of the employing member firm, NOT the broker-dealer who is accommodating the private securities transaction.

Without compensation—If the associated person has not received or will not receive compensation for the private securities transaction, the employing member must acknowledge that it has received written notification and may require the associated person to adhere to specified conditions during participation.

Transactions that the associated person enters into on behalf of immediate family members and for which the associated person receives no compensation are excluded from the definition of private securities transactions.

4.2.2.3   Political Contributions

Political contributions should never be used to procure business. All business should be awarded on the basis of merit only and not political favor gotten via contributions to political parties, elected individuals candidates, or third parties with connections to those with political affiliations. Industry rules regarding political contributions are intended to preserve investor confidence and market integrity.

4. 2. 2. 3. 1   *Registered Investment Advisers*

Rules within the Investment Advisers Act of 1940 are designed to deter what is commonly referred to as the practice of "pay to play" or "play for pay". In other words gaining political favor via contributions made to political parties, elected officials, or candidates.

If a political contribution to certain elected officials or candidates is made, an adviser may not provide advisory services to any government they represent for a fee for two years. Advisors are also prohibited from arranging payments via any other person (third party) to solicit advisory business, unless that third party satisfies the pay-to-play rules. When an advisor is seeking to provide or already providing government business, it may not solicit or coordinate contributions political parties, elected individuals, or candidates for office.

4. 2. 2. 3. 2   *Municipal Securities Dealers*

Recalling that the **Municipal Securities Rulemaking Board** (MSRB) was established as an SRO to enact and interpret rules relating to the underwriting and trading of municipal securities as well as advising municipal issuers, it should be noted they also have rules to prevent "pay to play"—MSRB Rule G-37. Because the MSRB has no enforcement capability, these rules would be enforced by FINRA.

The MSRB play for pay rule deals with the influence of political contributions on the selection of underwriters. The rule focuses on:

■ negotiated underwritings in which a municipal issuer selects an underwriter and negotiates a deal (not underwritings in which underwriters bid on a proposed new issue); and

■ financial advisory work in which a municipal issuer selects a municipal firm to help it structure a new issue.

Rule G-37 prohibits municipal firms from engaging in the municipal securities business noted above (negotiated underwritings/financial advisory work) with an issuer for two years after a contribution is made to an official of that issuer by:

■ the municipal firm;

■ a municipal finance professional (MFP) associated with the firm; or

■ any political action committee (PAC) controlled by the firm.

EXAMPLE   A municipal securities firm routinely makes political contributions to candidates in local municipalities. Later, it wants to take part in the underwriting of a new issue of municipal bonds in one of those municipalities. The municipality is requiring that bids be made by member firms in order for the municipality to select the underwriters. Because this isn't a negotiated underwriting the municipality would be allowed to submit a bid to participate in underwriting the issue of new bonds. Had it been a negotiated underwriting, the member firm would have been unable to negotiate with the municipality for a period of two years after the last contribution was made.

A municipal finance professional (MFP) is an associated person of a FINRA member firm engaged in municipal securities underwriting, trading, sales, financial advisory, research, investment advice, or any other activities that involve communication with public investors.

TAKE NOTE

Associated persons whose activities are limited solely to sales or have only clerical or ministerial functions are not MFPs.

Contributions of up to $250 per election are permitted to be made by municipal finance professionals (registered persons) eligible to vote for that official. The $250 de minimis exemption does not apply to contributions made by municipal firms.

4. 2. 2. 4   Gifts and Gratuities (Influencing or Rewarding Employees of Others)

Broker-dealers may not distribute business-related compensation (cash or noncash gifts or gratuities) to the employees of other member firms. However, a broker-dealer may give other firms' employees gratuities without violating the rules, provided:

- the compensation is not conditional on sales or promises of sales;
- it has the employing member's prior approval; and
- the compensation's total value does not exceed the annual limit set by the regulatory bodies (currently $100 per year).

TAKE NOTE

These rules permit occasional noncash expenditures that exceed the $100 limit, such as dinners, seminars, tickets or tickets to entertainment events. These are considered allowable business entertainment items. In addition, reminder advertising items such as pens, mouse pads and similar inexpensive items are also permitted. However, vacations or season tickets to cultural or sporting events are always violations.

EXAMPLE

Twice each year a mutual funds sales associate likes to sit down at a nice restaurant with a few broker-dealer representatives to discuss new funds his company is offering and explore possible suitable recommendations for their clients. These dinners can sometimes cost between $400 and $500. This would be permitted, as it is occasional and business is being discussed with the mutual fund sales associate present. In other words, an allowable business entertainment expense.

4. 2. 2. 4. 1   Noncash Compensation

FINRA is concerned about the potential conflicts of interest created when program sponsors, such as investment companies, provide incentives or rewards to representatives for selling the sponsor's products. These incentives are in the form of noncash compensation, which is subject to the following rules: an occasional meal or a ticket to a sporting event or the theater is acceptable as long as it is not conditioned on the achievement of a sales target. Payment or reimbursement by sponsors in connection with meetings held to train or educate representatives is acceptable as long as:

- the representative obtains the member firm's prior permission to attend;
- the location of the meeting is appropriate to the purpose of the meeting (e.g., an office of the sponsor or the member would be appropriate; a meeting held at posh hotel in the Bahamas is not);

■ there is no payment or reimbursement for a guest (e.g., a spouse) of the representative attending the meeting;

■ payment or reimbursement is not conditioned on the achievement of a sales target;

■ there is no payment or reimbursement for certain expenses incurred in connection with meetings, such as golf outings, cruises, tours, and similar types of entertainment; and

■ the member firm creates a record of all noncash compensation received by its representatives as well as the details of the meeting.

EXAMPLE

A mutual fund sales associate sends a registered representative two tickets for all of the home games of the RR's favorite sports team. The value of the two tickets is approximately $4,500. This would be considered a violation as it is not occasional and furthermore, there can be no assumption that the sales associate would be present at each game to discuss business nor would there be a reasonable need to do so that often.

QUICK QUIZ 4.B

LEARNING OBJECTIVES:

■ Distinguish between acceptable and unacceptable employee conduct

■ Identify reportable events for employees and broker / dealers

1. FINRA describes four sets of rules and codes in its manual. Which of the following is NOT one of them?

   A. Code of Arbitration Procedure
   B. Uniform Practice Code
   C. Code of Procedure
   D. Code of Business

2. FINRA's Conduct Rules dealing with outside business activity (OBA) of an associated person of a member firm require

   A. written notification to the employer
   B. written notification and consent of the employer
   C. written notification to the employer only in the case where the AP will be receiving compensation
   D. specific approval from the employer before the AP can make a passive investment

3. You overhear a discussion about a registered representative being disciplined because of *selling away*. Which of FINRA's Conduct Rules was violated?

   A. Outside business activity
   B. Accepting excessive non-cash compensation
   C. Private securities transactions
   D. Failure to direct the client's trade to the best available market

4. A broker-dealer may give other firms' employees gratuities without violating the rules, provided the compensation's total value does not exceed

   A. $50
   B. $100
   C. $250
   D. $500

5. One way that distributors of mutual funds attempt to encourage broker-dealers and their registered representatives to include their funds in recommendations to clients is to provide educational seminars. FINRA's Conduct Rules permit this activity as long as the sponsor does not

   A. promote their funds exclusively
   B. conduct the seminar on or near the premises of the distributor's office
   C. offer reimbursement for the travel expenses of the attendee's spouse
   D. offer reimbursement for the travel expenses for several representatives of the same broker-dealer

6. Regulators are concerned about the use of political influence to obtain business. This is particularly important with municipal securities because elected officials frequently are the people who select the underwriters for their community's financing. As a result, the MSRB issued Rule G-37 which, among other things,

   A. prohibits any political contributions
   B. prohibits municipal firms from engaging in negotiated underwritings with an issuer for two years after a contribution is made to an official of that issuer by a municipal securities dealer
   C. allows contributions up to $250 made by municipal finance professionals to persons the MFP is eligible to vote for
   D. is limited to issues where the underwriters must bid on the issue

7. A customer complaint against one of the firm's registered representatives involves allegations of misappropriation of funds or securities. The member firm must

   A. notify the FBI promptly
   B. temporarily suspend the representative
   C. notify FINRA within 10 business days
   D. maintain a copy of the complaint for 10 years

QUICK QUIZ ANSWERS AND RATIONALES

QUICK QUIZ 4.A

1. **B.** It is the National Adjudicatory Council (NAC) that has the responsibility for determining membership eligibility standards for FINRA members.

2. **D.** There are a number of reasons why application for registration as an associated person might be rejected. Among them are if he is under an SEC order or an order of a foreign financial regulator denying, suspending, or revoking his registration or barring him from association with a broker-dealer. Non-securities related misdemeanors, such as traffic violations, do not have to be reported. Zip+4 code being left out is not a cause for rejection and only a court injunction enjoining him from entering the securities business would be cause for rejection, not a domestic issue.

3. **A.** Registered broker-dealers must have **fingerprint records** made for most of their employees, and all directors, officers, and partners must submit those fingerprint cards to the U.S. attorney general for identification and processing.

4. **D.** If the SEC bars an associated person, no broker-dealer may allow that person to associate with it without the SEC's express permission.

5. **B.** When opening mail for the broker-dealer, it is inevitable that the receptionist will handle monies and securities from customers and as such, will need to be fingerprinted. Registration is not required.

6. **C.** The regulatory element requires that all registered persons complete a computer-based training session within 120 days of the person's second registration anniversary and every three years thereafter.

7. **A.** The continuing education firm element requires member firms to prepare an annual training plan. The training should take into account recent regulatory developments, the scope of the member's business activities, the performance of its personnel in the regulatory element, and its supervisory needs.

QUICK QUIZ 4.B

1. **D.** There is no FINRA Code of Business. FINRA's four sets of rules are the following: the Conduct Rules, the Code of Procedure, the Uniform Practice Code, and the Code of Arbitration.

2. **A.** If an associate person of a FINRA member firm wants to be employed by or accept compensation from an entity other than the member firm, that person must provide prior written notice to the member. Note that the employing member's permission is not required. Specifically excluded from the notification requirement is making passive investments, such as into limited partnership vehicles.

3. **C.** The Conduct Rules define a private securities transaction as any sale of securities outside an associated person's regular business and his employing member. Private securities transactions are also known as *selling away*.

4. **B.** Under the current rules, the cash gift that may be made without raising concern is $100 per person per year.

5. **C.** Training and educational seminars are an excellent way for mutual fund distributors to get their message across and potentially increase sales. Although expenses for representatives of a broker-dealer may be reimbursed, expenses of a spouse or other guest may not. The seminar must be held in an appropriate location and the company's office would certainly qualify.

6. **B.** Political contributions are permitted, but if made to an official of an issuer by the member firm in any amount, or by a municipal securities professional (MFP) in excess of the de minimis limit ($250), the firm is not permitted to engage in negotiated underwritings with that issuer for a period of two years.

7. **C.** Normally, reports of customer complaints are submitted to FINRA within 15 days of the end of each calendar quarter. However, when the complaint involves allegations of theft, misappropriation of funds or securities, or forgery, the member must immediately report this to FINRA within 10 business days. Records of complaints must be maintained for four years.

Common Abbreviations

ADR/ADS American depositary receipt (share)
AIR assumed interest rate
BA banker's acceptance
BD broker-dealer
BDC business development (growth) company
CD certificate of deposit
CDO collateralized debt obligation
CEO chief executive officer
CMO collateralized mortgage obligation
CMV current market value
COP Code of Procedure
CPI Consumer Price Index
CY current yield
DBCC District Business Conduct Committee
DEA designated examining authority
DJIA Dow Jones Industrial Average
DMM Designated Market Maker
EE Series EE savings bonds
EPS earnings per share
ERISA Employee Retirement Income Security Act of 1974
ETF exchange traded fund
FAC face-amount certificate
Fed Federal Reserve System
FDIC Federal Deposit Insurance Corporation
FGIC Financial Guaranty Insurance Company
FIFO first in, first out
FINRA Financial Industry Regulatory Authority
FNMA Federal National Mortgage Association
FOMC Federal Open Market Committee
FRB Federal Reserve Board
GNMA Government National Mortgage Association
GDP gross domestic product
GO general obligation bond
HH Series HH savings bond
HSA health savings account
IDR/IDB industrial development revenue bond

IPO initial public offering
IRA individual retirement account
IRC Internal Revenue Code
IRS Internal Revenue Service
JTIC joint tenants in common
JTWROS joint tenants with right of survivorship
LIFO last in, first out
MSRB Municipal Securities Rulemaking Board
Nasdaq National Association of Securities Dealers Automated Quotation system
NAV net asset value
NHA New Housing Authority
NL no load
NYSE New York Stock Exchange
OSJ office of supervisory jurisdiction
OTC over the counter
PE price-to-earnings ratio
PHA Public Housing Authority
POP public offering price
REIT real estate investment trust
RR registered representative
SAI statement of additional information
SEC Securities and Exchange Commission
SEP simplified employee pension plan
SIPC Securities Investor Protection Corporation
SRO self-regulatory organization
T+3 trade date plus three business days' settlement
TCPA Telephone Consumer Protection Act
TSA tax-sheltered annuity
UGMA/UTMA Uniform Gift (Transfers) to Minors Act
UIT unit investment trust
UPC Uniform Practice Code
YLD yield
YTC yield to call
YTM yield to maturity
ZR zero-coupon

Glossary

A

acceptance, waiver, and consent A process for settling a charge or complaint that is quicker and less formal than the regular complaint procedure. *Related item(s):* Code of Procedure.

account executive (AE) *See* registered representative.

accredited investor As defined in Rule 502 of Regulation D, any institution or individual meeting minimum net worth requirements for the purchase of securities qualifying under the Regulation D registration exemption.

An accredited investor is generally accepted to be one who:

- has a net worth of $1 million or more not including net equity in a primary residence; or
- has had an annual income of $200,000 or more during each of the two most recent years (or $300,000 jointly with a spouse) and who has a reasonable expectation of reaching the same income level during the current year.

accumulation stage The period during which contributions are made to an annuity account. *Related item(s):* accumulation unit; distribution stage.

accumulation unit An accounting measure used to determine an annuitant's proportionate interest in the insurer's separate account during an annuity's accumulation (deposit) stage. *Related item(s):* accumulation stage; annuity unit; separate account.

Act of 1933 *See* Securities Act of 1933.

Act of 1934 *See* Securities Exchange Act of 1934.

adjusted basis The value attributed to an asset or security that reflects any deductions taken on, or capital improvements to, the asset or security. Adjusted basis is used to compute the gain or loss on the sale or other disposition of the asset or security.

adjusted gross income (AGI) Earned income plus net passive income, portfolio income, and capital gains. *Related item(s):* tax liability.

administrator (1) A person authorized by a court of law to liquidate an intestate decedent's estate. (2) An official or agency that administers a state's securities laws.

ADR *See* American depositary receipt.

advertisement Any promotional material designed for use by newspapers, magazines, billboards, radio, television, telephone recording, or other public media where the firm has little control over the type of individuals exposed to the material. *Related item(s):* sales literature.

AE *See* registered representative.

affiliate (1) A person who directly or indirectly owns, controls, or holds with power to vote 10% or more of the outstanding voting securities of a company. (2) With respect to a direct participation program, any person who controls, is controlled by, or is under common control with the program's sponsor and includes any person who beneficially owns 50% or more of the equity interest in the sponsor. (3) Under the Investment Company Act of 1940, a person who has any type of control over an investment company's operations, which includes anyone with 5% or more of the outstanding voting securities of the investment company or any corporation of which the investment company holds 5% or more of outstanding securities. *Related item(s):* control person; insider.

agency basis *See* agency transaction.

agency issue A debt security issued by an authorized agency of the federal government. Such an issue is backed by the issuing agency itself, not by the full faith and credit of the U.S. government (except GNMA and Federal Import Export Bank issues). *Related item(s):* government security.

agency transaction A transaction in which a broker-dealer acts for the accounts of others by buying or selling securities on behalf of customers. *Syn.* agency basis. *Related item(s):* agent; broker; principal transaction.

agent (1) An individual or a firm that effects securities transactions for the accounts of others. (2) A person licensed by a state as a life insurance agent. (3) A securities salesperson who represents a broker-dealer or an issuer when selling or trying to sell securities to the investing public; this individual is considered an agent whether he actually receives or simply solicits orders. *Related item(s):* broker; broker-dealer; dealer; principal.

AGI *See* adjusted gross income.

agreement among underwriters The agreement that sets forth the terms under which each member of an underwriting syndicate will participate in a new issue offering and states the duties and responsibilities of the underwriting manager. *Related item(s):* syndicate; underwriting manager.

agreement of limited partnership The contract that establishes guidelines for the operation of a direct participation program, including the roles of the general and limited partners.

AIR *See* assumed interest rate.

all-or-none order (AON) An order that instructs the firm to execute the entire order. Firm does not have to execute immediately.

alternative order An order to execute either of two transactions—for example, placing a sell limit (above the market) and a sell stop (below the market) on the same stock. *Syn.* either/or order; one cancels other order.

American depositary receipt (ADR) A negotiable U.S. security certificate representing a given number of shares of stock in a foreign corporation. It is bought and sold in the American securities markets, just as stock is traded. *Syn.* American depositary share.

amortization (1) The paying off of debt in regular installments over a period of time. (2) The ratable deduction of certain capitalized expenditures over a specified period of time.

amortization of bond premium An accounting process whereby the initial cost of a bond purchased at a premium is decreased to reflect the basis of the bond as it approaches maturity. *Related item(s):* accretion of bond discount.

annual compliance review The annual meeting that all registered representatives and principals must attend, the purpose of which is to review compliance issues.

annuitant A person who receives an annuity contract's distribution.

annuitize To change an annuity contract from the accumulation (pay-in) stage to the distribution (pay-out) stage.

annuity A contract between an insurance company and an individual, generally guaranteeing lifetime income to the individual on whose life the contract is based in return for either a lump-sum or a periodic payment to the insurance company. The contract holder's objective is usually retirement income. *Related item(s):* deferred annuity; fixed annuity; immediate annuity; variable annuity.

annuity unit An accounting measure used to determine the amount of each payment during an annuity's distribution stage. The calculation takes into account the value of each accumulation unit and such other factors as assumed interest rate and mortality risk. *Related item(s):* accumulation unit; annuity; distribution stage.

anti-money laundering Programs developed under the Bank Secrecy Act to prevent and detect the act of "clean" money or money that has been laundered through legitimate businesses later being used for "dirty" purposes such as terrorist activities.

AON *See* all-or-none order.

AP *See* associated person of a member. appreciation The increase in an asset's value. approved plan *See* qualified retirement plan.

arbitration The arrangement whereby FINRA or a designated arbitration association hears and settles disagreements between members, member organizations, their employees, and customers.

ask An indication by a trader or a dealer of a willingness to sell a security or a commodity; the price at which an investor may buy from a broker-dealer. *Syn.* offer. *Related item(s):* bid; public offering price; quotation.

assessed value The value of a property as appraised by a taxing authority for the purpose of levying taxes.
Assessed value may equal market value or a stipulated percentage of market value. *Related item(s):* ad valorem tax.

asset (1) Anything that an individual or a corporation owns. (2) A balance sheet item expressing what a corporation owns.

asset allocation fund A mutual fund that splits its investment assets among stocks, bonds, and other vehicles in an attempt to provide a consistent return for the investor. *Related item(s):* mutual fund.

asset-backed security One whose value and income payments are backed by the expected cash flow from a specific pool of underlying assets. Pooling the assets into financial instruments allows them to be sold to investors more easily than selling them individually. This process is called securitization.

assignee A person who has acquired a beneficial interest in a limited partnership from a third party, but who is neither a substitute limited partner nor an assignee of record.

assignee of record A person who has acquired a beneficial interest in a limited partnership and whose interest has been recorded on the books of the partnership and is the subject of a written instrument of assignment.

assignment (1) A document accompanying or part of a stock certificate that is signed by the person named on the certificate for the purpose of transferring the certificate's title to another person's name. (2) The act of identifying and notifying an account holder that the option owner has exercised an option held short in that account. *Related item(s):* stock power.

associated person of a member (AP) Any employee, manager, director, officer, or partner of a member broker-dealer or another entity (e.g., issuer or bank) or any person controlling, controlled by, or in common control with that member. *Related item(s):* registered representative.

assumed interest rate (AIR) The net rate of investment return that must be credited to a variable life insurance policy to ensure that at all times the variable death benefit equals the amount of the death benefit. The AIR forms the basis for projecting payments, but it is not guaranteed.

at-the-close order *See* market-on-close order.

at-the-money The term used to describe an option when the underlying stock is trading precisely at the exercise price of the option. *Related item(s):* in-the-money; out-of-the-money.

at-the-opening order An order that specifies it is to be executed at the opening of the market of trading in that security or else it is to be canceled. The order will be executed at the opening price. *Related item(s):* market-on-close order.

auction market A market in which buyers enter competitive bids and sellers enter competitive offers simultaneously. The NYSE is an auction market. *Syn.* double auction market.

audited financial statement A financial statement of a program, a corporation, or an issuer (including the profit and loss statement, cash flow and source and application of revenues statement, and balance sheet) that has been examined and verified by an independent certified public accountant.

authorized stock The number of shares of stock that a corporation can issue. This number of shares is stipulated in the corporation's state-approved charter and may be changed by a vote of the corporation's stockholders.

authorizing resolution The document enabling a municipal or state government to issue securities. The resolution provides for the establishment of a revenue fund in which receipts or income are deposited.

automatic exercise Unless other instructions have been given, contracts that are in-the-money by a specified amount at expiration will automatically be exercised. The amount, determined by OCC, applies to both customer and institutional accounts.

average A price at a midpoint among a number of prices. Technical analysts frequently use averages as market indicators. *Related item(s):* index.

average basis An accounting method used when an investor has made multiple purchases at different prices of the same security; the method averages the purchase prices to calculate an investor's cost basis in shares being liquidated. The difference between the average cost basis and the selling price determines the investor's tax liability. *Related item(s):* first in, first out; last in, first out; share identification.

average price A step in determining a bond's yield to maturity. A bond's average price is calculated by adding its face value to the price paid for it and dividing the result by two.

B

BA *See* banker's acceptance.

back away The failure of a market maker to honor a firm bid and asked price. This violates the Conduct Rules.

back-end load A commission or sales fee that is charged when mutual fund shares or variable annuity contracts are redeemed. It declines annually, decreasing to zero over an extended holding period—up to eight years—as described in the prospectus. *Syn.* contingent-deferred sales load. *Related item(s):* front-end load.

balanced fund A mutual fund whose stated investment policy is to have at all times some portion of its investment assets in bonds and preferred stock, as well as in common stock, in an attempt to provide both growth and income. *Related item(s):* mutual fund.

balanced investment strategy A method of portfolio allocation and management aimed at balancing risk and return. A balanced portfolio may combine stocks, bonds, packaged products, and cash equivalents.

balance of payments (BOP) An international accounting record of all transactions made by one particular country with others during a certain time period; it compares the amount of foreign currency the country has taken in with the amount of its own currency it has paid out. *Related item(s):* balance of trade.

balance of trade The largest component of a country's balance of payments; it concerns the export and import of merchandise (not services). Debit items include imports, foreign aid, domestic spending abroad, and domestic investments abroad. Credit items include exports, foreign spending in the domestic economy, and foreign investments in the domestic economy. *Related item(s):* balance of payments.

balance sheet A report of a corporation's financial condition at a specific time.

balance sheet equation A formula stating that a corporation's assets equal the sum of its liabilities plus shareholders' equity.

balloon maturity A repayment schedule for an issue of bonds wherein a large number of the bonds come due at a prescribed time (normally at the final maturity date); a type of serial maturity. *Related item(s):* maturity date.

banker's acceptance (BA) A money market instrument used to finance international and domestic trade. A banker's acceptance is a check drawn on a bank by an importer or exporter of goods and represents the bank's conditional promise to pay the face amount of the note at maturity (normally less than three months).

bank guarantee letter The document supplied by a commercial bank in which the bank certifies that a put writer has sufficient funds on deposit at the bank to equal the aggregate exercise price of the put; this releases the option writer from the option margin requirement.

Bank Secrecy Act The act establishing the U.S. Treasury Department as the lead agency for developing regulation in connection with anti-money laundering programs, which require broker-dealers to establish internal compliance procedures to detect abuses.

bar chart A tool used by technical analysts to track the price movements of a commodity over several consecutive time periods. *Related item(s):* moving average chart; point-and-figure chart.

basis point A measure of a bond's yield, equal to 1/100 of 1% of yield. A bond whose yield increases from 5.0% to 5.5% is said to increase by 50 basis points. *Related item(s):* point.

basis quote The price of a security quoted in terms of the yield that the purchaser may expect to receive.

BD *See* broker-dealer.

bear An investor who acts on the belief that a security or the market is falling or will fall. *Related item(s):* bull.

bearer bond *See* coupon bond.

bear market A market in which prices of a certain group of securities are falling or are expected to fall. *See* bull market.

best efforts underwriting A new issue securities underwriting in which the underwriter acts as an agent for the issuer and puts forth its best efforts to sell as many shares as possible. The underwriter has no liability for unsold shares, unlike in a firm commitment underwriting. *Related item(s):* underwriting.

bid An indication by an investor, trader, or dealer of a willingness to buy a security; the price at which an investor may sell to a broker-dealer. *Related item(s):* offer; public offering price; quotation.

block trade In general, 10,000 shares of stock would be considered a block trade.

blue-chip stock The equity issues of financially stable, well-established companies that have demonstrated their ability to pay dividends in both good and bad times.

blue sky To register a securities offering in a particular state. *Related item(s):* blue-sky laws; registration by coordination; registration by filing; registration by qualification.

blue-sky laws The nickname for state regulations governing the securities industry. The term was coined in the early 1900s by a Kansas Supreme Court justice who wanted regulation to protect against "speculative schemes that have no more basis than so many feet of blue sky." *Related item(s):* Series 63; Uniform Securities Act.

board of directors (1) Individuals elected by stockholders to establish corporate management policies. A board of directors decides, among other issues, if and when dividends will be paid to stockholders. (2) The body that governs the NYSE. It is composed of 20 members elected by the NYSE general membership for a term of two years.

bona fide uote An offer from a broker-dealer to buy or sell securities. It indicates a willingness to execute a trade under the terms and conditions accompanying the quote. *Related item(s):* firm quote; nominal quote.

bond An issuing company's or government's legal obligation to repay the principal of a loan to bond investors at a specified future date. Bonds are usually issued with par, or face, values of $1,000, representing the amount of money borrowed. The issuer promises to pay a percentage of the par value as interest on the borrowed funds. The interest payment is stated on the face of the bond at issue.

bond counsel An attorney retained by a municipal issuer to give an opinion concerning the legality and tax-exempt status of a municipal issue. *Syn.* bond attorney. *Related item(s):* legal opinion of counsel.

bond fund A mutual fund whose investment objective is to provide stable income with minimal capital risk. It invests in income-producing instruments, which may include corporate, government, or municipal bonds. *Related item(s):* mutual fund.

bond quote One of a number of quotations listed in the financial press and most daily newspapers that provide representative bid prices from the previous day's bond market. Quotes for corporate and government bonds are percentages of the bonds' face values (usually $1,000). Corporate bonds are quoted in increments of 1/8, where a quote of 99 1/8 represents 99.125% of par ($1,000), or $991.25. Government bonds are quoted in 32nds. Municipal bonds may be quoted on a dollar basis or on a yield-to-maturity basis. *Related item(s):* quotation; stock quote.

bond rating An evaluation of the possibility of a bond issuer's default, based on an analysis of the issuer's financial condition and profit potential. Standard & Poor's, Moody's Investors Service, and Fitch Investors Service, among others, provide bond rating services.

bond ratio One of several tools used by bond analysts to assess the degree of safety offered by a corporation's bonds. It measures the percentage of the corporation's capitalization that is provided by long-term debt financing, calculated by dividing the total face value of the outstanding bonds by the total capitalization. *Syn.* debt ratio.

bond swap The sale of a bond and the simultaneous purchase of a different bond in a like amount. The technique is used to control tax liability, extend maturity, or update investment objectives. *Syn.* tax swap. *Related item(s):* wash sale.

bond yield The annual rate of return on a bond investment. Types of yield include nominal yield, current yield, yield to maturity, and yield to call. Their relationships vary according to whether the bond in question is at a discount, a premium, or at par. *Related item(s):* current yield; nominal yield.

book-entry security A security sold without delivery of a certificate. Evidence of ownership is maintained on records kept by a central agency; for example, the Treasury keeps records of Treasury bill purchasers. Transfer of ownership is recorded by entering the change on the books or electronic files. *Related item(s):* coupon bond; registered; registered as to principal only.

book value per share A measure of the net worth of each share of common stock. It is calculated by subtracting intangible assets and preferred stock from total net worth, then dividing the result by the number of shares of common outstanding. *Syn.* net tangible assets per share.

branch office Any location identified by any means to the public as a place where a registered broker-dealer conducts business.

breakeven point The point at which gains equal losses.

breakpoint The schedule of sales charge discounts mutual fund offers for lump-sum or cumulative investments.

breakpoint sale The sale of mutual fund shares in an amount just below the level at which the purchaser would qualify for reduced sales charges. This violates the Conduct Rules.

broad-based index An index designed to reflect the movement of the market as a whole. Examples include the S&P 100, the S&P 500, the Major Market Index, and the Value Line Composite Index. *Related item(s):* index.

broker (1) An individual or a firm that charges a fee or commission for executing buy and sell orders submitted by another individual or firm. (2) The role of a firm when it acts as an agent for a customer and charges the customer a commission for its services. *Related item(s):* agent; broker-dealer; dealer.

broker-dealer (BD) A person or firm in the business of buying and selling securities. A firm may act as both broker (agent) and dealer (principal), but not in the same transaction. Broker-dealers normally must register with the SEC, the appropriate SROs, and any state in which they do business. *Related item(s):* agent; broker; dealer; principal.

broker's loan Money loaned to a brokerage firm by a commercial bank or other lending institution for financing customers' margin account debit balances. *Related item(s):* call loan; rehypothecation.

bull An investor who acts on the belief that a security or the market is rising or will rise. *Related item(s):* bear.

bull market A market in which prices of a certain group of securities are rising or will rise. *Related item(s):* bear market.

business cycle A predictable long-term pattern of alternating periods of economic growth and decline. The cycle passes through four stages: expansion, peak, contraction, and trough.

business day A day on which financial markets are open for trading. Saturdays, Sundays, and legal holidays are not considered business days.

buyer's option A settlement contract that calls for delivery and payment according to a number of days specified by the buyer. *Related item(s):* regular way; seller's option.

buy-in The procedure that the buyer of a security follows when the seller fails to complete the contract by delivering the security. The buyer closes the contract by buying the security in the open market and charging the account of the seller for transaction fees and any loss caused by changes in the markets. *Related item(s):* sell-out.

buying power The amount of fully margined securities that a margin client may purchase using only the cash, securities, and special memorandum account balance and without depositing additional equity.

buy stop order An order to buy a security that is entered at a price above the current offering price and that is triggered when the market price touches or goes through the buy stop price.

C

call (1) An option contract giving the owner the right to buy a specified amount of an underlying security at a specified price within a specified time. (2) The act of exercising a call option. *Related item(s):* put.

callable bond A type of bond issued with a provision allowing the issuer to redeem the bond before maturity at a predetermined price. *Related item(s):* call price.

callable preferred stock A type of preferred stock issued with a provision allowing the corporation to call in the stock at a certain price and retire it. *Related item(s):* call price; preferred stock.

call buyer An investor who pays a premium for an option contract and receives, for a specified time, the right to buy the underlying security at a specified price. *Related item(s):* call writer; put buyer; put writer.

call date The date, specified in the prospectus of every callable security, after which the security's issuer has the option to redeem the issue at par or at par plus a premium.

call feature *See* call provision.

call loan A collateralized loan of a brokerage firm having no maturity date that may be called (terminated) at any time. The loan has a fluctuating interest rate that is recomputed daily. Generally, the loan is payable on demand the day after it is contracted. If not called, the loan is automatically renewed for another day. *Related item(s):* broker's loan.

call loan rate The rate of interest a brokerage firm charges its margin account clients on their debit balances.

call price The price, usually a premium over the issue's par value, at which preferred stocks or bonds may be redeemed before an issue's maturity.

call protection A provision in a bond indenture stating that the issue is noncallable for a certain period of time (e.g., 5 years or 10 years) after the original issue date. *Related item(s):* call provision.

call provision The written agreement between an issuing corporation and its bondholders or preferred stockholders giving the corporation the option to redeem its senior securities at a specified price before maturity and under certain conditions. *Syn.* call feature.

call risk The potential for a bond to be called before maturity, leaving the investor without the bond's current income. Because this is more likely to occur during times of falling interest rates, the investor may not be able to reinvest the principal at a comparable rate of return.

call writer An investor who receives a premium and takes on, for a specified time, the obligation to sell the underlying security at a specified price at the call buyer's discretion. *Related item(s)*: call buyer; put buyer; put writer.

capital Accumulated money or goods available for use in producing more money or goods.

capital appreciation A rise in an asset's market price.

capital asset All tangible property, including securities, real estate, and other property, held for the long term.

capital contribution The amount of a participant's investment in a direct participation program, not including units purchased by the sponsors.

capital gain The profit realized when a capital asset is sold for a higher price than the purchase price. *Related item(s)*: capital loss; long-term gain.

capitalization The sum of a corporation's long-term debt, stock, and surpluses. *Syn.* invested capital. *Related item(s)*: capital structure.

capital loss The loss incurred when a capital asset is sold for a lower price than the purchase price. *Related item(s)*: capital gain; long-term loss.

capital market The segment of the securities market that deals in instruments with more than one year to maturity—that is, long-term debt and equity securities.

capital risk The potential for an investor to lose all money invested owing to circumstances unrelated to an issuer's financial strength. For example, derivative instruments such as options carry risk independent of the underlying securities' changing value. *Related item(s)*: derivative.

capital stock All of a corporation's outstanding preferred stock and common stock listed at par value.

capital structure The composition of long-term funds (equity and debt) a corporation has as a source for financing. *Related item(s)*: capitalization.

capital surplus The money a corporation receives in excess of the stated value of stock at the time of first sale. *Syn.* paid-in capital; paid-in surplus. *Related item(s)*: par.

capping Placing selling pressure on a stock in an attempt to keep its price low or to move its price lower; this violates the Conduct Rules.

carried interest A sharing arrangement in an oil and gas direct participation program whereby the general partner shares the tangible drilling costs with the limited partners but pays no part of the intangible drilling costs. *Related item(s)*: sharing arrangement.

cash account An account in which the customer is required by the SEC's Regulation T to pay in full for securities purchased not later than two days after the standard payment period set by the Uniform Practice Code. *Syn.* special cash account.

cash dividend Money paid to a corporation's stockholders out of the corporation's current earnings or accumulated profits. The board of directors must declare all dividends.

cash equivalent A security that may be readily converted into cash. Examples include Treasury bills, certificates of deposit, and money market instruments and funds.

cash flow The money received by a business minus the money paid out. Cash flow is also equal to net income plus depreciation or depletion.

cashiering department The department within a brokerage firm that delivers securities and money to and receives securities and money from other firms and clients of the brokerage firm. *Syn.* security cage.

cash trade *See* cash transaction.

cash transaction A settlement contract that calls for delivery and payment on the same day the trade is executed. Payment is due by 2:30 pm ET or within 30 minutes of the trade if it occurs after 2:00 pm ET. *Syn.* cash trade. *Related item(s)*: regular way; settlement date.

CBOE *See* Chicago Board Options Exchange.

CD *See* negotiable certificate of deposit.

certificate of deposit (CD) *See* negotiable certificate of deposit.

CHB *See* commission house broker.

Chicago Board Options Exchange (CBOE) The self-regulatory organization with jurisdiction over all writing and trading of standardized options and related contracts listed on that exchange. Also, the first national securities exchange for the trading of listed options.

Chicago Stock Exchange (CHX) Regional exchange that provides a listed market for smaller businesses and new enterprises. In 1949, the exchange merged with the St. Louis, Cleveland, and Minneapolis/St. Paul exchanges to form the Midwest Stock Exchange, but in 1993, the original name was reinstated. *Related item(s)*: regional exchange.

churning Excessive trading in a customer's account by a registered representative who ignores the customer's interests and seeks only to increase commissions. This violates the Conduct Rules. *Syn.* overtrading.

class Options of the same type (i.e., all calls or all puts) on the same underlying security. *Related item(s)*: series; type.

Class A share A class of mutual fund share issued with a front-end sales load. A mutual fund offers different classes of shares to allow investors to choose the type of sales charge they will pay. *Related item(s):* Class B share; Class C share; Class D share; front-end load.

Class B share A class of mutual fund share issued with a back-end load. A mutual fund offers different classes of shares to allow investors to choose the type of sales charge they will pay. *Related item(s):* back-end load; Class A share; Class C share; Class D share.

Class C share A class of mutual fund share issued with a level load. A mutual fund offers different classes of shares to allow investors to choose the type of sales charge they will pay. *Related item(s):* Class A share; Class B share; Class D share; level load.

Class D share A class of mutual fund share issued with both a level load and a back-end load. A mutual fund offers different classes of shares to allow investors to choose the type of sales charge they will pay. *Related item(s):* back-end load; Class A share; Class B share; Class C share; level load.

clearing agency An intermediary between the buy and sell sides in a securities transaction that receives and delivers payments and securities. Any organization that fills this function, including a securities depository but not including a Federal Reserve Bank, is considered a clearing agency.

clearing broker-dealer A broker-dealer that clears its own trades as well as those of introducing brokers. A clearing broker-dealer may hold customers' securities and cash. *Syn.* carrying broker.

close The price of the last transaction for a particular security on a particular day.

closed-end investment company An investment company that issues a fixed number of shares in an actively-managed portfolio of securities. The shares may be of several classes; they are traded in the secondary marketplace, either on an exchange or over the counter. The market price of the shares is determined by supply and demand and not by net asset value. *Syn.* publicly traded fund. *Related item(s):* dual-purpose fund; mutual fund.

closed-end management company An investment company that issues a fixed number of shares in an actively-managed portfolio of securities. The shares may be of several classes; they are traded in the secondary marketplace, either on an exchange or over the counter. The shares' market price is determined by supply and demand, not by net asset value. *Syn.* publicly traded fund. *Related item(s):* dual-purpose fund.

closing date The date designated by the general partners in a direct participation program as the date when sales of units in the program cease; typically the offering period extends for one year.

closing purchase An options transaction in which the seller buys back an option in the same series; the two transactions effectively cancel each other out, and

the position is liquidated. *Related item(s):* closing sale; opening purchase.

closing range The relatively narrow range of prices at which transactions take place during the final minutes of the trading day. *Related item(s):* close.

closing sale An options transaction in which the buyer sells an option in the same series; the two transactions effectively cancel each other out, and the position is liquidated. *Related item(s):* closing purchase; opening sale.

CMO *See* collateralized mortgage obligation.

CMV *See* current market value.

Code of Arbitration Procedure The formal method of handling securities-related disputes or clearing controversies between members, public customers, clearing corporations, or clearing banks. Any claim, dispute, or controversy between member firms or associated persons must be submitted to arbitration.

Code of Procedure (COP) The formal procedure for handling trade practice complaints involving violations of the Conduct Rules. The Department of Enforcement (DOE) is the first body to hear and judge complaints.

The National Adjudicatory Council handles appeals and review of DOE decisions.

coincident indicator A measurable economic factor that varies directly and simultaneously with the business cycle, thus indicating the current state of the economy. Examples include nonagricultural employment, personal income, and industrial production. *Related item(s):* lagging indicator; leading indicator.

collateral Certain assets set aside and pledged to a lender for the duration of a loan. If the borrower fails to meet obligations to pay principal or interest, the lender has claim to the assets.

collateralized mortgage obligation (CMO) A mortgage-backed corporate security. Unlike pass-through obligations issued by FNMA and GNMA, its yield is not guaranteed, and it does not have the federal government's backing. These issues attempt to return interest and principal at a predetermined rate.

collection ratio (1) For corporations, a rough measure of the length of time accounts receivable have been outstanding. It is calculated by multiplying the receivables by 360 and dividing the result by net sales. (2) For municipal bonds, a means of detecting deteriorating credit conditions; it is calculated by dividing taxes collected by taxes assessed.

combination fund An equity mutual fund that attempts to combine the objectives of growth and current yield by dividing its portfolio between companies that show long-term growth potential and companies that pay high dividends. *Related item(s):* mutual fund.

combined account A customer account that has cash and long and short margin positions in different securities. *Syn.* mixed account.

commercial bank An institution that is in the business of accepting deposits and making business loans. Commercial banks may not underwrite corporate securities or most municipal bonds. *Related item(s):* investment banker.

commercial paper An unsecured, short-term promissory note issued by a corporation for financing accounts receivable and inventories. It is usually issued at a discount reflecting prevailing market interest rates. Maturities range up to 270 days.

commingling (1) The combining by a brokerage firm of one customer's securities with another customer's securities and pledging them as joint collateral for a bank loan; unless authorized by the customers, this violates SEC Rule 15c2-1. (2) The combining by a brokerage firm of customer securities with firm securities and pledging them as joint collateral for a bank loan; this practice is prohibited.

commission A service charge an agent assesses in return for arranging a security's purchase or sale. A commission must be fair and reasonable, considering all the relevant factors of the transaction. *Syn.* sales charge. *Related item(s):* markup.

commissioner The state official with jurisdiction over insurance transactions.

commission house broker (CHB) A member of an exchange who is eligible to execute orders for customers of a member firm on the floor of the exchange. *Syn.* floor broker.

Committee on Uniform Securities Identification Procedures (CUSIP) A committee that assigns identification numbers and codes to all securities to be used when recording all buy and sell orders.

common stock A security that represents ownership in a corporation. Holders of common stock exercise control by electing a board of directors and voting on corporate policy. *Related item(s):* equity; preferred stock.

communications with the public FINRA categorizes public communications into three categories: retail, institutional, and correspondence. *See* retail communications, institutional communications, and correspondence.

compliance department The department within a brokerage firm that oversees the firm's trading and market-making activities. It ensures that the firm's employees and officers abide by the rules and regulations of the SEC, exchanges, and SROs.

Conduct Rules Regulations designed to ensure that FINRA member firms and their representatives follow fair and ethical trade practices when dealing with the public. The rules complement and broaden the Securities Act of 1933, the Securities Exchange Act of 1934, and the Investment Company Act of 1940.

conduit theory A means for an investment company to avoid taxation on net investment income distributed to shareholders. If a mutual fund acts as a conduit for the distribution of net investment income, it may qualify as a regulated investment company and be taxed only on the income the fund retains. *Syn.* pipeline theory.

confirmation A printed document that states the trade date, settlement date, and money due from or owed to a customer. It is sent or given to the customer on or before the settlement date. *Related item(s):* duplicate confirmation.

constructive receipt The date on which the Internal Revenue Service considers that a taxpayer receives dividends or other income.

Consumer Price Index (CPI) A measure of price changes in consumer goods and services used to identify periods of inflation or deflation.

consumption A term used by Keynesian economists to refer to the purchase by household units of newly produced goods and services.

contemporaneous trader A person who enters a trade at or near the same time and in the same security as a person who has inside information. The contemporaneous trader may bring suit against the inside trader. *Related item(s):* Insider Trading and Securities Fraud Enforcement Act of 1988.

contingent deferred sales load *See* back-end load.

contingent order An order that is conditional upon the execution of a previous order and that will be executed only after the first order is filled.

contra broker The broker on the buy side of a sell order or on the sell side of a buy order.

contraction A period of general economic decline—one of the business cycle's four stages. *Related item(s):* business cycle.

contractionary policy A monetary policy that decreases the money supply, usually with the intention of raising interest rates and combating inflation.

control (controlling, controlled by, under common control with) The power to direct or affect the direction of a company's management and policies, whether through the ownership of voting securities, by contract, or otherwise. Control is presumed to exist if a person, directly or indirectly, owns, controls, holds with the power to vote, or holds proxies representing at least 10% of a company's voting securities.

control person (1) A director, an officer, or another affiliate of an issuer. (2) A stockholder who owns at least 10% of any class of a corporation's outstanding securities. *Related item(s):* affiliate; insider.

control security Any security owned by a director, an officer, or another affiliate of the issuer or by a stockholder who owns at least 10% of any class of a corporation's outstanding securities. Who owns a security, not the security itself, determines whether it is a control security.

conversion parity Two securities, one of which may be converted into the other, of equal dollar value. A convertible security holder can calculate parity to help decide whether converting would lead to gain or loss.

conversion price The dollar amount of a convertible security's par value that is exchangeable for one share of common stock.

conversion privilege A feature the issuer adds to a security that allows the holder to change the security into shares of common stock. This makes the security attractive to investors and, therefore, more marketable. *Related item(s):* convertible bond; convertible preferred stock.

conversion rate *See* conversion ratio.

conversion ratio The number of shares of common stock per par value amount that the holder would receive for converting a convertible bond or preferred share. *Syn.* conversion rate.

conversion value The total market value of common stock into which a senior security is convertible.

convertible bond A debt security, usually in the form of a debenture, that may be exchanged for equity securities of the issuing corporation at specified prices or rates. *Related item(s):* debenture.

convertible preferred stock An equity security that may be exchanged for common stock at specified prices or rates. Dividends may be cumulative or noncumulative. *Related item(s):* cumulative preferred stock; noncumulative preferred stock; preferred stock.

cooling-off period The period (a minimum of 20 days) between a registration statement's filing date and the registration's effective date. In practice, the period varies in length.

COP *See* Code of Procedure.

corporate account An account held in a corporation's name. The corporate agreement, signed when the account is opened, specifies which officers are authorized to trade in the account. In addition to standard margin account documents, a corporation must provide a copy of its charter and bylaws authorizing a margin account.

corporate bond A debt security issued by a corporation. A corporate bond typically has a par value of $1,000, is taxable, has a term maturity, and is traded on a major exchange.

corporation The most common form of business organization, in which the organization's total worth is divided into shares of stock, each share representing a unit of ownership. A corporation is characterized by a continuous life span and its owners' limited liability.

correspondence FINRA defines this category of communications with the public as any written (including electronic) communication that is distributed or made available to 25 or fewer retail investors within any 30-calendar-day period.

cost basis The price paid for an asset, including any commissions or fees, used to calculate capital gains or losses when the asset is sold.

coterminous A term used to describe municipal entities that share the same boundaries. For example, a municipality's school district and fire district may issue debt separately although the debt is backed by revenues from the same taxpayers. *Related item(s):* overlapping debt.

coupon bond A debt obligation with attached coupons representing semiannual interest payments. The holder submits the coupons to the trustee to receive the interest payments. The issuer keeps no record of the purchaser, and the purchaser's name is not printed on the certificate. *Syn.* bearer bond. *Related item(s):* book-entry security; registered; registered as to principal only.

coupon yield *See* nominal yield.

covenant A component of a debt issue's trust indenture that identifies bondholders' rights and other provisions. Examples include rate covenants that establish a minimum revenue coverage for a bond; insurance covenants that require insurance on a project; and maintenance covenants that require maintenance on a facility constructed by the proceeds of a bond issue.

covered call writer An investor who sells a call option while owning the underlying security or some other asset that guarantees the ability to deliver if the call is exercised.

covered put writer An investor who sells a put option while owning an asset that guarantees the ability to pay if the put is exercised (e.g., cash in the account).

CPI *See* Consumer Price Index.

CR *See* credit balance.

credit agreement A component of a customer's margin account agreement, outlining the conditions of the credit arrangement between broker and customer.

credit balance (CR) The amount of money remaining in a customer's account after all commitments have been paid in full. *Syn.* credit record; credit register. *Related item(s):* debit balance.

credit department *See* margin department.

creditor Any broker or dealer, member of a national securities exchange, or person associated with a broker-dealer involved in extending credit to customers.

credit risk The degree of probability that a bond's issuer will default in the payment of either principal or interest. *Syn.* default risk; financial risk.

CTR *See* currency transaction report.

cum rights A term describing stock trading with rights. *Related item(s):* ex-rights.

cumulative preferred stock An equity security that offers the holder any unpaid dividends in arrears. These dividends accumulate and must be paid to the cumulative preferred stockholder before any dividends may be paid to the common stockholders. *Related item(s):* convertible preferred stock; noncumulative preferred stock; preferred stock.

cumulative voting A voting procedure that permits stockholders either to cast all of their votes for any one candidate or to cast their total number of votes in any proportion they choose. This results in greater representation for minority stockholders. *Related item(s):* statutory voting.

currency transaction report (CTR) A report filed by financial institutions to the IRS for deposits of any currency on a single day of more than $10,000.

current assets Cash and other assets that are expected to be converted into cash within the next 12 months. Examples include such liquid items as cash and equivalents, accounts receivable, inventory, and prepaid expenses.

current liabilities A corporation's debt obligations due for payment within the next 12 months. Examples include accounts payable, accrued wages payable, and current long-term debt.

current market value (CMV) The worth of the securities in an account. The market value of listed securities is based on the closing prices on the previous business day. *Syn.* long market value. *Related item(s):* market value.

current price *See* public offering price.

current ratio A measure of a corporation's liquidity; that is, its ability to transfer assets into cash to meet current short-term obligations. It is calculated by dividing total current assets by total current liabilities. *Syn.* working capital ratio.

current yield The annual rate of return on a security, calculated by dividing the interest or dividends paid by the security's current market price. *Related item(s):* bond yield.

CUSIP *See* Committee on Uniform Securities Identification Procedures.

custodial account An account in which a custodian enters trades on behalf of the beneficial owner, often a minor. *Related item(s):* custodian.

custodian An institution or a person responsible for making all investment, management, and distribution decisions in an account maintained in the best interests of another. Mutual funds have custodians responsible for safeguarding certificates and performing clerical duties. *Related item(s):* mutual fund custodian.

customer Any person who opens a trading account with a broker-dealer. A customer may be classified in terms of account ownership, trading authorization, payment method, or types of securities traded.

customer agreement A document that a customer must sign when opening a margin account with a broker-dealer; it allows the firm to liquidate all or a portion of the account if the customer fails to meet a margin call.

customer ledger The accounting record that lists separately all customer cash and margin accounts carried by a firm.

customer statement A document showing a customer's trading activity, positions, and account balance. The SEC requires that customer statements be sent quarterly, but customers generally receive them monthly.

cyclical industry A fundamental analysis term for an industry that is sensitive to the business cycle and price changes. Most cyclical industries produce durable goods, such as raw materials and heavy equipment.

D

dated date The date on which interest on a new bond issue begins to accrue.

day order An order that is valid only until the close of trading on the day it is entered; if it is not executed by the close of trading, it is canceled.

day trader A trader in securities who opens all positions after the opening of the market and offsets or closes out all positions before the close of the market on the same day.

dealer (1) An individual or a firm engaged in the business of buying and selling securities for its own account, either directly or through a broker. (2) The role of a firm when it acts as a principal and charges the customer a markup or markdown. *Syn.* principal. *Related item(s):* broker; broker-dealer.

dealer paper Short-term, unsecured promissory notes that the issuer sells through a dealer rather than directly to the public.

debenture A debt obligation backed by the issuing corporation's general credit. *Syn.* unsecured bond.

debit balance (DR) The amount of money a customer owes a brokerage firm. *Syn.* debit record; debit register. *Related item(s):* credit balance.

debit register *See* debit balance.

debt financing Raising money for working capital or for capital expenditures by selling bonds, bills, or notes to individual or institutional investors. In return for the money lent, the investors become creditors and receive the issuer's promise to repay principal and interest on the debt. *Related item(s):* equity financing.

debt security A security representing an investor's loan to an issuer such as a corporation, a municipality, the federal government, or a federal agency. In return for the loan, the issuer promises to repay the debt on a specified date and to pay interest. *Related item(s):* equity security.

debt service The schedule for repayment of interest and principal (or the scheduled sinking fund contribution) on an outstanding debt. *Related item(s):* sinking fund.

debt-to-equity ratio The ratio of total long-term debt to total stockholders' equity; it is used to measure leverage.

declaration date The date on which a corporation announces an upcoming dividend's amount, payment date, and record date.

default The failure to pay interest or principal promptly when due.

default risk *See* credit risk.

defensive investment strategy A method of portfolio allocation and management aimed at minimizing the risk of losing principal. Defensive investors place a high percentage of their investable assets in bonds, cash equivalents, and stocks that are less volatile than average.

deferred annuity An annuity contract that delays payment of income, installments, or a lump sum until the investor elects to receive it. *Related item(s):* annuity.

deferred compensation plan A nonqualified retirement plan whereby the employee defers receiving current compensation in favor of a larger payout at retirement (or in the case of disability or death).

deficiency letter The SEC's notification of additions or corrections that a prospective issuer must make to a registration statement before the SEC will clear the offering for distribution. *Syn.* bedbug letter.

defined benefit plan A qualified retirement plan that specifies the total amount of money that the employee will receive at retirement.

defined contribution plan A qualified retirement plan that specifies the amount of money that the employer will contribute annually to the plan.

deflation A persistent and measurable fall in the general level of prices. *Related item(s):* inflation.

delivery The change in ownership or in control of a security in exchange for cash. Delivery takes place on the settlement date.

demand A consumer's desire and willingness to pay for a good or service. *Related item(s):* supply.

demand deposit A sum of money left with a bank (or borrowed from a bank and left on deposit) that the depositing customer has the right to withdraw immediately. *Related item(s):* time deposit.

depletion A tax deduction that compensates a business for the decreasing supply of the natural resource that provides its income (oil, gas, coal, gold, or other nonrenewable resource). There are two ways to calculate depletion: cost depletion and percentage depletion. *Related item(s):* cost depletion; percentage depletion.

depreciation (1) A tax deduction that compensates a business for the cost of certain tangible assets. (2) A decrease in the value of a particular currency relative to other currencies.

depreciation expense A bookkeeping entry of a noncash expense charged against earnings to recover the cost of an asset over its useful life.

depression A prolonged period of general economic decline.

derivative An investment vehicle, the value of which is based on another security's value. Futures contracts, forward contracts, and options are among the most common types of derivatives. Institutional investors generally use derivatives to increase overall portfolio return or to hedge portfolio risk.

designated market maker (DMM) Previously known as specialists, they are exchange members who are assigned to securities on the trading floor and are charged with keeping a fair and orderly market in those securities while providing liquidity to the marketplace.

devaluation A substantial fall in a currency's value, compared with the value of gold or to the value of another country's currency.

developmental drilling program A limited partnership that drills for oil, gas, or minerals in areas of proven reserves or near existing fields. *Related item(s):* exploratory drilling program; income program; step-out well.

dilution A reduction in earnings per share of common stock. Dilution occurs through the issuance of additional shares of common stock and the conversion of convertible securities.

direct participation program (DPP) A business organized so as to pass all income, gains, losses, and tax benefits to its owners, the investors; the business is usually structured as a limited partnership. Examples include oil and gas programs, real estate programs, agricultural programs, cattle programs, condominium securities, and Subchapter S corporate offerings. *Syn.* program.

discount The difference between the lower price paid for a security and the security's face amount at issue.

discount bond A bond that sells at a lower price than its face value. *Related item(s):* par.

discount rate The interest rate charged by the 12 Federal Reserve Banks for short-term loans made to member banks.

discretion The authority given to someone other than an account's beneficial owner to make investment decisions for the account concerning the security, the number of shares or units, and whether to buy or sell. The authority to decide only timing or price does not constitute discretion. *Related item(s):* limited power of attorney.

discretionary account An account in which the customer has given the registered representative authority to enter transactions at the representative's discretion.

disposable income (DI) The sum that people divide between spending and personal savings. *Related item(s):* personal income.

disproportionate sharing A sharing arrangement whereby the sponsor in an oil and gas direct participation program pays a portion of the program's costs but receives a disproportionately higher percentage of its revenues. *Related item(s):* sharing arrangement.

distribution Any cash or other property distributed to shareholders or general partners that arises from their interests in the business, investment company, or partnership.

distribution stage The period during which an individual receives distributions from an annuity account. *Syn.* payout stage. *Related item(s):* accumulation stage; accumulation unit.

diversification A risk management technique that mixes a wide variety of investments within a portfolio, thus minimizing the impact of any one security on overall portfolio performance.

diversified common stock fund A mutual fund that invests its assets in a wide range of common stocks. The fund's objectives may be growth, income, or a combination of both. *Related item(s):* growth fund; mutual fund.

diversified investment company As defined by the Investment Company Act of 1940, an investment company that meets certain standards as to the percentage of assets invested. These companies use diversification to manage risk. *Related item(s):* management company; nondiversified investment company; 75-5-10 test.

diversified management company As defined by the Investment Company Act of 1940, a management company that meets certain standards for percentage of assets invested. These companies use diversification to manage risk. *Related item(s):* management company; 75-5-10 test.

dividend A distribution of a corporation's earnings. Dividends may be in the form of cash, stock, or property. The board of directors must declare all dividends. *Syn.* stock dividend. *Related item(s):* cash dividend; dividend yield; property dividend.

dividend department The department within a brokerage firm that is responsible for crediting client accounts with dividends and interest payments on client securities held in the firm's name.

dividend disbursing agent (DDA) The person responsible for making the required dividend distributions to the broker-dealer's dividend department.

dividend payout ratio A measure of a corporation's policy of paying cash dividends, calculated by dividing the dividends paid on common stock by the net income available for common stockholders. The ratio is the complement of the retained earnings ratio.

dividends per share The dollar amount of cash dividends paid on each common share during one year.

dividend yield The annual rate of return on a common or preferred stock investment. The yield is calculated by dividing the annual dividend by the stock's purchase price. *Related item(s):* current yield; dividend.

DJIA *See* Dow Jones Industrial Average.

dollar cost averaging A system of buying mutual fund shares in fixed dollar amounts at regular fixed intervals, regardless of the share's price. The investor purchases more shares when prices are low and fewer shares when prices are high, thus lowering the average cost per share over time.

donor A person who makes a gift of money or securities to another. Once the gift is donated, the donor gives up all rights to it. Gifts of securities to minors under the Uniform Gifts to Minors Act provide tax advantages to the donor. *Related item(s):* Uniform Gifts to Minors Act.

don't know (DK) A response to a confirmation received from a broker-dealer indicating a lack of information about, or record of, the transaction.

Dow Jones averages The most widely quoted and oldest measures of change in stock prices. Each of the four averages is based on the prices of a limited number of stocks in a particular category. *Related item(s):* average; Dow Jones Industrial Average.

Dow Jones Composite Average (DJCA) A market indicator composed of the 65 stocks that make up the Dow Jones Industrial, Transportation, and Utilities Averages. *Related item(s):* average; Dow Jones Industrial Average; Dow Jones Transportation Average; Dow Jones Utilities Average.

Dow Jones Industrial Average (DJIA) The most widely used market indicator, composed of 30 large, actively traded issues of industrial stocks. *Related item(s):* average.

Dow Jones Transportation Average (DJTA) A market indicator composed of 20 transportation stocks. *Related item(s):* average; Dow Jones Composite Average; Dow Jones Industrial Average; Dow Jones Utilities Average.

Dow Jones Utilities Average (DJUA) A market indicator composed of 15 utilities stocks. *Related item(s):* average; Dow Jones Composite Average; Dow Jones Industrial Average; Dow Jones Transportation Average.

down tick *See* minus tick.

DPP *See* direct participation program.

DR *See* debit balance.

due bill A printed statement showing the obligation of a seller to deliver securities or rights to the purchaser. A due bill is also used as a pledge to deliver dividends when the transaction occurs after the record date.

due diligence The careful investigation by the underwriters that is necessary to ensure that all material information pertinent to an issue has been disclosed to prospective investors.

duplicate confirmation A copy of a customer's confirmation that a brokerage firm sends to an agent or an attorney if the customer requests it in writing. In addition, if the customer is an employee of another broker-dealer, SRO regulations may require a duplicate confirmation to be sent to the employing broker-dealer. *Related item(s):* confirmation.

E

earned income Income derived from active participation in a trade or business, including wages, salary, tips, commissions, and bonuses. *Related item(s):* portfolio income; unearned income.

earnings per share (EPS) A corporation's net income available for common stock divided by its number of shares of common stock outstanding. *Syn.* primary earnings per share.

earnings per share fully diluted A corporation's earnings per share calculated by assuming that all convertible securities have been converted. *Related item(s):* earnings per share.

economic risk The potential for international developments and domestic events to trigger losses in securities investments.

effective date The date the registration of an issue of securities becomes effective, allowing the underwriters to sell the newly issued securities to the public and to confirm sales to investors who have given indications of interest.

Employee Retirement Income Security Act of 1974 (ERISA) The law that governs the operation of most corporate pension and benefit plans. The law eased pension eligibility rules, set up the Pension Benefit Guaranty Corporation, and established guidelines for the management of pension funds. Corporate retirement plans established under ERISA qualify for favorable tax treatment for employers and participants. *Syn.* Pension Reform Act.

endorsement The signature on the back of a stock or bond certificate by the person named on the certificate as the owner. An owner must endorse certificates when transferring them to another person. *Related item(s):* assignment.

EPS *See* earnings per share.

EQ *See* equity.

equipment-leasing limited partnership A direct participation program that purchases equipment for leasing to other businesses on a long-term basis. Tax-sheltered income is the primary objective of such a partnership.

equipment trust certificate A debt obligation backed by equipment. The title to the equipment is held by an independent trustee (usually a bank), not the issuing company. Equipment trust certificates are generally issued by transportation companies such as railroads. *Syn.* equipment bond; equipment note.

equity (EQ) Common and preferred stockholders' ownership interests in a corporation. *Related item(s):* common stock; preferred stock.

equity financing Raising money for working capital or for capital expenditures by selling common or preferred stock to individual or institutional investors.

In return for the money paid, the investors receive ownership interests in the corporation. *Related item(s):* debt financing.

equity option A security representing the right to buy or sell common stock at a specified price within a specified time. *Related item(s):* option.

equity security A security representing ownership in a corporation or another enterprise. Examples of equity securities include:

- common and preferred stock; and

- put and call options on equity securities.

ERISA *See* Employee Retirement Income Security Act of 1974.

escrow agreement The certificate provided by an approved bank that guarantees that the indicated securities are on deposit at that bank. An investor who writes a call option and can present an escrow agreement is considered covered and does not need to meet margin requirements.

eurobond A long-term debt instrument of a government or corporation that is denominated in the currency of the issuer's country but is issued and sold in a different country.

eurodollar U.S. currency held in banks outside the United States.

excess equity (EE) The value of money or securities in a margin account that is in excess of the federal requirement. *Syn.* margin excess; Regulation T excess.

exchange Any organization, association, or group of persons that maintains or provides a marketplace in which securities may be bought and sold. An exchange need not be a physical place, and several strictly electronic exchanges do business around the world.

Exchange Act *See* Securities Exchange Act of 1934.

exchange-listed security A security that has met certain requirements and has been admitted to full trading privileges on an exchange. The NYSE and regional exchanges set listing requirements for volume of shares outstanding, corporate earnings, and other characteristics. Exchange-listed securities may also be traded in the third market, the market for institutional investors.

exchange market All of the exchanges on which listed securities are traded.

exchange privilege A feature offered by a mutual fund allowing an individual to transfer an investment in one fund to another fund under the same sponsor without incurring an additional sales charge.

exchange rate *See* foreign exchange rate.

exchange traded fund (ETF) An investment company legally classified as an open-end company or unit investment trust (UIT), but differing from traditional open-end companies (mutual funds) and UITs. An ETF issues shares in large blocks that are known as Creation Units. Those who purchase Creation Units are frequently large institutional traders or investors. The Creation Units can then be split up and sold as individual shares in the secondary markets allowing individual investors to purchase shares.

ex-date The first date on which a security is traded that the buyer is not entitled to receive distributions previously declared. *Syn.* ex-dividend date.

ex-dividend date *See* ex-date.

executor A person given fiduciary authorization to manage the affairs of a decedent's estate. An executor's authority is established by the decedent's last will.

exempt security A security exempt from the registration requirements (although not from the antifraud requirements) of the Securities Act of 1933. Examples include U.S. government securities and municipal securities.

exempt transaction A transaction that does not trigger a state's registration and advertising requirements under the Uniform Securities Act. Examples of exempt transactions include:

■ nonissuer transactions in outstanding securities (normal market trading);

■ transactions with financial institutions;

■ unsolicited transactions; and

■ private placement transactions.
No transaction is exempt from the Uniform Securities Act's antifraud provisions.

exercise To effect the transaction offered by an option, a right, or a warrant. For example, an equity call holder exercises a call by buying 100 shares of the underlying stock at the agreed-upon price within the agreed-upon time period.

exercise price The cost per share at which an option or a warrant holder may buy or sell the underlying security. *Syn.* strike price.

expansion A period of increased business activity throughout an economy—one of the four stages of the business cycle. *Syn.* recovery. *Related item(s):* business cycle.

expansionary policy A monetary policy that increases the money supply, usually with the intention of lowering interest rates and combating deflation.

expense ratio A ratio for comparing a mutual fund's efficiency by dividing the fund's expenses by its net assets.

expiration cycle A set of four expiration months for a class of listed options. An option may have expiration dates of January, April, July, and October (JAJO); February, May, August, and November (FMAN); or March, June, September, and December (MJSD).

expiration date The specified date on which an option buyer no longer has the rights specified in the option contract.

exploratory drilling program A limited partnership that aims to locate and recover undiscovered reserves of oil, gas, or minerals. These programs are considered highly risky investments. *Syn.* wildcatting. *Related*

item(s): developmental drilling program; income program.

exploratory well A well drilled either in search of an undiscovered pool of oil or gas or with the hope of substantially extending the limits of an existing pool of oil or gas.

F

FAC *See* face-amount certificate company.

face-amount certificate company (FAC) An investment company that issues certificates obligating it to pay an investor a stated amount of money (the face amount) on a specific future date. The investor pays into the certificate in periodic payments or in a lump sum.

face value *See* par.

fail to deliver A situation where the broker-dealer on the sell side of a transaction or contract does not deliver the specified securities to the broker-dealer on the buy side. *Syn.* broker fail; fails; fails to deliver; failure to deliver.

fail to receive A situation where the broker-dealer on the buy side of a transaction or contract does not receive the specified securities from the broker-dealer on the sell side. *Syn.* fails; fails to receive; failure to receive.

Fannie Mae *See* Federal National Mortgage Association.

Farm Credit Administration (FCA) The government agency that coordinates the activities of the banks in the Farm Credit System. *Related item(s):* Farm Credit System.

Farm Credit System (FCS) An organization of 37 privately owned banks that provide credit services to farmers and mortgages on farm property. Included in the system are the Federal Land Banks, Federal Intermediate Credit Banks, and Banks for Cooperatives. *Related item(s):* Federal Intermediate Credit Bank.

FCA *See* Farm Credit Administration.

FCO *See* foreign currency option.

FCS *See* Farm Credit System.

FDIC *See* Federal Deposit Insurance Corporation.

Fed *See* Federal Reserve System.

Fed call *See* margin call.

federal call *See* margin call.

Federal Deposit Insurance Corporation (FDIC) The government agency that provides deposit insurance for member banks and prevents bank and thrift failures.

federal funds The reserves of banks and certain other institutions greater than the reserve requirements or excess reserves. These funds are available immediately.

federal funds rate The interest rate charged by one institution lending federal funds to another.

Federal Home Loan Bank (FHLB) A government-regulated organization that operates a credit reserve system for the nation's savings and loan associations.

Federal Home Loan Mortgage Corporation (FHLMC) A publicly traded corporation that promotes the nationwide secondary market in mortgages by issuing mortgage-backed pass-through debt certificates. *Syn.* Freddie Mac.

Federal Intermediate Credit Bank (FICB) One of 12 banks that provide short-term financing to farmers as part of the Farm Credit System.

Federal National Mortgage Association (FNMA) A publicly held corporation that purchases conventional mortgages and mortgages from government agencies, including the Federal Housing Administration, Department of Veterans Affairs, and Farmers Home Administration. *Syn.* Fannie Mae.

Federal Open Market Committee (FOMC) A committee that makes decisions concerning the Fed's operations to control the money supply.

Federal Reserve Board (FRB) A seven-member group that directs the operations of the Federal Reserve System. The president appoints board members, subject to Congressional approval.

Federal Reserve System The central bank system of the United States. Its primary responsibility is to regulate the flow of money and credit.

FHLB *See* Federal Home Loan Bank.

FHLMC *See* Federal Home Loan Mortgage Corporation.

FICB *See* Federal Intermediate Credit Bank.

fictitious quotation A bid or an offer published before being identified by source and verified as legitimate. A fictitious quote may create the appearance of trading activity where none exists; this violates the Conduct Rules.

fidelity bond Insurance coverage required by the self-regulatory organizations for all employees, officers, and partners of member firms to protect clients against acts of lost securities, fraudulent trading, and check forgery. *Syn.* surety bond.

fiduciary A person legally appointed and authorized to hold assets in trust for another person and manage those assets for that person's benefit.

filing *See* registration by filing.

filing date The day on which an issuer submits to the SEC the registration statement for a new securities issue.

fill-or-kill order (FOK) An order that instructs the floor broker to fill the entire order immediately; if the entire order cannot be executed immediately, it is canceled.

final prospectus The legal document that states a new issue security's price, delivery date, and underwriting spread as well as other material information. It must be given to every investor who purchases a new issue of registered securities. *Syn.* prospectus.

Financial Guaranty Insurance Corporation (FGIC) An insurance company that offers insurance on the timely payment of interest and principal on municipal issues and unit investment trusts.

financial risk *See* credit risk.

firewall A descriptive name also referred to as an information barrier for the division within a brokerage firm that prevents insider information from passing from corporate advisers to investment traders, who could make use of the information to reap illicit profits. *Related item(s):* Insider Trading and Securities Fraud Enforcement Act of 1988.

firm quote The actual price at which a trading unit of a security (such as 100 shares of stock or five bonds) may be bought or sold. All quotes are firm quotes unless otherwise indicated. *Related item(s):* bona fide quote; nominal quote.

first in, first out (FIFO) An accounting method used to assess a company's inventory, in which it is assumed that the first goods acquired are the first to be sold. The same method is used by the IRS to determine cost basis for tax purposes. *Related item(s):* average basis; last in, first out; share identification.

fiscal policy The federal tax and spending policies set by Congress or the president. These policies affect tax rates, interest rates, and government spending in an effort to control the economy. *Related item(s):* monetary policy.

fixed annuity An insurance contract in which the insurance company makes fixed dollar payments to the annuitant for the term of the contract, usually until the annuitant dies. The insurance company guarantees both earnings and principal. *Syn.* fixed dollar annuity; guaranteed dollar annuity. *Related item(s):* annuity; variable annuity.

fixed asset A tangible, physical property used in the course of a corporation's everyday operations; it includes buildings, equipment, and land.

fixed dollar annuity *See* fixed annuity.

fixed unit investment trust An investment company that invests in a portfolio of securities in which no changes are permissible.

flat A term used to describe bonds traded without accrued interest. They are traded at the agreed-upon market price only. *Related item(s):* accrued interest.

flat yield curve A chart showing the yields of bonds with short maturities as equal to the yields of bonds with long maturities. *Syn.* even yield curve. *Related item(s):* inverted yield curve; normal yield curve; yield curve.

floor broker *See* commission house broker.

floor trader An exchange member who executes transactions from the floor of the exchange only for his own account. *Syn.* local.

flow of funds The schedule of payments disbursed from the proceeds of a facility financed by a revenue bond. The flow of funds determines the order in which the operating expenses, debt service, and other expenses are paid. Typically, the priority is (1) operations and maintenance, (2) debt service, (3) debt service reserve,

(4) reserve maintenance, (5) renewal and replacement, and (6) surplus. *Related item(s):* debt service reserve fund.

flow-through A term that describes the way income, deductions, and credits resulting from the activities of a business are applied to individual taxes and expenses as though each incurred the income and deductions directly. *Related item(s):* limited partnership.

FNMA *See* Federal National Mortgage Association.

FOK *See* fill-or-kill order.

FOMC *See* Federal Open Market Committee.

foreign currency Money issued by a country other than the one in which the investor resides. Options and futures contracts on numerous foreign currencies are traded on U.S. exchanges.

foreign currency option (FCO) A security representing the right to buy or sell a specified amount of a foreign currency. *Related item(s):* option.

foreign exchange rate The price of one country's currency in terms of another currency. *Syn.* exchange rate.

foreign fund *See* specialized fund.

forward pricing The valuation process for mutual fund shares, whereby an order to purchase or redeem shares is executed at the price determined by the portfolio valuation calculated after the order is received. Portfolio valuations occur at least once per business day.

401(k) plan A tax-deferred defined contribution retirement plan offered by an employer.

403(b) plan A tax-deferred annuity retirement plan available to employees of public schools and certain nonprofit organizations.

fractional share A portion of a whole share of stock. Mutual fund shares are frequently issued in fractional amounts. Fractional shares used to be generated when corporations declared stock dividends, merged, or voted to split stock, but today it is more common for corporations to issue the cash equivalent of fractional shares.

fraud The deliberate concealment, misrepresentation, or omission of material information or the truth to deceive or manipulate another party for unlawful or unfair gain.

FRB *See* Federal Reserve Board.

Freddie Mac *See* Federal Home Loan Mortgage Corporation.

free credit balance The cash funds in customer accounts. Broker-dealers must notify customers of their free credit balances at least quarterly.

freeriding Buying and immediately selling securities without making payment. This practice violates the SEC's Regulation T.

freeriding and withholding The failure of a member participating in the distribution of a hot issue to make a bona fide public offering at the public offering price. This practice violates the Conduct Rules. *Related item(s):* hot issue.

front-end fee The expenses paid for services rendered during a direct participation program's organization or acquisition phase, including front-end organization and offering expenses, acquisition fees and expenses, and any other similar fees designated by the sponsor.

front-end load A mutual fund commission or sales fee that is charged at the time shares are purchased. The load is added to the share's net asset value when calculating the public offering price. *Related item(s):* back-end load.

frozen account An account requiring cash in advance before a buy order is executed and securities in hand before a sell order is executed. An account holder under such restrictions has violated the SEC's Regulation T.

Full Disclosure Act *See* Securities Act of 1933.

full power of attorney A written authorization for someone other than an account's beneficial owner to make deposits and withdrawals and to execute trades in the account. *Related item(s):* limited power of attorney.

full trading authorization An authorization, usually provided by a full power of attorney, for someone other than the customer to have full trading privileges in an account. *Related item(s):* limited trading authorization.

fully registered bond A debt issue that prints the bondholder's name on the certificate. The issuer's transfer agent maintains the records and sends principal and interest payments directly to the investor. *Related item(s):* registered; registered as to principal only.

functional allocation A sharing arrangement whereby the investors in an oil and gas direct participation program are responsible for intangible costs and the sponsor is responsible for tangible costs; revenues are shared. *Related item(s):* sharing arrangement.

funded debt All long-term debt financing of a corporation.

funding An ERISA guideline stipulating that retirement plan assets must be segregated from other corporate assets.

fund manager *See* portfolio manager.

fungible Interchangeable, owing to identical characteristics or value. A security is fungible if it can be substituted or exchanged for another security.

G

GDP *See* gross domestic product.

general account The account that holds all of an insurer's assets other than those in separate accounts. The general account holds the contributions paid for traditional life insurance contracts. *Related item(s):* separate account.

general obligation bond (GO) A municipal debt issue backed by the full faith, credit, and taxing power of the issuer for payment of interest and principal. *Syn.* full faith and credit bond. *Related item(s):* double-barreled bond; revenue bond.

general partner (GP) An active investor in a direct participation program who is personally liable for all debts of the program and who manages the business of the program. The GP's duties include making decisions that bind the partnership; buying and selling property; managing property and money; supervising all aspects of the business; and maintaining a 1% financial interest in the partnership. *Related item(s):* limited partner.

general partnership (GP) An association of two or more entities formed to conduct a business jointly. The partnership does not require documents for formation, and the general partners are jointly and severally liable for the partnership's liabilities. *Related item(s):* limited partnership.

General Securities Principal *See* Series 24.

General Securities Representative *See* Series 7.

generic advertising Communications with the public that promote securities as investments but that do not refer to particular securities. *Syn.* institutional advertising.

Ginnie Mae *See* Government National Mortgage Association.

Glass-Steagall Act of 1933 Federal legislation that forbids commercial banks to underwrite securities and forbids investment bankers to open deposit accounts or make commercial loans. *Syn.* banking act.

GNMA *See* Government National Mortgage Association.

GNP *See* gross domestic product.

GO *See* general obligation bond.

good delivery A term describing a security that is negotiable, in compliance with the contract of the sale, and ready to be transferred from seller to purchaser.

good til canceled order (GTC) An order that is left on the order book until it is either executed or canceled. *Syn.* open order.

goodwill An intangible asset that represents the value that a firm's business reputation adds to its book value.

Government National Mortgage Association (GNMA) A wholly government-owned corporation that issues pass-through mortgage debt certificates backed by the full faith and credit of the U.S. government. *Syn.* Ginnie Mae.

government security A debt obligation of the U.S. government, backed by its full faith, credit, and taxing power, and regarded as having no risk of default. The government issues short-term Treasury bills, medium-term Treasury notes, and long-term Treasury bonds. *Related item(s):* agency issue.

GP *See* general partner; general partnership.

green shoe option A provision of an issue's registration statement that allows an underwriter to buy extra shares from the issuer (thus increasing the size of the offering) if public demand proves exceptionally strong. The term derives from the Green Shoe Manufacturing Company, which first used the technique.

gross domestic product (GDP) The total value of goods and services produced in a country during one year. It includes consumption, government purchases, investments, and exports minus imports.

gross income All income of a taxpayer, from whatever source derived.

gross proceeds The total of the initial invested capital in a direct participation program contributed by all of the original and additional limited partners.

gross revenues All money received by a business from its operations. The term typically does not include interest income or income from the sale, refinancing, or other disposition of properties.

growth fund A diversified common stock fund that has capital appreciation as its primary goal. It invests in companies that reinvest most of their earnings for expansion, research, or development. *Related item(s):* diversified common stock fund; mutual fund.

growth industry An industry that is growing faster than the economy as a whole as a result of technological changes, new products, or changing consumer tastes.

growth stock A relatively speculative issue that is believed to offer significant potential for capital gains. It often pays low dividends and sells at a high price/earnings ratio.

GTC *See* good til canceled order.

guaranteed bond A debt obligation issued with a promise from a corporation other than the issuing corporation to maintain payments of principal and interest.

guaranteed dollar annuity *See* fixed annuity.

guaranteed stock An equity security, generally a preferred stock, issued with a promise from a corporation other than the issuing corporation to maintain dividend payments. The stock still represents ownership in the issuing corporation, but it is considered a dual security.

guardian A fiduciary who manages the assets of a minor or an incompetent for that person's benefit. *Related item(s):* fiduciary.

H

hedge An investment made to reduce the risk of adverse price movements in a security. Normally, a hedge consists of a protecting position in a related security. *Related item(s):* long hedge.

high The highest price a security reaches during a specified period of time. *Related item(s):* low.

holder The owner of a security. *Related item(s):* long.

holding company A company organized to invest in and manage other corporations.

holding period A time period signifying how long the owner possesses a security. It starts the day after a purchase and ends on the day of the sale.

hold in street name A securities transaction settlement and delivery procedure whereby a customer's securities are transferred into the broker-dealer's name and held by the broker-dealer. Although the broker-dealer is the nominal owner, the customer is the beneficial owner. *Related item(s): transfer and hold in safekeeping; transfer and ship.*

hot issue A new issue that sells or is anticipated to sell at a premium over the public offering price. *Related item(s): freeriding and withholding.*

HR-10 plan *See Keogh plan.*

hypothecation Pledging to a broker-dealer securities bought on margin as collateral for the margin loan. *Related item(s): rehypothecation.*

I

IDC *See intangible drilling cost.*

identified security The particular security designated for sale by an investor holding identical securities with different acquisition dates and cost bases. This allows the investor to control the amount of capital gain or loss incurred through the sale.

immediate annuity An insurance contract purchased for a single premium that starts to pay the annuitant immediately following its purchase. *Related item(s): annuity.*

immediate family A parent, mother- or father-in-law, husband or wife, child, sibling, or other relative supported financially by a person associated with the securities industry.

immediate-or-cancel order (IOC) An order that instructs the floor broker to execute it immediately, in full or in part. Any portion of the order that remains unexecuted is canceled.

income bond A debt obligation that promises to repay principal in full at maturity. Interest is paid only if the corporation's earnings are sufficient to meet the interest payment and if the board of directors declares the interest payment. Income bonds are usually traded flat. *Syn. adjustment bond. Related item(s): flat.*

income fund A mutual fund that seeks to provide stable current income by investing in securities that pay interest or dividends. *Related item(s): mutual fund.*

income program A limited partnership that buys and markets proven reserves of oil and gas: it buys the value of the oil in the ground. *Related item(s): developmental drilling program; exploratory drilling program.*

income statement The summary of a corporation's revenues and expenses for a specific fiscal period.

index A comparison of current prices to some baseline, such as prices on a particular date. Indexes are frequently used in technical analysis. *Related item(s): average.*

index option A security representing the right to receive in cash the difference between the underlying value of a market index and the strike price of the option. The investor speculates on the direction, degree, and timing of the change in the numerical value of the index. *Related item(s): capped index option.*

individual retirement account (IRA) A retirement investing tool for employed individuals that allows an annual contribution of 100% of earned income up to a maximum annual allowable limit. Some or all of the contribution may be deductible from current taxes, depending on the individual's adjusted gross income and coverage by employer-sponsored qualified retirement plans. *Related item(s): Keogh plan; nonqualified retirement plan; qualified retirement plan; simplified employee pension plan.*

industrial development bond (IDB) A debt security issued by a municipal authority, which uses the proceeds to finance the construction or purchase of facilities to be leased or purchased by a private company. The bonds are backed by the credit of the private company, which is ultimately responsible for principal and interest payments. *Syn. industrial revenue bond.*

industrial revenue bond (IRB) *See industrial development bond.*

industry fund *See sector fund.*

inflation A persistent and measurable rise in the general level of prices. *Related item(s): deflation.*

inflation risk *See purchasing power risk.*

information barrier A descriptive name also referred to as a "firewall" for the division within a brokerage firm that prevents insider information from passing from corporate advisers to investment traders, who could make use of the information to reap illicit profits. *Related item(s): Insider Trading and Securities Fraud Enforcement Act of 1988.*

informer bounty (award) An award paid in connection for original information concerning any violation of securities law. Under Dodd-Frank legislation, awards may range from 10% to 30% of amounts recovered.

initial margin requirement The amount of equity a customer must deposit when making a new purchase in a margin account. The SEC's Regulation T requirement for equity securities is currently 50% of the purchase price. The initial minimum requirement is a deposit of $2,000 but not more than 100% of the purchase price. *Related item(s): margin; margin call.*

initial public offering (IPO) A corporation's first sale of common stock to the public. *Related item(s): new issue market; public offering.*

in-part call The redemption of a certain portion of a bond issue at the request of the issuer. *Related item(s): in-whole call.*

inside information Material information that has not been disseminated to, or is not readily available to, the general public.

inside market The best (highest) bid price at which an OTC stock may be sold, and the best (lowest) ask price at which the same stock may be bought in the inter-dealer market. *Related item(s):* affiliate; control person.

insider Any person who possesses or has access to material nonpublic information about a corporation. Insiders include directors, officers, and stockholders who own at least 10% of any class of equity security of a corporation.

Insider Trading and Securities Fraud Enforcement Act of 1988 Legislation that defines what constitutes the illicit use of nonpublic information in making securities trades and the liabilities and penalties that apply. *Syn.* Insider Trading Act. *Related item(s):* Chinese wall; insider.

institutional account An account held for the benefit of others. Examples of institutional accounts include banks, trusts, pension and profit-sharing plans, mutual funds, and insurance companies.

institutional communication FINRA defines this category of communications with the public as any written (including electronic) communication that is distributed or made available only to institutional investors, but does not include a member's internal communications (i.e., internal memos).

institutional investor A person or organization that trades securities in large enough share quantities or dollar amounts that it qualifies for preferential treatment such as lower commissions. Institutional investors are covered by fewer protective regulations because it is assumed that they are more knowledgeable and better able to protect themselves. Examples would include another member firm, bank or savings and loan, insurance company, registered investment company, government entity, or any entity with $50 million or more in total assets.

intangible asset A property owned that is not physical, such as a formula, a copyright, or goodwill. *Related item(s):* goodwill.

intangible drilling cost (IDC) In an oil and gas limited partnership, a tax-deductible cost; usually this is for a nonphysical asset, such as labor or fuel, which does not depreciate. The cost may be expensed in the year incurred, or deductions may be amortized over the life of the well. *Syn.* intangible drilling development expense.

interbank market An unregulated, decentralized, international market in which the various major currencies of the world are traded.

interest The charge for the privilege of borrowing money, usually expressed as an annual percentage rate.

interest rate option A security representing the right to buy or sell government debt securities. The federal deficit has created a large market in securities that are sensitive to changes in interest rates; the investor can profit from fluctuations in interest rates and can hedge the risks created by the fluctuations.

interest rate risk The risk associated with investments relating to the sensitivity of price or value to fluctuation in the current level of interest rates; also, the risk that involves the competitive cost of money. This term is generally associated with bond prices, but it applies to all investments. In bonds, prices carry interest risk because if bond prices rise, outstanding bonds will not remain competitive unless their yields and prices adjust to reflect the current market.

Internal Revenue Code (IRC) The legislation that defines tax liabilities and deductions for U.S. taxpayers.

Internal Revenue Service (IRS) The U.S. government agency responsible for collecting most federal taxes and for administering tax rules and regulations.

interstate offering An issue of securities registered with the SEC sold to residents of states other than the state in which the issuer does business.

in-the-money The term used to describe an option that has intrinsic value, such as a call option when the stock is selling above the exercise price or a put option when the stock is selling below the exercise price. *Related item(s):* at-the-money; intrinsic value; out-of-the-money.

intrastate offering An issue of securities exempt from SEC registration, available to companies that do business in one state and sell their securities only to residents of that same state. *Related item(s):* Rule 147.

intrinsic value The potential profit to be made from exercising an option. A call option is said to have intrinsic value when the underlying stock is trading above the exercise price. *Related item(s):* time value.

investment adviser (1) Any person who makes investment recommendations in return for a flat fee or a percentage of assets managed. (2) For an investment company, the individual who bears the day-to-day responsibility of investing the cash and securities held in the fund's portfolio in accordance with objectives stated in the fund's prospectus.

Investment Advisers Act of 1940 Legislation which governs who must register with the SEC as an investment adviser. *Related item(s):* investment adviser.

investment banker An institution in the business of raising capital for corporations and municipalities. An investment banker may not accept deposits or make commercial loans. *Syn.* investment bank.

investment banking business A broker, dealer, or municipal or government securities dealer that underwrites or distributes new issues of securities as a dealer or that buys and sells securities for the accounts of others as a broker. *Syn.* investment securities business.

investment company A company engaged in the business of pooling investors' money and trading in securities for them. Examples include face-amount certificate companies, unit investment trusts, and management companies.

Investment Company Act of 1940 Congressional legislation regulating companies that invest and reinvest in securities. The act requires an investment company engaged in interstate commerce to register with the SEC.

investment grade security A security to which the rating services (e.g., Standard & Poor's and Moody's) have assigned a rating of BBB/Baa or above.

investment objective Any goal a client hopes to achieve through investing. Examples include current income, capital growth, and preservation of capital.

investment value The market price at which a convertible security (usually a debenture) would sell if it were not converted into common stock. *Related item(s):* conversion value; convertible bond; debenture.

investor The purchaser of an asset or security with the intent of profiting from the transaction.

in-whole call The redemption of a bond issue in its entirety at the option of the issuer, as opposed to its redemption based on a lottery held by an independent trustee. *Related item(s):* in-part call.

IOC *See* immediate-or-cancel order.

IPO *See* initial public offering.

IRA *See* individual retirement account.

IRA rollover The reinvestment of assets that an individual receives as a distribution from a qualified tax-deferred retirement plan into an individual retirement account within 60 days of receiving the distribution.

The individual may reinvest either the entire sum or a portion of the sum, although any portion not reinvested is taxed as ordinary income. *Related item(s):* individual retirement account; IRA transfer.

IRA transfer The direct reinvestment of retirement assets from one qualified tax-deferred retirement plan to an individual retirement account. The account owner never takes possession of the assets, but directs that they be transferred directly from the existing plan custodian to the new plan custodian. *Related item(s):* individual retirement account; IRA rollover.

IRC *See* Internal Revenue Code.

irrevocable stock power *See* stock power.

issued stock Equity securities authorized by the issuer's registration statement and distributed to the public. *Related item(s):* outstanding stock; treasury stock.

issuer The entity, such as a corporation or municipality, that offers or proposes to offer its securities for sale.

J

joint account An account in which two or more individuals possess some form of control over the account and may transact business in the account. The account must be designated as either tenants in common or joint tenants with right of survivorship. *Related item(s):* tenants in common; joint tenants with right of survivorship.

joint life with last survivor An annuity payout option that covers two or more people, with annuity payments continuing as long as one of the annuitants remains alive.

joint tenants with right of survivorship (JTWROS) A form of joint ownership of an account whereby a deceased tenant's fractional interest in the account passes to the surviving tenant(s). It is used almost exclusively by husbands and wives. *Related item(s):* tenants in common.

joint venture The cooperation of two or more individuals or enterprises in a specific business enterprise rather than in a continuing relationship—as in a partnership.

JTWROS *See* joint tenants with right of survivorship.

junior lien debt A bond backed by the same collateral backing a previous issue and having a subordinate claim to the collateral in the event of default. *Related item(s):* closed-end covenant; open-end covenant.

K

Keogh plan A qualified tax-deferred retirement plan for persons who are self-employed and unincorporated or who earn extra income through personal services aside from their regular employment. *Syn.* HR-10 plan. *Related item(s):* individual retirement account; nonqualified retirement plan; qualified retirement plan.

Keynesian economics The theory that active government intervention in the marketplace is the best method of ensuring economic growth and stability.

know your customer rule *See* Rule 405.

L

lagging indicator A measurable economic factor that changes after the economy has started to follow a particular pattern or trend. Lagging indicators are believed to confirm long-term trends. Examples include average duration of unemployment, corporate profits, and labor cost per unit of output. *Related item(s):* coincident indicator; leading indicator.

last in, first out (LIFO) An accounting method used to assess a corporation's inventory in which it is assumed that the last goods acquired are the first to be sold. The method is used to determine cost basis for tax purposes; the IRS designates last in, first out as the order in which sales or withdrawals from an investment are made. *Related item(s):* average basis; first in, first out; share identification.

leading indicator A measurable economic factor that changes before the economy starts to follow a particular pattern or trend. Leading indicators are believed to predict changes in the economy. Examples include new orders for durable goods, slowdowns in deliveries by vendors, and numbers of building permits issued. *Related item(s):* coincident indicator; lagging indicator.

LEAPS *See* long-term equity option.

lease rental bond A debt security issued by a municipal authority to raise funds for new construction with the understanding that the finished structure will be rented to the authority and that the rental payments will finance the bond payments.

legal list The selection of securities that a state agency (usually a state banking or insurance commission) determines to be appropriate investments for fiduciary accounts, such as mutual savings banks, pension funds, and insurance companies.

legal opinion of counsel The statement of a bond attorney affirming that an issue is a municipal issue and that interest is exempt from federal taxation. Each municipal bond certificate must be accompanied by a legal opinion of counsel. *Related item(s):* ex-legal; qualified legal opinion; unqualified legal opinion.

legislative risk The potential for an investor to be adversely affected by changes in investment or tax laws.

letter of intent (LOI) A signed agreement allowing an investor to buy mutual fund shares at a lower overall sales charge, based on the total dollar amount of the intended investment. A letter of intent is valid only if the investor completes the terms of the agreement within 13 months of signing the agreement. A letter of intent may be backdated 90 days. *Syn.* statement of intention.

level debt service A schedule for debt repayment whereby principal and interest payments remain essentially constant from year to year over the life of the issue. *Related item(s):* decreasing debt service.

level load A mutual fund sales fee charged annually based on the net asset value of a share. A 12b-1 asset-based fee is an example of a level load. *Related item(s):* back-end load; Class C share; Class D share; front-end load.

leverage Using borrowed capital to increase investment return. *Syn.* trading on the equity.

liability A legal obligation to pay a debt owed. Current liabilities are debts payable within 12 months. Long-term liabilities are debts payable over a period of more than 12 months.

life annuity/straight life An annuity payout option that pays a monthly check over the annuitant's lifetime.

life annuity with period certain An annuity payout option that guarantees the annuitant a monthly check for a certain period and thereafter until the annuitant's death. If the annuitant dies before the period expires, the payments go to the annuitant's named beneficiary.

life contingency An annuity payout option that provides a death benefit during the accumulation stage. If the annuitant dies during this period, a full contribution is made to the account, which is paid to the annuitant's named beneficiary.

LIFO *See* last in, first out.

limited liability An investor's right to limit potential losses to no more than the amount invested. Equity shareholders, such as corporate stockholders and limited partners, have limited liability.

limited partner (LP) An investor in a direct participation program who does not participate in the management or control of the program and whose liability for partnership debts is limited to the amount invested in the program. *Related item(s):* general partner; participant; passive investor.

limited partnership (LP) An association of two or more partners formed to conduct a business jointly and in which one or more of the partners is liable only to the extent of the amount of money invested. Limited partners do not receive dividends but enjoy direct flow-through of income and expenses. *Related item(s):* flow-through; general partnership.

limited partnership agreement The contract between a partnership's limited and general partners that provides the guidelines for partnership operation and states the rights and responsibilities of each partner.

limited power of attorney A written authorization for someone other than an account's beneficial owner to make certain investment decisions regarding transactions in the account. *Related item(s):* discretion; full power of attorney.

limited tax bond A general obligation municipal debt security issued by a municipality whose taxing power is limited to a specified maximum rate.

limited trading authorization An authorization, usually provided by a limited power of attorney, for someone other than the customer to have trading privileges in an account. These privileges are limited to purchases and sales; withdrawal of assets is not authorized. *Related item(s):* full trading authorization.

limit order An order that instructs the floor broker to buy a specified security below a certain price or to sell a specified security above a certain price. *Syn.* or better order. *Related item(s):* stop limit order; stop order.

liquidation priority In the case of a corporation's liquidation, the order that is strictly followed for paying off creditors and stockholders:
1. Unpaid wages
2. Taxes
3. Secured claims (mortgages)
4. Secured liabilities (bonds)
5. Unsecured liabilities (debentures) and general creditors
6. Subordinated debt
7. Preferred stockholders
8. Common stockholders

liquidity The ease with which an asset may be converted to cash in the marketplace. A large number of buyers and sellers and a high volume of trading activity provide high liquidity.

liquidity risk The potential that an investor might not be able to sell an investment as and when desired. *Syn.* marketability risk.

listed option An option contract that may be bought and sold on a national securities exchange in a continuous secondary market. Listed options carry standardized strike prices and expiration dates. *Syn.* standardized option. *Related item(s):* OTC option.

listed security A stock, a bond, or another security that satisfies certain minimum requirements and is traded on a regional or national securities exchange such as the New York Stock Exchange.

LMV *See* current market value.

loan consent agreement An optional contract between a brokerage firm and a margin customer that permits the firm to lend the margined securities to other brokers; the contract is part of the margin agreement. *Syn.* consent to lend agreement.

LOI *See* letter of intent.

long The term used to describe the owning of a security, contract, or commodity. For example, a common stock owner is said to have a long position in the stock. *Related item(s):* short.

long hedge Buying puts as protection against a decline in the value of a long securities or actuals position. *Related item(s):* hedge.

long market value (LMV) *See* current market value.

long-term equity option An option contract that has a longer expiration than traditional equity option contracts. The most common long-term equity option is the CBOE's long-term equity anticipation security (LEAPS).

long-term gain The profit earned on the sale of a capital asset that has been owned for more than 12 months. *Related item(s):* capital gain; capital loss; long-term loss.

long-term loss The loss realized on the sale of a capital asset that has been owned for more than 12 months. *Related item(s):* capital gain; capital loss; long-term gain.

loss carryover A capital loss incurred during one tax year that is carried over to the next year or later years for use as a capital loss deduction. *Related item(s):* capital loss.

low The lowest price a security or commodity reaches during a specified period. *Related item(s):* high.

LP *See* limited partner; limited partnership.

M

maintenance call *See* margin maintenance call.

maintenance covenant A provision of a municipal revenue bond's trust indenture that helps ensure the safety of the issue by promising to keep the facility and equipment in good working order. *Related item(s):* insurance covenant; rate covenant.

maintenance requirement *See* margin maintenance requirement.

make a market To stand ready to buy or sell a particular security as a dealer for its own account. A market maker accepts the risk of holding the position in the security. *Related item(s):* market maker.

management company An investment company that trades various types of securities in a portfolio in accordance with specific objectives stated in the prospectus. *Related item(s):* closed-end management company; diversified management company; mutual fund; nondiversified management company.

management fee The payment to the sponsor of a direct participation program for managing and administering the program. The fee is capped at about 5% of the program's gross revenues.

managing partner The general partner of a direct participation program that selects the investments and operates the partnership.

mandatory call The redemption of a bond by an issuer authorized in the trust indenture and based on a predetermined schedule or event. *Related item(s):* catastrophe call; partial call.

margin The amount of equity contributed by a customer as a percentage of the current market value of the securities held in a margin account. *Related item(s):* equity; initial margin requirement; margin call; Regulation T.

margin account A customer account in which a brokerage firm lends the customer part of the purchase price of securities. *Related item(s):* cash account; Regulation T.

margin call The Federal Reserve Board's demand that a customer deposit a specified amount of money or securities when a purchase is made in a margin account; the amount is expressed as a percentage of the market value of the securities at the time of purchase. The deposit must be made within one payment period. *Syn.* Fed call; federal call; federal margin; Reg T call; T call. *Related item(s):* initial margin requirement; margin.

margin department The department within a brokerage firm that computes the amount of money clients must deposit in margin and cash accounts. *Syn.* credit department.

margin excess *See* excess equity.

margin maintenance call A demand that a margin customer deposit money or securities when the customer's equity falls below the margin maintenance requirement set by the broker-dealer or the SRO the broker dealer reports to. *Syn.* house maintenance call; maintenance call; FINRA maintenance call.

margin maintenance requirement The minimum equity that must be held in a margin account, determined by the broker-dealer and the SRO the broker-dealer reports to. The amount of equity required varies with the type of security bought on margin, and the broker-dealer's house requirement is usually higher than that set by the SRO. *Syn.* house maintenance requirement; maintenance requirement; FINRA maintenance requirement.

margin risk The potential that a margin customer will be required to deposit additional cash if his security positions are subject to adverse price movements.

margin security A security that is eligible for purchase on margin, including any registered security, OTC margin stock or bond, or Nasdaq Global Select or Global Market security. A firm is permitted to lend money to help customers purchase these securities and may accept these securities as collateral for margin purchases. *Syn.* eligible security. *Related item(s):* nonmargin security; OTC margin security.

markdown The difference between the highest current bid price among dealers and the lower price that a dealer pays to a customer.

marketability The ease with which a security may be bought or sold; having a readily available market for trading.

market maker A dealer willing to accept the risk of holding a particular security in its own account to facilitate trading in that security. *Related item(s):* make a market.

market not held order *See* not held order

market-on-close order An order that specifies it is to be executed at the close. The order will be executed at the closing price. *Syn.* at-the-close order. *Related item(s):* at-the-opening order.

market order An order to be executed immediately at the best available price. A market order is the only order that guarantees execution. *Syn.* unrestricted order.

market risk The potential for an investor to experience losses owing to day-to-day fluctuations in the prices at which securities may be bought or sold. *Related item(s):* systemic risk.

market value The price at which investors buy or sell a share of common stock or a bond at a given time. Market value is determined by buyers' and sellers' interaction. *Related item(s):* current market value.

mark to market To adjust the value of the securities in an account to the current market value of those securities; used to calculate the market value and equity in a margin account.

markup The difference between the lowest current offering price among dealers and the higher price a dealer charges a customer.

material information Any fact that could affect an investor's decision to trade a security.

maturity date The date on which a bond's principal is repaid to the investor and interest payments cease. *Related item(s):* par; principal.

member firm A broker-dealer in which at least one of the principal officers is a member of an exchange, a self-regulatory organization or a clearing corporation.

mini-options Option contracts that overlay only 10 shares of the underlying security instead of 100 shares as is the case for standard options contracts.

minimum margin requirement *See* margin maintenance requirement.

minor rule violation (MRV) In instances where the Department of Enforcement considers a violation minor and the respondent does not dispute the allegation, the Department of Enforcement may prepare and request that the respondent sign an MRV letter, accepting a finding of violation. Once the respondent signs an MRV letter, the settlement is final.

minus tick A security transaction's execution price that is below the previous execution price, by a minimum amount. *Syn.* down tick. *Related item(s):* plus tick; tick; zero-minus tick.

monetary policy The Federal Reserve Board's actions that determine the size and rate of the money supply's growth, which, in turn, affect interest rates. *Related item(s):* fiscal policy.

money laundering The act of cleaning money gotten from illegitimate businesses through three stages known as placement, layering, and integration for the purpose of hiding the money's origin in anticipation of its later use for both legitimate and illegitimate purposes.

money market The securities market that deals in short-term debt. Money market instruments are liquid forms of debt that mature in less than one year. Treasury bills make up the bulk of money market instruments.

money market fund A mutual fund that invests in short-term debt instruments. The fund's objective is to earn interest while maintaining a stable net asset value of $1 per share. Generally sold with no load, the fund may also offer draft-writing privileges and low opening investments. *Related item(s):* mutual fund.

Moody's Investors Service One of the best known investment rating agencies in the United States. A subsidiary of Dun & Bradstreet, Moody's rates bonds, commercial paper, preferred and common stocks, and municipal short-term issues. *Related item(s):* bond rating; Standard & Poor's Corporation.

mortgage bond A debt obligation secured by a property pledge. It represents a lien or mortgage against the issuing corporation's properties and real estate assets.

MSRB *See* Municipal Securities Rulemaking Board.

municipal bond A debt security issued by a state, a municipality, or another subdivision (such as a school, a park, or a sanitation or other local taxing district) to finance its capital expenditures. Such expenditures might include the construction of highways, public works, or school buildings. *Syn.* municipal security.

municipal bond fund A mutual fund that invests in municipal bonds and operates either as a unit investment trust or as an open-end fund. The fund's objective is to maximize federally tax-exempt income. *Related item(s):* mutual fund; unit investment trust.

municipal note A short-term municipal security issued in anticipation of funds from another source. *Related item(s):* municipal security.

Municipal Securities Rulemaking Board (MSRB) A self-regulatory organization that regulates the issuance and trading of municipal securities. The Board functions under the Securities and Exchange Commission's supervision; it has no enforcement powers. *Related item(s):* Securities Acts Amendments of 1975.

municipal security *See* municipal bond.

mutual fund An investment company that continuously offers new equity shares in an actively managed portfolio of securities. All shareholders participate in the fund's gains or losses. The shares are redeemable on any business day at the net asset value. Each mutual fund's portfolio is invested to match the objective stated in the prospectus. *Syn.* open-end investment company; open-end management company. *Related item(s):* asset allocation fund; balanced fund; net asset value.

mutual fund custodian A national bank, a stock exchange member firm, a trust company, or another qualified institution that physically safeguards the securities a mutual fund holds. It does not manage the fund's investments; its function is solely clerical.

N

naked The position of an option investor who writes a call or a put on a security he does not own. *Syn.* uncovered.

naked call writer An investor who writes a call option without owning the underlying stock or other related assets that would enable the investor to deliver the stock should the option be exercised. *Syn.* uncovered call writer. *Related item(s):* naked put writer.

naked put writer An investor who writes a put option without owning the underlying stock or other related assets that would enable the investor to purchase the stock should the option be exercised. *Syn.* uncovered put writer. *Related item(s):* naked call writer.

narrow-based index An index that is designed to reflect the movement of a market segment, such as a group of stocks in one industry or a specific type of investment. Examples include the Technology Index and the Gold/Silver Index. *Related item(s):* broad-based index; index.

Nasdaq National Association of Securities Dealers Automated Quotation system.

National Market System (Regulation NMS) A broad sweeping SEC regulation designed to bring trading and reporting uniformity to U.S. securities markets. *Related item(s):* order protection rule; minimum incre- ment price rule.

National Securities Clearing Corporation (NSCC) An organization that acts as a medium through which member brokerage firms and exchanges reconcile accounts with each other.

NAV *See* net asset value.

NAV of fund The net total of a mutual fund's assets and li- abilities; used to calculate the price of new fund shares.

NAV per share The value of a mutual fund share, calculated by dividing the fund's total net asset value by the number of shares outstanding.

negotiability A characteristic of a security that permits the owner to assign, give, transfer, or sell it to another person without a third party's permission.

negotiable certificate of deposit (CD) An unsecured promissory note issued with a minimum face value of $100,000. It evidences a time deposit of funds with the issuing bank and is guaranteed by the bank.

net asset value (NAV) A mutual fund share's value, calculated once a day, based on the closing market price for each security in the fund's portfolio. It is computed by deducting the fund's liabilities from the portfolio's total assets and dividing this amount by the number of shares outstanding. *Related item(s):* mutual fund.

net change The difference between a security's closing price on the trading day reported and the previous day's closing price. In over-the-counter transactions, the term refers to the difference between the closing bids.

net current asset value per share The calculation of book value per share that excludes all fixed assets. *Related item(s):* book value per share.

net debt per capita A measure of the ability of a municipality to meet its debt obligations; it compares the debt issued by the municipality to its property values.

net direct debt The amount of debt obligations of a municipality, including general obligation bonds and notes and short-term notes. Self-supported debt from revenue bond issues is not included in the calculation.

net domestic product A measure of the annual economic output of a nation adjusted to account for depreciation. It is calculated by subtracting the amount of depreciation from the gross domestic product. *Related item(s):* gross domestic product.

net income to net sales *See* net profit ratio.

net investment income The source of an investment company's dividend payments. It is calculated by subtracting the company's operating expenses from the total dividends and interest the company receives from the securities in its portfolio.

net profit margin *See* net profit ratio.

net profit ratio A measure of a corporation's relative profitability. It is calculated by dividing aftertax income by net sales. *Syn.* net income to net sales; net profit margin; net profits to sales; profit after taxes; profit ratio.

net profits to sales *See* net profit ratio.

net tangible assets per share *See* book value per share.

net total debt The sum of the debt obligations of a municipality, calculated by adding the municipality's net direct debt to its overlapping debt. *Related item(s):* net direct debt; overlapping debt.

net worth The amount by which assets exceed liabilities. *Syn.* owners' equity; shareholders' equity; stockholders' equity.

new account form The form that must be filled out for each new account opened with a brokerage firm.

The form specifies, at a minimum, the account owner, trading authorization, payment method, and types of securities appropriate for the customer.

new construction program A real estate direct participation program that aims to provide capital appreciation from building new property.

New Housing Authority bond (NHA) A municipal special revenue bond backed by the U.S. government and issued by a local public housing authority to develop and improve low-income housing. *Syn.* Housing Authority bond; Public Housing Authority bond.

new issue market The securities market for shares in privately owned businesses that are raising capital by selling common stock to the public for the first time. *Syn.* primary market. *Related item(s):* initial public offering; secondary market.

New Issues Act *See* Securities Act of 1933.

New York Stock Exchange (NYSE) The largest stock exchange in the United States.

New York Stock Exchange Composite Index Index of common stocks listed on the NYSE, based on the price of each stock weighted by its total value of shares outstanding. *Syn.* NYSE Index.

NH *See* not held order.

NHA *See* New Housing Authority bond.

no-load fund A mutual fund whose shares are sold without a commission or sales charge. The investment company distributes the shares directly. *Related item(s):* mutual fund; net asset value; sales load.

nominal owner The person in whose name securities are registered if that person is other than the beneficial owner. This is a brokerage firm's role when customer securities are registered in street name.

nominal yield The interest rate stated on the face of a bond that represents the percentage of interest the issuer pays on the bond's face value. *Syn.* coupon rate; stated yield. *Related item(s):* bond yield.

nonaccredited investor An investor not meeting the net worth requirements of Regulation D. Nonaccredited investors are counted for purposes of the 35-investor limitation for Regulation D private placements. *Related item(s):* accredited investor; private placement; Regulation D.

nonaffiliate A buyer of an unregistered public offering security who has no management or major ownership interest in the company being acquired. Nonaffiliates may sell this stock only after a specified holding period.

noncumulative preferred stock An equity security that does not have to pay any dividends in arrears to the holder. *Related item(s):* convertible preferred stock; cumulative preferred stock; preferred stock.

nondiscrimination In a qualified retirement plan, a formula for calculating contributions and benefits that must be applied uniformly so as to ensure that all employees receive fair and equitable treatment. *Related item(s):* qualified retirement plan.

nondiversified investment company A management company that does not meet the diversification requirements of the Investment Company Act of 1940. These companies are not restricted in the choice of securities or by the concentration of interest they have in those securities. *Related item(s):* diversified investment company; management company; mutual fund.

nonequity option A security representing the right to buy or sell an investment instrument other than a common stock at a specified price within a specified period. Examples of such investment instruments include foreign currencies, indexes, and interest rates. *Related item(s):* equity option; foreign currency option; index option; interest rate option; option.

nonmargin security A security that must be purchased in a cash account, that must be paid for in full, and that may not be used as collateral for a loan. Examples include put and call options, rights, insurance contracts, and new issues. *Related item(s):* margin security.

nonqualified retirement plan A corporate retirement plan that does not meet the standards set by the Employee Retirement Income Security Act of 1974. Contributions to a nonqualified plan are not tax deductible. *Related item(s):* qualified retirement plan.

nonsystematic risk Company-specific risk.

normal yield curve A chart showing long-term debt instruments having higher yields than short-term debt instruments. *Syn.* positive yield curve. *Related item(s):* flat yield curve; inverted yield curve; yield curve.

note A short-term debt security, usually maturing in five years or less. *Related item(s):* Treasury note.

not held order (NH) An order that gives the floor broker discretion as to the price and timing of the order's execution. Not held orders are often entered for large amounts of a security. *Syn.* market NH; market not held order.

notification *See* registration by filing.

NSCC *See* National Securities Clearing Corporation.

numbered account An account titled with something other than the customer's name. The title might be a number, symbol, or special title. The customer must sign a form designating account ownership.

NYSE *See* New York Stock Exchange.

O

OCC *See* Options Clearing Corporation.

OCC Disclosure Document *See* options disclosure document.

odd lot An amount of a security that is less than the normal unit of trading for that security. Generally, an odd lot is fewer than 100 shares of stock or five bonds. *Related item(s):* round lot.

offer Under the Uniform Securities Act, any attempt to solicit a purchase or sale in a security for value. *Related item(s):* bid; public offering price; quotation; ask.

offering circular An abbreviated prospectus used by corporations issuing less than $5 million of stock. The SEC's Regulation A allows these offerings an exemption from the full registration requirements of the 1933 Act. *Related item(s):* Regulation A.

oil and gas direct participation program A direct participation program formed to locate new oil and gas reserves, develop existing reserves, or generate income from producing wells. A high return is the primary objective of such a program. *Syn.* oil and gas limited partnership.

oil depletion allowance An accounting procedure that reduces the taxable portion of revenues from the sale of oil to compensate for the decreased supply of oil in the ground. Depletion is the natural resource counterpart of depreciation.

omnibus account An account opened in the name of an investment adviser or a broker-dealer for the benefit of its customers. The firm carrying the account does not receive disclosure of the individual customers' names or holdings and does not maintain records for the individual customers. *Syn.* special omnibus account.

open-end investment company *See* mutual fund.

opening purchase Entering the options market by buying calls or puts. *Related item(s):* closing sale; opening sale.

opening sale Entering the options market by selling calls or puts. *Related item(s):* closing purchase; opening purchase.

open-market operations The buying and selling of securities (primarily government or agency debt) by the Federal Open Market Committee to effect control of the money supply. These transactions increase or decrease the level of bank reserves available for lending.

open order *See* good til canceled order.

operating expenses (1) The day-to-day costs incurred in running a business. (2) In an oil and gas program, any production or leasehold expense incurred in the operation of a producing lease, including district expense; direct out-of-pocket expenses for labor, materials, and supplies; and those shares of taxes and transportation charges not borne by overriding royalty interests.

operating income The profit realized from one year of operation of a business.

option A security that represents the right to buy or sell a specified amount of an underlying security—such as a stock, bond, or futures contract—at a specified price within a specified time. The purchaser acquires a right, and the seller assumes an obligation.

option agreement The document a customer must sign within 15 days of being approved for options trading. In it, the customer agrees to abide by the rules of the options exchanges and not to exceed position or exercise limits.

option contract adjustment An adjustment made automatically to the terms of an option on the ex-dividend date when a stock pays a stock dividend or if there is a stock split or a reverse split.

options account A customer account in which the customer has received approval to trade options.

Options Clearing Corporation (OCC) The organization that issues options, standardizes option contracts, and guarantees their performance. The OCC made secondary trading possible by creating fungible option contracts.

options disclosure document A publication of the Options Clearing Corporation that outlines the risks and rewards of investing in options. The document must be given to each customer at the time of opening an options account and must accompany any options sales literature sent to a customer. *Syn.* OCC Disclosure Document.

order department The department within a brokerage firm that transmits orders to the proper market for execution and returns confirmations to the appropriate representative. *Syn.* order room; wire room.

order memorandum The form completed by a registered representative that contains customer instructions regarding an order's placement. The memorandum contains such information as the customer's name and account number, a description of the security, the type of transaction (e.g., buy, sell, or sell short), and any special instructions (such as time or price limits). *Syn.* order ticket.

order room *See* order department.

order ticket *See* order memorandum.

ordinary income Earnings other than capital gain.

OTC Bulletin Board An electronic quotation system for equity securities that are not listed on a national exchange or included in the Nasdaq system.

OTC margin security A security that is not traded on a national exchange but that has been designated by the Federal Reserve Board as eligible for trading on margin. The Fed publishes a list of such securities. *Related item(s):* margin security.

OTC market The security exchange system in which broker-dealers negotiate directly with one another rather than through an auction on an exchange floor. The trading takes place over computer and telephone net-works that link brokers and dealers around the world. Both listed and OTC securities, as well as municipal and U.S. government securities, trade in the OTC market.

OTC option An option contract that is not listed on an exchange. All contract terms are negotiated between buyer and seller. *Syn.* nonstandard option. *Related item(s):* listed option.

out-of-the-money The term used to describe an option that has no intrinsic value, such as a call option when the stock is selling below the exercise price or a put option when the stock is selling above the exercise price. *Related item(s):* at-the-money; in-the-money; intrinsic value.

outstanding stock Equity securities issued by a corporation and in the hands of the public; issued stock that the issuer has not reacquired. *Related item(s):* treasury stock.

overbought A technical analysis term for a market in which more and stronger buying has occurred than the fundamentals justify. *Related item(s):* oversold.

overlapping debt A condition resulting when property in a municipality is subject to multiple taxing authorities or tax districts, each having tax collection powers and recourse to the residents of that municipality. *Related item(s):* coterminous.

oversold A technical analysis term for a market in which more and stronger selling has occurred than the fundamentals justify. *Related item(s):* overbought.

P

par The dollar amount the issuer assigns to a security. For an equity security, par is usually a small dollar amount that bears no relationship to the security's market price. For a debt security, par is the amount repaid to the investor when the bond matures, usually $1,000. *Syn.* face value; principal; stated value. *Related item(s):* capital surplus; maturity date.

parity In an exchange market, a situation in which all brokers bidding have equal standing and the winning bid is awarded by a random drawing. *Related item(s):* precedence; priority.

parity price of common The dollar amount at which a common stock is equal in value to its corresponding convertible security. It is calculated by dividing the convertible security's market value by its conversion ratio.

parity price of convertible The dollar amount at which a convertible security is equal in value to its corresponding common stock. It is calculated by multiplying the market price of the common stock by its conversion ratio.

partial call The redemption by an issuer of a portion of an outstanding bond issue before the maturity date. *Related item(s):* catastrophe call; mandatory call.

participating preferred stock An equity security that offers the holder a share of corporate earnings remaining after all senior securities have been paid a fixed dividend. The payment is made in addition to the fixed dividend stated on the certificate and may be cumulative or noncumulative. *Related item(s):* convertible preferred stock; cumulative preferred stock; noncumulative preferred stock; preferred stock.

participation The provision of the Employee Retirement Income Security Act of 1974 requiring that all employees in a qualified retirement plan be covered within a reasonable time of their dates of hire.

partnership A form of business organization in which two or more individuals manage the business and are equally and personally liable for its debts.

partnership account An account that empowers the individual members of a partnership to act on the behalf of the partnership as a whole.

partnership management fee The amount payable to the general partners of a limited partnership or to other persons for managing the day-to-day partnership operations. *Syn.* program management fee; property management fee.

par value The dollar amount assigned to a security by the issuer. For an equity security, par value is usually a small dollar amount that bears no relationship to the security's market price. For a debt security, par value is the amount repaid to the investor when the bond matures, usually $1,000. *Syn.* face value; principal; stated value. *Related item(s):* capital surplus; discount bond; premium bond.

passive income Earnings derived from a rental property, limited partnership, or other enterprise in which the individual is not actively involved. Passive income, therefore, does not include earnings from wages or active business participation, nor does it include income from dividends, interest, and capital gains. *Related item(s):* passive loss; unearned income.

passive investor *See* limited partner.

passive loss A loss incurred through a rental property, limited partnership, or other enterprise in which the individual is not actively involved. Passive losses may be used to offset passive income only, not wage or portfolio income. *Related item(s):* passive income.

pass-through certificate A security representing an interest in a pool of conventional, VA, Farmers Home Administration, or other agency mortgages. The pool receives the principal and interest payments, and it passes through to each certificate holder. Payments may or may not be guaranteed. *Related item(s):* Federal National Mortgage Association; Government National Mortgage Association.

payment date The day on which a declared dividend is paid to all stockholders owning shares on the record date.

payment period As defined by the Federal Reserve Board's Regulation T, the period corresponding to the regular way settlement period.

payout stage *See* distribution stage.

payroll deduction plan A retirement plan whereby an employee authorizes a deduction from his check on a regular basis. The plan may be qualified, such as a 401(k) plan, or nonqualified.

P/E *See* price-to-earnings ratio.

peak The end of a period of increasing business activity throughout the economy, one of the four stages of the business cycle. *Syn.* prosperity. *Related item(s):* business cycle.

pension plan A contract between an individual and an employer, a labor union, a government entity, or another institution that provides for the distribution of pension benefits at retirement.

P/E ratio *See* price-to-earnings ratio.

person As defined in securities law, an individual, a corporation, a partnership, an association, a fund, a joint stock company, an unincorporated organization, a trust, a government, or a political subdivision of a government.

personal income (PI) An individual's total earnings derived from wages, passive business enterprises, and investments. *Related item(s):* disposable income.

plan custodian An institution retained by an investment company to perform clerical duties. The custodian's responsibilities include safeguarding plan assets, sending out customer confirmations, and issuing shares. *Related item(s):* custodian; mutual fund custodian.

plus tick A security transaction's execution price that is above the previous execution price by a minimum amount. *Syn.* uptick. *Related item(s):* minus tick; tick; zero-plus tick.

point A measure of a bond's price; $10 or 1% of the par value of $1,000. *Related item(s):* basis point.

POP *See* public offering price.

portfolio income Earnings from interest, dividends, and all nonbusiness investments. *Related item(s):* earned income; passive income; unearned income.

portfolio manager The entity responsible for investing a mutual fund's assets, implementing its investment strategy, and managing day-to-day portfolio trading. *Syn.* fund manager.

position The amount of a security either owned (a long position) or owed (a short position) by an individual or a dealer. Dealers take long positions in specific securities to maintain inventories and thereby facilitate trading.

position limit The rule established by options exchanges that prohibits an investor from having a net long or short position of more than a specific number of contracts on the same side of the market.

power of substitution *See* stock power.

preemptive right A stockholder's legal right to maintain her proportionate ownership by purchasing newly issued shares before the new stock is offered to the public. *Related item(s):* right.

preferred stock An equity security that represents ownership in a corporation. It is issued with a stated dividend, which must be paid before dividends are paid to common stockholders. It generally carries no voting rights. *Related item(s):* callable preferred stock; convertible preferred stock; cumulative preferred stock.

preferred stock fund A mutual fund whose investment objective is to provide stable income with minimal capital risk. It invests in income-producing instruments such as preferred stock. *Related item(s):* bond fund.

preliminary prospectus An abbreviated prospectus that is distributed while the SEC is reviewing an issuer's registration statement. It contains all of the essential facts about the forthcoming offering except the underwriting spread, final public offering price, and date on which the shares will be delivered. *Syn.* red herring.

premium (1) The amount of cash that an option buyer pays to an option seller. (2) The difference between the higher price paid for a security and the security's face amount at issue. *Related item(s):* discount.

premium bond A bond that sells at a higher price than its face value. *Related item(s):* discount bond; par value.

price-to-earnings ratio (P/E) A tool for comparing the prices of different common stocks by assessing how much the market is willing to pay for a share of each corporation's earnings. It is calculated by dividing the current market price of a stock by the earnings per share.

price risk The potential that the value of a currency or commodity will change between the signing of a delivery contract and the time delivery is made. The futures markets serve to manage price risk.

primary distribution *See* primary offering.

primary market *See* new issue market.

primary offering An offering in which the proceeds of the underwriting go to the issuing corporation, agency, or municipality. The issuer seeks to increase its capitalization either by selling shares of stock, representing ownership, or by selling bonds, representing loans to the issuer. *Syn.* primary distribution.

prime rate The interest rate that commercial banks charge their prime or most creditworthy customers, generally large corporations.

principal A person who trades for his own account in the primary or secondary market. Also, a dealer.

principal transaction A transaction in which a broker-dealer either buys securities from customers and takes them into its own inventory or sells securities to customers from its inventory. *Related item(s)*: agency transaction; agent; broker; dealer; principal.

priority In an exchange market, the ranking of bids and offers according to the first person to bid or offer at a given price. Therefore, only one individual or firm can have priority. *Related item(s)*: parity; precedence.

private placement An offering of new issue securities that complies with Regulation D of the Securities Act of 1933. According to Regulation D, a security generally is not required to be registered with the SEC if it is offered to no more than 35 nonaccredited investors or to an unlimited number of accredited investors. *Related item(s)*: Regulation D.

productive well An oil or gas well that produces mineral resources that may be marketed commercially. *Related item(s)*: dry hole.

profitability The ability to generate a level of income and gain in excess of expenses.

profit-sharing plan An employee benefit plan established and maintained by an employer whereby the employees receive a share of the business's profits. The money may be paid directly to the employees or deferred until retirement. A combination of both approaches is also possible.

progressive tax A tax that takes a larger percentage of the income of high-income earners than that of low-income earners. An example is the graduated income tax. *Related item(s)*: regressive tax.

property dividend A distribution made by a corporation to its stockholders of securities it owns in other corporations or of its products. *Related item(s)*: dividend.

prospectus *See* final prospectus.

Prospectus Act *See* Securities Act of 1933.

proxy A limited power of attorney from a stockholder authorizing another person to vote on stockholder issues according to the first stockholder's instructions. To vote on corporate matters, a stockholder must either attend the annual meeting or vote by proxy.

proxy department The department within a brokerage firm that is responsible for sending proxy statements to customers whose securities are held in the firm's name, and for mailing financial reports received from issuers to their stockholders.

prudent investor rule A legal maxim that restricts discretion in a fiduciary account to only those investments that a reasonable and prudent person might make.

publicly traded fund *See* closed-end investment company.

public offering The sale of an issue of common stock, either by a corporation going public or by an offering of additional shares. *Related item(s)*: initial public offering.

public offering price (POP) (1) The price of new shares that is established in the issuing corporation's prospectus. (2) The price to investors for mutual fund

shares, equal to the net asset value plus the sales charge. *Related item(s)*: ask; bid; mutual fund; net asset value.

purchasing power risk The potential that, because of inflation, a certain amount of money will not purchase as much in the future as it does today. *Syn.* inflation risk.

put (1) An option contract giving the owner the right to sell a certain amount of an underlying security at a specified price within a specified time. (2) The act of exercising a put option. *Related item(s)*: call.

put bond A debt security requiring the issuer to purchase the security at the holder's discretion or within a prescribed time. *Syn.* tender bond.

put buyer An investor who pays a premium for an option contract and receives, for a specified time, the right to sell the underlying security at a specified price. *Related item(s)*: call buyer; call writer; put writer.

put writer An investor who receives a premium and takes on, for a specified time, the obligation to buy the underlying security at a specified price at the put buyer's discretion. *Related item(s)*: call buyer; call writer; put buyer.

Q

qualification *See* registration by qualification.

qualified legal opinion The statement of a bond attorney affirming the validity of a new municipal bond issue but expressing reservations about its quality. *Related item(s)*: legal opinion of counsel; unqualified legal opinion.

qualified retirement plan A corporate retirement plan that meets the standards set by the Employee Retirement Income Security Act of 1974. Contributions to a qualified plan are tax deductible. *Syn.* approved plan. *Related item(s)*: individual retirement account; Keogh plan; nonqualified retirement plan.

quotation The price or bid a market maker or broker-dealer offers for a particular security. *Syn.* quote. *Related item(s)*: ask; bid; bond quote; stock quote.

quote *See* quotation.

R

range A security's low price and high price for a particular trading period, such as the close of a day's trading, the opening of a day's trading, or a day, month, or year. *Syn.* opening range.

rating An evaluation of a corporate or municipal bond's relative safety, according to the issuer's ability to re- pay principal and make interest payments. Bonds are rated by various organizations, such as Standard & Poor's and Moody's. Ratings range from AAA or Aaa (the highest) to C or D, which represents a company in default.

rating service A company, such as Moody's or Standard & Poor's, that rates various debt and preferred stock issues for safety of payment of principal, interest, or dividends. The issuing company or municipality pays a fee for the rating. *Related item(s):* bond rating; rating.

raw land program A real estate direct participation program that aims to provide capital appreciation by investing in undeveloped land.

real estate investment trust (REIT) A corporation or trust that uses the pooled capital of many investors to invest in direct ownership of either income property or mortgage loans. These investments offer tax benefits in addition to interest and capital gains distributions.

real estate limited partnership A direct participation program formed to build new structures, generate income from existing property, or profit from the capital appreciation of undeveloped land. Growth potential, income distributions, and tax shelter are the most important benefits of such a program.

realized gain The amount a taxpayer earns when he sells an asset. *Related item(s):* unrealized gain.

recapitalization Changing the capital structure of a corporation by issuing, converting, or redeeming securities.

recession A general economic decline lasting from 6 to 18 months.

record date The date a corporation's board of directors establishes that determines which of its stockholders are entitled to receive dividends or rights distributions.

recovery *See* expansion.

redeemable security A security that the issuer redeems upon the holder's request. Examples include shares in an open-end investment company and Treasury notes.

redemption The return of an investor's principal in a security, such as a bond, preferred stock, or mutual fund shares. By law, redemption of mutual fund shares must occur within seven days of receiving the investor's request for redemption.

red herring *See* preliminary prospectus.

refinancing Issuing equity, the proceeds of which are used to retire debt.

refunding Retiring an outstanding bond issue at maturity using money from the sale of a new offering. *Related item(s):* advance refunding.

registered Describes a security that prints the owner's name on the certificate. The owner's name is stored in records kept by the issuer or a transfer agent.

registered as to principal only The term describing a bond that prints the owner's name on the certificate, but that has unregistered coupons payable to the bearer. *Syn.* partially registered. *Related item(s):* coupon bond; fully registered bond; registered.

Registered Options Principal (ROP) The officer or partner of a brokerage firm who approves, in writing, accounts in which options transactions are permitted.

registered principal An associated person of a member firm who manages or supervises the firm's investment banking or securities business. This includes any indi-

vidual who trains associated persons and who solicits business.

Unless the member firm is a sole proprietorship, it must employ at least two registered principals, one of whom must be registered as a general securities principal and one of whom must be registered as a financial and operations principal. If the firm does options business with the public, it must employ at least one Registered Options Principal.

registered representative (RR) An associated person engaged in the investment banking or securities business. This includes any individual who supervises, solicits, or conducts business in securities or who trains people to supervise, solicit, or conduct business in securities.

Anyone employed by a brokerage firm who is not a principal and who is not engaged in clerical or brokerage administration is subject to registration and exam licensing as a registered representative. *Syn.* account executive; stockbroker. *Related item(s):* associated person of a member.

registrar The independent organization or part of a corporation responsible for accounting for all of the issuer's outstanding stock and certifying that its bonds constitute legal debt.

registration by coordination A process that allows a security to be sold in a state. It is available to an issuer that files for the security's registration under the Securities Act of 1933 and files duplicates of the registration documents with the state administrator. The state registration becomes effective at the same time the federal registration statement becomes effective.

registration by filing A process that allows a security to be sold in a state. Previously referred to as *registration by notification*, it is available to an issuer who files for the security's registration under the Securities Act of 1933, meets minimum net worth and certain other requirements, and notifies the state of this eligibility by filing certain documents with the state administrator. The state registration becomes effective at the same time the federal registration statement becomes effective.

registration by notification *See* registration by filing.

registration by qualification A process that allows a security to be sold in a state. It is available to an issuer who files for the security's registration with the state administrator; meets minimum net worth, disclosure, and other requirements; and files appropriate registration fees. The state registration becomes effective when the legal document that discloses all pertinent information concerning an offering of a security and its issuer is filed. It is submitted to the SEC in accordance with the requirements of the Securities Act of 1933, and it forms the basis of the final prospectus distributed to investors.

regressive tax A tax that takes a larger percentage of the income of low-income earners than that of high-income earners. Examples include gasoline tax and cigarette tax. *Related item(s)*: progressive tax.

Reg T *See* Regulation T.

Reg T call *See* margin call.

regular way A settlement contract that calls for delivery and payment within a standard payment period from the date of the trade. The Uniform Practice Code sets the standard payment period. The type of security being traded determines the amount of time allowed for regular way settlement. *Related item(s)*: cash transaction; settlement date.

Regulation A The provision of the Securities Act of 1933 that exempts from registration small public offerings valued at no more than $5 million worth of securities issued during a 12-month period.

Regulation D The provision of the Securities Act of 1933 that exempts from registration offerings sold to a maximum of 35 nonaccredited investors during a 12-month period. *Related item(s)*: private placement.

Regulation NMS (National Market System) A broad sweeping SEC regulation designed to bring trading and reporting uniformity to U.S. securities markets. *Related item(s)*: order protection rule; minimum increments rule.

Regulation SP Regulation enacted by the SEC to protect the privacy of customer information, particularly non-public personal information. Your firm must provide a privacy notice describing its privacy policies to customers whenever a new account is opened and annually thereafter. The notice must provide customers a reasonable means to opt out of the disclosure of the customer's nonpublic personal information to unaffiliated third parties.

Regulation T The Federal Reserve Board regulation that governs customer cash accounts and the amount of credit that brokerage firms and dealers may extend to customers for the purchase of securities. Regulation T currently sets the loan value of marginable securities at 50% and the payment deadline at two days beyond regular way settlement. *Syn.* Reg T. *Related item(s)*: Regulation U.

Regulation U The Federal Reserve Board regulation that governs loans by banks for the purchase of securities. Call loans are exempt from Regulation U. *Related item(s)*: broker's loan; call loan; Regulation T.

rehypothecation The pledging of a client's securities as collateral for a bank loan. Brokerage firms may rehypothecate up to 140% of the value of their customers' securities to finance margin loans to customers. *Related item(s)*: hypothecation.

REIT *See* real estate investment trust.

repo *See* repurchase agreement.

repurchase agreement A sale of securities with an attendant agreement to repurchase them at a higher price on an agreed-upon future date; the difference between the sale price and the repurchase price represents the interest earned by the investor. Repos are considered money market instruments and are used to raise short-term capital and as instruments of monetary policy. *Syn.* repo. *Related item(s)*: reverse repurchase agreement.

reserve requirement The percentage of depositors' money that the Federal Reserve Board requires a commercial bank to keep on deposit in the form of cash or in its vault. *Syn.* reserves.

residual claim The right of a common stockholder to corporate assets in the event that the corporation ceases to exist. A common stockholder may claim assets only after the claims of all creditors and other security holders have been satisfied.

resistance level A technical analysis term describing the top of a stock's historical trading range. *Related item(s)*: breakout; support level.

restricted account A margin account in which the equity is less than the Regulation T initial requirement. *Related item(s)*: equity; initial margin requirement; margin account; retention requirement.

restricted security An unregistered, nonexempt security acquired either directly or indirectly from the issuer, or an affiliate of the issuer, in a transaction that does not involve a public offering. *Related item(s)*: holding period; Rule 144.

retail communications FINRA defines this category of communications with the public as any written (including electronic) communication that is distributed or made available to more than 25 retail investors within any 30 calendar-day period. A retail investor is any person other than an institutional investor, regardless of whether the person has an account with the member firm or not.

retained earnings The amount of a corporation's net income that remains after all dividends have been paid to preferred and common stockholders. *Syn.* earned surplus; reinvested earnings.

retirement account A customer account established to provide retirement funds.

retiring bonds Ending an issuer's debt obligation by calling the outstanding bonds, by purchasing bonds in the open market, or by repaying bondholders the principal amount at maturity.

return on investment (ROI) The profit or loss resulting from a security transaction, often expressed as an annual percentage rate.

revenue bond A municipal debt issue whose interest and principal are payable only from the specific earnings of an income-producing public project. *Related item(s)*: double-barreled bond; general obligation bond; municipal bond; special revenue bond.

reverse churning The unsuitable practice of placing a client who trades infrequently in a fee-based account rather than a commission based account that would be more appropriate. *Related item:* churning

reverse repurchase agreement A purchase of securities with an attendant agreement to resell them at a higher price on an agreed-upon future date; the difference between the purchase price and the resale price represents the interest earned by the investor. The purchaser initiates the deal. *Syn.* reverse repo. *Related item(s):* repurchase agreement.

reverse split A reduction in the number of a corporation's shares outstanding that increases the par value of its stock or its earnings per share. The market value of the total number of shares remains the same. *Related item(s):* stock split.

right A security representing a stockholder's entitlement to the first opportunity to purchase new shares issued by the corporation at a predetermined price (normally less than the current market price) in proportion to the number of shares already owned. Rights are issued for a short time only, after which they expire. *Syn.* subscription right; subscription right certificate. *Related item(s):* preemptive right; rights offering.

right of accumulation A benefit offered by a mutual fund that allows the investor to qualify for reduced sales loads on additional purchases according to the fund account's total dollar value.

rights offering An issue of new shares of stock accompanied by the opportunity for each stockholder to maintain a proportionate ownership by purchasing additional shares in the corporation before the shares are offered to the public. *Related item(s):* right.

ROI *See* return on investment.

rollover The transfer of funds from one qualified retirement plan to another qualified retirement plan. If this is not done within a specified time period, the funds are taxed as ordinary income.

ROP *See* Registered Options Principal.

round lot A security's normal unit of trading, which is generally 100 shares of stock or five bonds. *Related item(s):* odd lot.

Rule 144 SEC rule requiring that persons who hold control or restricted securities sell them only in limited quantities, and that all sales of restricted stock by control persons must be reported to the SEC by filing a Form 144, "Notice of Proposed Sale of Securities." *Related item(s):* control security; restricted security.

Rule 147 SEC rule that provides exemption from the registration statement and prospectus requirements of the 1933 Act for securities offered and sold exclusively intrastate.

Rule 405 NYSE rule requiring that each member organization exercise due diligence to learn the essential facts about every customer. *Syn.* know your customer rule.

Rule 415 SEC rule governing shelf offerings. The rule allows an issuer to sell limited portions of a new issue over a three-year period. *Related item(s):* shelf offering.

Rule 504 SEC rule providing that an offering of less than $1 million during any 12-month period may be exempt from full registration. The rule does not restrict the number of accredited or nonaccredited purchasers.

Rule 505 SEC rule providing that an offering of $1 million to $5 million during any 12-month period may be exempt from full registration. The rule restricts the number of nonaccredited purchasers to 35 but does not restrict the number of accredited purchasers.

Rule 506 SEC rule providing that an offering of more than $5 million during any 12-month period may be exempt from full registration. The rule restricts the number of nonaccredited purchasers to 35 but does not restrict the number of accredited purchasers.

S

SAR *See* suspicious activity report.

sale *See* sell.

sales charge *See* commission.

sales literature Any written material a firm distributes to customers or the public in a controlled manner. Examples include circulars, research reports, form letters, market letters, performance reports, and text used for seminars. *Related item(s):* advertisement; market letter.

sales load The amount added to a mutual fund share's net asset value to arrive at the offering price. *Related item(s):* mutual fund; net asset value; no-load fund.

Sallie Mae *See* Student Loan Marketing Association.

S&P *See* Standard & Poor's Corporation.

S&P 100 *See* Standard & Poor's 100 Stock Index.

S&P 500 *See* Standard & Poor's Composite Index of 500 Stocks.

savings bond A government debt security that is not negotiable or transferable and that may not be used as collateral. *Related item(s):* Series EE bond; Series HH bond.

SEC *See* Securities and Exchange Commission.

secondary distribution (1) A distribution, with a prospectus, that involves securities owned by major stockholders (typically founders or principal owners of a corporation). The sale proceeds go to the sellers of the stock, not to the issuer. *Syn.* registered secondary distribution. (2) A procedure for trading very large blocks of shares of stock whereby the trade is executed off the floor of an exchange after the market closes.

secondary market The market in which securities are bought and sold subsequently to their being sold to the public for the first time. *Related item(s):* new issue market.

secondary offering A sale of securities in which one or more major stockholders in a company sell all or a large portion of their holdings; the underwriting proceeds are paid to the stockholders rather than to the corporation. Typically, such an offering occurs when the founder of a business (and perhaps some of the original financial backers) determines that there is more to be gained by going public than by staying private. The offering does not increase the number of shares of stock outstanding. *Related item(s):* secondary distribution.

sector fund A mutual fund whose investment objective is to capitalize on the return potential provided by investing primarily in a particular industry or sector of the economy. *Syn.* industry fund; specialized fund.

secured bond A debt security backed by identifiable assets set aside as collateral. In the event that the issuer defaults on payment, the bondholders may lay claim to the collateral. *Related item(s):* debenture.

Securities Act of 1933 Federal legislation requiring the full and fair disclosure of all material information about the issuance of new securities. *Syn.* Act of 1933; Full Disclosure Act; New Issues Act; Prospectus Act; Trust in Securities Act; Truth in Securities Act.

Securities Acts Amendments of 1975 Federal legislation that established the Municipal Securities Rulemaking Board. *Related item(s):* Municipal Securities Rulemaking Board.

Securities and Exchange Commission (SEC) Commission created by Congress to regulate the securities markets and protect investors. It is composed of five commissioners appointed by the president of the United States and approved by the Senate. The SEC enforces, among other acts, the Securities Act of 1933, the Securities Exchange Act of 1934, the Trust Indenture Act of 1939, the Investment Company Act of 1940, and the Investment Advisers Act of 1940.

Securities Exchange Act of 1934 Federal legislation that established the Securities and Exchange Commission. The act aims to protect investors by regulating the exchanges, the over-the-counter market, the extension of credit by the Federal Reserve Board, broker-dealers, insider transactions, trading activities, client accounts, and net capital. *Syn.* Act of 1934; Exchange Act.

Securities Investor Protection Corporation (SIPC) A nonprofit membership corporation created by an act of Congress to protect clients of brokerage firms that are forced into bankruptcy. Membership is composed of all brokers and dealers registered under the Securities Exchange Act of 1934. SIPC provides brokerage firm customers up to $500,000 coverage for cash and securities held by the firms (although cash coverage is limited to $250,000).

security Other than an insurance policy or a fixed annuity, any piece of securitized paper that can be traded for value. Under the Act of 1934, this includes any note, stock, bond, investment contract, debenture, certificate of interest in a profit-sharing or partnership agreement, certificate of deposit, collateral trust certificate, preorganization certificate, option on a security, or other instrument of investment commonly known as a *security*.

segregation Holding customer-owned securities separate from securities owned by other customers and securities owned by the brokerage firm. *Related item(s):* commingling.

selection risk The potential for loss on an investment owing to the particular security chosen performing poorly in spite of good overall market or industry performance.

self-regulatory organization (SRO) One of eight organizations accountable to the SEC for the enforcement of federal securities laws and the supervision of securities practices within an assigned field of jurisdiction. For example, the Financial Industry Regulatory Authority regulates trading on the NYSE and the over-the-counter market; the Municipal Securities Rulemaking Board supervises state and municipal securities; and certain exchanges, such as the Chicago Board Options Exchange, act as self-regulatory bodies to promote ethical conduct and standard trading practices.

sell To convey ownership of a security or another asset for money or value. This includes giving or delivering a security with or as a bonus for a purchase of securities, a gift of assessable stock, and selling or offering a warrant or right to purchase or subscribe to another security.

Not included in the definition is a bona fide pledge or loan or a stock dividend if nothing of value is given by the stockholders for the dividend. *Syn.* sale.

seller *See* writer.

seller's option A settlement contract that calls for delivery and payment according to a number of days specified by the seller. *Related item(s):* buyer's option.

sell out The procedure that the seller of a security follows when the buyer fails to complete the contract by accepting delivery of the security. The seller closes the contract by selling the security in the open market and charging the account of the buyer for transaction fees and any loss caused by changes in the market. *Related item(s):* buy-in.

sell stop order An order to sell a security that is entered at a price below the current market price and that is triggered when the market price touches or goes through the sell stop price.

senior lien debt A bond issue that shares the same collateral as is backing other issues but that has a prior claim to the collateral in the event of default.

senior security A security that grants its holder a prior claim to the issuer's assets over the claims of another security's holders. For example, a bond is a senior security over common stock.

SEP *See* simplified employee pension plan.

separate account The account that holds funds paid by variable annuity contract holders. The funds are kept separate from the insurer's general account and are invested in a portfolio of securities that match the contract holders' objectives. *Related item(s):* accumulation unit; annuity; general account.

separately identifiable department or division A department of a bank that engages in the business of buying or selling municipal securities under the direct supervision of an officer of the bank. Such a department is classified by the Municipal Securities Rulemaking Board as a municipal securities dealer and must comply with MSRB regulations. *Related item(s):* Rule G-1.

Separate Trading of Registered Interest and Principal of Securities (STRIPS) A zero-coupon bond issued and backed by the Treasury Department. *Related item(s):* zero-coupon bond.

SEP-IRA *See* simplified employee pension plan.

serial bond A debt security issued with a maturity schedule in which parts of the outstanding issue mature at intervals until the entire balance has been repaid. Most municipal bonds are serial bonds. *Related item(s):* maturity date; series bond.

series Options of the same class that have the same exercise price and the same expiration date. *Related item(s):* class; type.

series bond A debt security issued in a series of public offerings spread over an extended time period. All the bonds in the series have the same priority claim against assets. *Related item(s):* serial bond.

Series EE bond A nonmarketable, interest-bearing U.S. government savings bond issued at a discount from par. Interest on Series EE bonds is exempt from state and local taxes. *Related item(s):* savings bond; Series HH bond.

Series HH bond A nonmarketable, interest-bearing U.S. government savings bond issued at par and purchased only by trading in Series EE bonds at maturity. Interest on Series HH bonds is exempt from state and local taxes. *Related item(s):* savings bond; Series EE bond.

Series 6 The investment company/variable contract products limited representative license, which entitles the holder to sell mutual funds and variable annuities and is used by many firms that sell primarily insurance-related products. The Series 6 can serve as the prerequisite for the Series 26 license.

Series 63 The uniform securities agent state law exam, which entitles the successful candidate to sell securities and give investment advice in those states that require Series 63 registration. *Related item(s):* blue-sky laws; Uniform Securities Act.

Series 7 The general securities registered representative license, which entitles the holder to sell all types of securities products, with the exception of commodities futures (which requires a Series 3 license). The Series 7 is the most comprehensive of the FINRA representa-

tive licenses and serves as a prerequisite for most of the principals examinations.

Series 24 The General Securities Principal License, which entitles the holder to supervise the business of a broker-dealer. A Series 7 or a Series 62 qualification is a prerequisite for this license.

settlement The completion of a trade through the delivery of a security or commodity and the payment of cash or other consideration.

settlement date The date on which ownership changes between buyer and seller. The Uniform Practice Code standardizes settlement provisions. *Related item(s):* cash transaction; regular way.

share identification An accounting method that identifies the specific shares selected for liquidation in the event that an investor wishes to liquidate shares. The difference between the buying and selling prices determines the investor's tax liability.

sharing arrangement A method of allocating the responsibility for expenses and the right to share in revenues among the sponsor and limited partners in a direct participation program. *Related item(s):* carried interest; disproportionate sharing; functional allocation; net operating profits interest; overriding royalty interest; reversionary working interest.

shelf offering An SEC provision allowing an issuer to register a new issue security without selling the entire issue at once. The issuer may sell limited portions of the issuer over a three-year period without reregistering the security or incurring penalties. *Related item(s):* Rule 415.

short The term used to describe the selling of a security, contract, or commodity that the seller does not own. For example, an investor who borrows shares of stock from a broker-dealer and sells them on the open market is said to have a *short position* in the stock. *Related item(s):* long.

short sale The sale of a security that the seller does not own, or any sale consummated by the delivery of a security borrowed by or for the account of the seller.

short-term capital gain The profit realized on the sale of an asset that has been owned for 12 months or less. *Related item(s):* capital gain; capital loss; short-term capital loss.

short-term capital loss The loss incurred on the sale of a capital asset that has been owned for 12 months or less. *Related item(s):* capital gain; capital loss; short-term capital gain.

simplified arbitration An expedient method of settling disputes involving claims not exceeding $50,000, whereby a panel of arbitrators reviews the evidence and renders a decision. All awards are made within 30 business days. *Related item(s):* arbitration.

simplified employee pension plan (SEP) A qualified retirement plan designed for employers with 25 or fewer employees. Contributions made to each employee's individual retirement account grow tax deferred until retirement. *Related item(s):* individual retirement account.

single account An account in which only one individual has control over the investments and may transact business.

SIPC *See* Securities Investor Protection Corporation.

SLMA *See* Student Loan Marketing Association.

SMA *See* special memorandum account.

solvency The ability of a corporation both to meet its long-term fixed expenses and to have adequate money for long-term expansion and growth.

specialized fund *See* sector fund.

special memorandum account (SMA) A notation on a customer's general or margin account indicating that funds are credited to the account on a memo basis; the account is used much like a line of credit with a bank. An SMA preserves the customer's right to use excess equity. *Syn.* special miscellaneous account.

special situation fund A mutual fund whose objective is to capitalize on the profit potential of corporations in nonrecurring circumstances, such as those undergoing reorganizations or being considered as takeover candidates.

speculation Trading a commodity or security with a higher-than-average risk in return for a higher-than-average profit potential. The trade is effected solely for the purpose of profiting from it and not as a means of hedging or protecting other positions.

speculator One who trades a commodity or security with a higher than average risk in return for a higher than average profit potential. *Related item(s):* speculation.

spin-off A type of divestiture where a parent company sells all of the shares of a subsidiary or distributes new shares of a company or division it owns to create a new company.

split offering A public offering of securities that combines aspects of both a primary and a secondary offering. A portion of the issue is a primary offering, the proceeds of which go to the issuing corporation; the remainder of the issue is a secondary offering, the proceeds of which go to the selling stockholders. *Syn.* combined distribution. *Related item(s):* primary offering; secondary offering.

sponsor A person who is instrumental in organizing, selling, or managing a limited partnership.

spousal account A separate individual retirement account established for a nonworking spouse. Contributions to the account made by the working spouse grow tax deferred until withdrawal. *Related item(s):* individual retirement account.

spread In a quotation, the difference between a security's bid and ask prices.

SRO *See* self-regulatory organization.

stagflation A period of high unemployment in the economy accompanied by a general rise in prices. *Related item(s):* deflation; inflation.

Standard & Poor's Composite Index of 500 Stocks (S&P 500) A value-weighted index that offers broad coverage of the securities market. It is composed of 400 industrial stocks, 40 financial stocks, 40 public utility stocks, and 20 transportation stocks. The index is owned and compiled by Standard & Poor's Corporation. *Related item(s):* index; Standard & Poor's Corporation; Standard & Poor's 100 Stock Index.

Standard & Poor's Corporation (S&P) A company that rates stocks and corporate and municipal bonds according to risk profiles and that produces and tracks the S&P indexes. The company also publishes a variety of financial and investment reports. *Related item(s):* bond rating; Moody's Investors Service; rating; Standard & Poor's 100 Stock Index; Standard & Poor's Composite Index of 500 Stocks.

Standard & Poor's 100 Stock Index (S&P 100) A value-weighted index composed of 100 blue-chip stocks. The index is owned and compiled by Standard & Poor's Corporation. *Related item(s):* index; Standard & Poor's Corporation; Standard & Poor's Composite Index of 500 Stocks.

Standard and Poor's Composite Index of 500 Stocks (S&P 500) A value-weighted index that offers broad coverage of the securities market. It is composed of 400 industrial stocks, 40 financial stocks, 40 public utility stocks, and 20 transportation stocks. The index is owned and compiled by Standard & Poor's Corporation. *Related item(s):* index; Standard & Poor's Corporation; Standard & Poor's 100 Stock Index.

stated yield *See* nominal yield.

statutory disqualification Prohibiting a person from associating with a self-regulatory organization because the person has been expelled, barred, or suspended from association with a member of an SRO; has had his registration suspended, denied or revoked by the SEC; has been the cause of someone else being suspended, barred, or having their license revoked; has been convicted of certain crimes; or has falsified an application or a report that he must file with or on behalf of a membership organization.

statutory voting A voting procedure that permits stockholders to cast one vote per share owned for each position. The procedure tends to benefit majority stockholders. *Related item(s):* cumulative voting.

stock ahead The term used to describe the inability to fill a limit order at a specific price because other orders at the same price were entered previously.

stockbroker *See* registered representative.

stock certificate Written evidence of ownership in a corporation.

stock dividend *See* dividend.

stock loan agreement The document that an institutional customer must sign when the broker-dealer borrows stock from the customer's account; the document specifies the terms of the loan and the rights of both parties.

stock power A standard form that duplicates the back of a stock certificate and is used for transferring the stock to the new owner's name. A separate stock power is used if a security's registered owner does not have the certificate available for signature endorsement. *Syn.* irrevocable stock power; power of substitution. *Related item(s):* assignment.

stock quote A list of representative prices bid and asked for a stock during a particular trading day. Stocks are quoted in points, where one point equals $1. Stock quotes are listed in the financial press and most daily newspapers. *Related item(s):* bond quote.

stock split An increase in the number of a corporation's outstanding shares, which decreases its stock's par value. The market value of the total number of shares remains the same. The proportional reductions in orders held on the books for a split stock are calculated by dividing the stock's market price by the fraction that represents the split.

stop limit order A customer order that becomes a limit order when the market price of the security reaches or passes a specific price. *Related item(s):* limit order; stop order.

stop order (1) A directive from the SEC that suspends the sale of new issue securities to the public when fraud is suspected or filing materials are deficient. (2) A customer order that becomes a market order when the market price of the security reaches or passes a specific price. *Related item(s):* limit order; market order; stop limit order.

strike price *See* exercise price.

STRIPS *See* Separate Trading of Registered Interest and Principal of Securities.

Student Loan Marketing Association (SLMA) A publicly owned corporation that purchases student loans from financial institutions and packages them for sale in the secondary market, thereby increasing the availability of money for educational loans. *Syn.* Sal- lie Mae.

subject quote A securities quotation that does not represent an actual offer to buy or sell but is tentative, subject to reconfirmation by the broker-dealer. *Related item(s):* bona fide quote; firm quote; nominal quote; workout quote.

subordinated debenture A debt obligation backed by the general credit of the issuing corporation that has claims to interest and principal subordinated to ordinary debentures and all other liabilities. *Related item(s):* debenture.

subordinated debt financing A form of long-term capitalization used by broker-dealers in which the claims of lenders are subordinated to the claims of other creditors. Subordinated financing is considered part of the broker-dealer's capital structure and is added to net worth when computing its net capital.

subordinated loan A loan to a broker-dealer in which the lender agrees to subordinate its claim to the claims of the firm's other creditors.

suitability A determination made by a registered representative as to whether a particular security matches a customer's objectives and financial capability. The representative must have enough information about the customer to make this judgment. *Related item(s):* Rule 405.

supply The total amount of a good or service available for purchase by consumers. *Related item(s):* demand.

support level A technical analysis term describing the bottom of a stock's historical trading range. *Related item(s):* breakout; resistance level.

suspicious activity report (SAR) A report filed by broker-dealers and financial institutions when investor behavior is detected that is commercially illogical and serves no apparent purpose. The filing threshold for a SAR is $5,000.

systematic risk The potential for a security to decrease in value owing to its inherent tendency to move together with all securities of the same type. Neither diversification nor any other investment strategy can eliminate this risk. *Related item(s):* market risk.

T

taxability The risk of the erosion of investment income through taxation.

taxable gain The portion of a sale or distribution of mutual fund shares subject to taxation.

tax basis The amount that a limited partner has invested in a partnership.

tax credit An amount that can be subtracted from a tax liability, often in connection with real estate development, energy conservation, and research and development programs. Every dollar of tax credit reduces the amount of tax due, dollar for dollar. *Related item(s):* deduction.

tax-equivalent yield The rate of return a taxable bond must earn before taxes in order to equal the tax-exempt earnings on a municipal bond. This number varies with the investor's tax bracket.

taxes per capita *See* taxes per person.

taxes per person A measure of the tax burden of a municipality's population, calculated by dividing the municipality's tax receipts by its population. *Syn.* taxes per capita.

tax-exempt bond fund A mutual fund whose investment objective is to provide maximum tax-free income. It invests primarily in municipal bonds and short-term debt. *Syn.* tax-free bond fund.

tax-free bond fund *See* tax-exempt bond fund.

tax liability The amount of tax payable on earnings, usually calculated by subtracting standard and item- ized deductions and personal exemptions from adjusted gross income, then multiplying by the tax rate. *Related item(s)*: adjusted gross income.

T-bill *See* Treasury bill.

T-bond *See* Treasury bond.

T-call *See* margin call.

Telephone Consumer Protection Act of 1991 (TCPA) Federal legislation restricting the use of telephone lines for solicitation purposes. A company soliciting sales via telephone, facsimile, or email must disclose its name and address to the called party and must not call any person who has requested not to be called.

tenants in common (TIC) A form of joint ownership of an account whereby a deceased tenant's fractional interest in the account is retained by his estate. *Related item(s)*: joint tenants with right of survivorship.

tender offer An offer to buy securities for cash or for cash plus securities.

term bond *See* term maturity.

term maturity A repayment schedule for a bond issue in which the entire issue comes due on a single date. *Syn.* term bond. *Related item(s)*: maturity date.

third-party account (1) A customer account for which the owner has given power of attorney to a third party. (2) A customer account opened by an adult naming a minor as beneficial owner. (3) A customer account opened for another adult. This type of account is prohibited.

tick A minimum upward or downward movement in the price of a security. *Related item(s)*: minus tick; plus tick.

time deposit A sum of money left with a bank (or borrowed from a bank and left on deposit) that the depositing customer has agreed not to withdraw for a specified time period or without a specified amount of notice. *Related item(s)*: demand deposit.

time value The amount an investor pays for an option above its intrinsic value; it reflects the amount of time left until expiration. The amount is calculated by subtracting the intrinsic value from the premium paid. *Related item(s)*: intrinsic value.

timing risk The potential for an investor to incur a loss as a result of buying or selling a particular security at an unfavorable time.

T-note *See* Treasury note.

total capitalization The sum of a corporation's long-term debt, stock accounts, and capital in excess of par.

trade confirmation A printed document that contains details of a transaction, including the settlement date and amount of money due from or owed to a customer. It must be sent to the customer on or before the settlement date.

trade date The date on which a securities transaction is executed.

trading authorization *See* full trading authorization; limited trading authorization.

trading halt A pause in the trading of a particular security on one or more exchanges, usually in anticipation of a news announcement or to correct an order imbalance. During a trading halt, open orders may be canceled and options may be exercised.

transfer agent A person or corporation responsible for recording the names and holdings of registered security owners, seeing that certificates are signed by the appropriate corporate officers, affixing the corporate seal, and delivering securities to the new owners.

transfer and hold in safekeeping A securities buy order settlement and delivery procedure whereby the securities bought are transferred to the customer's name but are held by the broker-dealer. *Related item(s)*: hold in street name; transfer and ship.

transfer and ship A securities buy order settlement and delivery procedure whereby the securities bought are transferred to the customer's name and sent to the customer. *Related item(s)*: hold in street name; transfer and hold in safekeeping.

Treasury bill A marketable U.S. government debt security with a maturity of less than one year. Treasury bills are issued through a competitive bidding process at a discount from par; they have no fixed interest rate. *Syn.* T bill.

Treasury bond A marketable, fixed-interest U.S. government debt security with a maturity of more than 10 years. *Syn.* T bond.

Treasury note A marketable, fixed-interest U.S. government debt security with a maturity of between two and 10 years. *Syn.* T note.

Treasury receipt The generic term for a zero-coupon bond issued by a brokerage firm and collateralized by the Treasury securities a custodian holds in escrow for the investor.

treasury stock Equity securities that the issuing corporation has issued and repurchased from the public at the current market price. *Related item(s)*: issued stock; outstanding stock.

trendline A tool used by technical analysts to trace a security's movement by connecting the reaction lows in an upward trend or the rally highs in a downward trend.

trough The end of a period of declining business activity throughout the economy, one of the four stages of the business cycle. *Related item(s)*: business cycle.

trustee A person legally appointed to act on a beneficiary's behalf.

Trust Indenture Act of 1939 The legislation requiring that all publicly offered, nonexempt debt securities be registered under the Securities Act of 1933 and be issued under a trust indenture that protects the bondholders.

12b-1 asset-based fees An Investment Company Act of 1940 provision that allows a mutual fund to collect a fee for the promotion or sale of or another activity connected with the distribution of its shares. The fee must be reasonable (typically .25% to 1% of net assets managed).

type A term that classifies an option as a call or a put. *Related item(s):* class; series.

U

UGMA *See* Uniform Gift to Minors Act.

UIT *See* unit investment trust.

uncovered *See* naked.

uncovered call writer *See* naked call writer.

uncovered put writer *See* naked put writer.

underlying securities The securities that are bought or sold when an option, right, or warrant is exercised.

underwriter An investment banker that works with an issuer to help bring a security to the market and sell it to the public.

underwriting The procedure by which investment bankers channel investment capital from investors to corporations and municipalities that are issuing securities.

underwriting compensation The amount paid to a broker-dealer firm for its involvement in offering and selling securities.

underwriting manager The brokerage firm responsible for organizing a syndicate, preparing the issue, negotiating with the issuer and underwriters, and allocating stock to the selling group. *Syn.* manager of the syndicate; managing underwriter; syndicate manager. *Related item(s):* agreement among underwriters; syndicate.

unearned income Income derived from investments and other sources not related to employment services.

Examples of unearned income include interest from a savings account, bond interest, and dividends from stock. *Related item(s):* earned income; passive income; portfolio income.

Uniform Gift to Minors Act (UGMA) Legislation that permits a gift of money or securities to be given to a minor and held in a custodial account that an adult manages for the minor's benefit. Income and capital gains transferred to a minor's name are taxed at a lower rate. *Related item(s):* Uniform Transfers to Minors Act.

Uniform Securities Act (USA) Model legislation for securities industry regulation at the state level. Each state may adopt the legislation in its entirety or it may

adapt it (within limits) to suit its needs. *Related item(s):* blue-sky laws; Series 63.

Uniform Transfers to Minors Act (UTMA) Legislation adopted in some states that permits a gift of money or securities to be given to a minor and held in a custodial account that an adult manages for the minor's benefit until the minor reaches a certain age (not necessarily the age of majority). *Related item(s):* Uniform Gifts to Minors Act.

unit A share in the ownership of a direct participation program that entitles the investor to an interest in the program's net income, net loss, and distributions.

unit investment trust (UIT) An investment company that sells redeemable shares in a professionally selected portfolio of securities. It is organized under a trust indenture, not a corporate charter. *Related item(s):* fixed unit investment trust; unit of beneficial interest.

unit of beneficial interest A redeemable share in a unit investment trust, representing ownership of an undivided interest in the underlying portfolio. *Syn.* share of beneficial interest. *Related item(s):* unit investment trust.

unrealized gain The amount by which a security appreciates in value before it is sold. Until it is sold, the investor does not actually possess the sale proceeds. *Related item(s):* realized gain.

unsecured bond *See* debenture.

uptick *See* plus tick.

USA *See* Uniform Securities Act.

Utilities Average *See* Dow Jones Utilities Average.

UTMA *See* Uniform Transfers to Minors Act.

V

variable annuity An insurance contract in which, at the end of the accumulation stage, the insurance company guarantees a minimum total payment to the annuitant. The performance of a separate account, generally invested in equity securities, determines the amount of this total payment. *Related item(s):* accumulation stage; annuity; fixed annuity; separate account.

vesting (1) An ERISA guideline stipulating that an employee must be entitled to his entire retirement benefits within a certain period of time even if he no longer works for the employer. (2) The amount of time that an employee must work before retirement or before benefit plan contributions made by the employer become the employee's property without penalty. The IRS and the Employee Retirement Income Security Act of 1974 set minimum requirements for vesting in a qualified plan.

volatility The magnitude and frequency of changes in the price of a security or commodity within a given time period.

voting right A stockholder's right to vote for members of the board of directors and on matters of corporate policy—particularly the issuance of senior securities, stock splits and substantial changes in the corporation's business. A variation of this right is extended to variable annuity contract holders and mutual fund shareholders, who may vote on material policy issues.

W

warrant A security that gives the holder the right to purchase securities from the warrant issuer at a stipulated subscription price. Warrants are usually long-term instruments with expiration dates years in the future.

wash sale Selling a security at a loss for tax purposes and, within 30 days before or after, purchasing the same or a substantially identical security. The IRS disallows the claimed loss. *Related item(s):* bond swap.

wildcatting *See* exploratory drilling program.

Wilshire 5,000 Equity Index A value-weighted market indicator composed of 5,000 exchange-listed and over-the-counter common stocks. It is the broadest measure of the market. *Related item(s):* index.

wire room *See* order department.

working capital A measure of a corporation's liquidity; that is, its ability to transfer assets into cash to meet current short-term obligations. It is calculated by subtracting total current liabilities from total current assets.

writer The seller of an option contract. An option writer takes on the obligation to buy or sell the underlying security if and when the option buyer exercises the option. *Syn.* seller.

Y

yield The rate of return on an investment, usually expressed as an annual percentage rate. *Related item(s):* current yield; dividend yield; nominal yield.

yield-based option A security representing the right to receive, in cash, the difference between the current yield of an underlying U.S. government security and the strike price of the option. A yield-based option is used to speculate on or hedge against the risk associated with fluctuating interest rates; its strike price represents the anticipated yield of the underlying debt security.

yield curve A graphic representation of the actual or projected yields of fixed-income securities in relation to their maturities. *Related item(s):* flat yield curve; inverted yield curve.

yield to call (YTC) The rate of return on a bond that accounts for the difference between the bond's acquisition cost and its proceeds, including interest income, calculated to the earliest date that the bond may be called by the issuing corporation. *Related item(s):* bond yield.

yield to maturity (YTM) The rate of return on a bond that accounts for the difference between the bond's acquisition cost and its maturity proceeds, including interest income. *Related item(s):* bond yield.

YTC *See* yield to call.

YTM *See* yield to maturity.

Z

zero-coupon bond A corporate or municipal debt security traded at a deep discount from face value. The bond pays no interest; rather, it may be redeemed at maturity for its full face value. It may be issued at a discount, or it may be stripped of its coupons and repackaged.

zero-minus tick A security transaction's execution price that is equal to the price of the last sale but lower than the last different price. *Related item(s):* minus tick; plus tick; zero-plus tick.

zero-plus tick A security transaction's execution price that is equal to the price of the last sale but higher than the last different price. *Related item(s):* minus tick; plus tick; zero-minus tick.

Index

Notes

Notes

Notes

Notes

Notes